Understanding Exodus

Understanding Exodus

A Holistic Commentary on Exodus 1–11

SECOND EDITION

Moshe Greenberg

Edited and with a Foreword by
Jeffrey H. Tigay

CASCADE *Books* · Eugene, Oregon

UNDERSTANDING EXODUS
A Holistic Commentary on Exodus 1–11
Second Edition

Copyright © 2013 Evelyn Greenberg. All rights reserved. Except for brief quotations in critical publications or reviews, no part of this book may be reproduced in any manner without prior written permission from the publisher. Write: Permissions, Wipf and Stock Publishers, 199 W. 8th Ave., Suite 3, Eugene, OR 97401.

Cascade Books
A Division of Wipf and Stock Publishers
199 W. 8th Ave., Suite 3
Eugene, OR 97401

www.wipfandstock.com

ISBN 13: 978-1-62032-732-6

Cataloging-in-Publication data:

Greenberg, Moshe.

Understanding Exodus : a holistic commentary on Exodus 1–11 / Moshe Greenberg ; second edition, edited and with a foreword by Jeffrey H. Tigay.

xxiv + 192 p. ; 23 cm.

ISBN 13: 978-1-62032-732-6

Note: First edition 1969

1. Bible. Exodus—Commentaries. I. Tigay, Jeffrey H. II. Title.

BS1245.3 G7 2013

Manufactured in the USA

Contents

Foreword | vii
Preface to the Second Edition | xvii
Acknowledgments | xix
Abbreviations | xxi

Purpose and Method | 1
Exodus in the Context of Torah | 7

I. The Prologue | 15
    How the Israelites Became Enslaved (1:1–22) | 15
        The Movement of the Story | 15
        Themes and Structure | 26
    The Life of Moses before His Call (2:1–25) | 30
        The Movement of the Story | 30
        Themes and Structure | 45
    The Prologue: General Considerations | 48
        The Preliminary Nature of Chapters 1–2 | 48
        Two Progressions | 49
        The Redactional Process | 50

II. Moses' Commissioning | 56
    The Revelation at the Bush (3:1—4:17) | 56
        The Movement of the Story | 56
        Themes and Structure | 74
        Composition and Redaction | 81
    The Return to Egypt (4:18–26) | 86
        The Movement of the Story | 86
        Themes and Structure | 92
        The Redactional Process | 94

Execution and Rebuff (4:27—6:1) | 96
    The Movement of the Story | 96
    Themes and Structure | 100
    Composition and Redaction | 102
The Commission Renewed (6:2—7:13) | 103
    The Movement of the Story | 103
    Themes and Structure | 113
    The Literary Problem of 6:2—7:13: Its Relation to 3:1—6:1 | 115

III. The Plagues of Egypt | 120
    The Movement of the Story (7:14—11:10) | 120
    Themes and Structure | 135
    The Redactional Process | 147

Excursus: Exodus and History: Preliminary Reflections | 155
Appendix: Questions for Uncovering the Message
    of a Biblical Text | 165
Bibliography | 167
Scripture Index | 175
Index of Ancient and Premodern Sources | 189

Foreword

Moshe Greenberg (1928–2010) was one of the most profound and influential biblical scholars of the second half of the twentieth century. The first Jewish biblical scholar appointed to a position in a secular university in post-war America, Greenberg had an important influence on the development of biblical scholarship. Previously, in America the teaching of what Christians call the Old Testament was largely in the hands of Protestant scholars who taught it as something separate from the Jewish tradition. Greenberg brought to the field a thorough mastery of both Jewish and ancient Near Eastern sources as well as rigorous philology, literary-critical insight, and theological sensitivity.

Greenberg had a broad impact due to his lifelong commitment to sharing the results of scholarship beyond the academy. He published articles in newspapers and magazines and, in addition to his full-time university teaching, often taught courses to rabbinical students at the seminaries of the Conservative/Masorti movement in the United States and Israel. He wrote frequently for Jewish educators about teaching the Bible and, after settling in Israel, served as an advisor to Israel's Ministry of Education on how to bring the results of modern scholarship into the required teaching of the Bible in public schools. He served on the Jewish Publication Society's Bible translation committee and, with Shmuel Ahituv, founded *Miqra LeYisrael*, a visionary series of Hebrew commentaries on the Bible, written in Hebrew and addressed to the educated public at large. In his theological writings Greenberg argued that a critical reading of the Bible can be harmonized with Jewish tradition and with religious veneration for the Bible, that faith and criticism can coexist without being sealed off in separate compartments of the mind.[1] His ideal was

---

1. See "A Faith-ful Jewish Critical Interpretation of the Bible," in *Judaism and Modernity: The Religious Philosophy of David Hartman*, ed. J. W. Malino (Aldershot, UK: Ashgate, 2004) 210–15.

the "sober believer" whose faith does not prevent an open-eyed, critical examination of both life and tradition. He argued that a Scripture-based religion can and must avoid fundamentalism by being selective and critical in its reliance on tradition and by re-prioritizing values.

Greenberg devoted most of his attention to the phenomenology of biblical law and religion, the role of the Bible in Jewish thought, and the theory and practice of interpreting biblical texts.[2] One of his most important contributions was his "holistic" method of interpretation, about which we shall have more to say below.

Born in Philadelphia in 1928 and raised in a Hebrew-speaking, Zionist home, Greenberg pursued his doctoral studies at the University of Pennsylvania, where he studied Bible and Assyriology with the Semitist E. A. Speiser and received his Ph.D. in 1954. Simultaneously, he studied Bible and postbiblical Judaica at the Jewish Theological Seminary of America in New York with H. L. Ginsberg, Saul Lieberman, Abraham J. Heschel, and Shalom Spiegel and was ordained there as a rabbi the same year. In addition, he was strongly influenced by the studies of the Israeli scholar Yehezkel Kaufmann in biblical thought and religion.[3] He taught the Bible and Judaica at the University of Pennsylvania from 1954 until1970, when he and his family settled in Israel where he was a professor of Bible at the Hebrew University until retiring in 1996. He died in Jerusalem in 2010.

Greenberg received many honors throughout his career. He was known as an extraordinary teacher—meticulous, methodical, and intellectually inspiring—and, in 1968, won the Danforth Foundation's Harbison Award for Gifted Teaching. He was elected as a fellow of the American Academy of Arts and Sciences and the American Academy of Jewish Research. He was awarded Guggenheim and other research fellowships and received the Biblical Archeology Society's publication Award for his commentary on Ezekiel. In 1994 the State of Israel

---

2. Many of his most notable essays were gathered together in his *Studies in the Bible and Jewish Thought* (Philadelphia: Jewish Publication Society, 1995). A bibliography of his publications to 1997, along with a biographical appreciation of him, may be found in *Tehilla le-Moshe: Biblical and Judaic Studies in Honor of Moshe Greenberg*, ed. M. Cogan, B. L. Eichler, and J. H. Tigay (Winona Lake, IN: Eisenbrauns, 1997) ix–xxxviii. Subsequent publications are listed in RAMBI (The Index of Articles on Jewish Studies of the Jewish National and University Library); online: http://jnul.huji.ac.il/rambi/.

3. Greenberg published an abridgement and translation of vols. 1–7 of Kaufmann's *Toledot ha'Emuna haYisre'elit*, under the title *The Religion of Israel* (Chicago: University of Chicago Press, 1960; reprinted, Jerusalem: Sefer VeSefel, 2003).

awarded him *Pras Yisrael* (the Israel Prize) in Bible, Israel's highest award for personal achievement and public service, and in 1996 he received the Hebrew University's Rothberg Prize for Jewish Education.

Understanding Exodus

Greenberg began his work on the book of Exodus in response to a request from the Melton Research Center of the Jewish Theological Seminary that he write a book that would help American Jewish religious school teachers incorporate the results of modern biblical scholarship in their teaching of Exodus.[4] Deeply committed to Jewish education, Greenberg accepted the assignment and began, in the spring of 1965, by offering a seminar on Exodus to a small group of teachers who were tasked with preparing lesson plans on the basis of his lectures. I had the privilege of being a member of that group. It was in this seminar that Greenberg began to develop what he would later call the "holistic method," and we could see his creativity in bloom as he applied his method to the text. After the conclusion of the seminar an edited version of his lectures, accompanied by the lesson plans, was disseminated by the Melton Center while Greenberg continued his research on Exodus. In 1969 he published *Understanding Exodus*, covering Exodus 1–11.[5] It was at once an aid to teachers and an innovative, substantial contribution to scholarship, acutely sensitive to methodology and brimming with interpretive insights.

Incorporating modern scholarship would naturally include the results of biblical criticism, particularly the Documentary Hypothesis. According to this theory, the Torah was not composed all at once but, rather, was the work of a compiler, or compilers (known as redactors),[6] who wove together four earlier documents, each by a separate author, that

---

4. See Greenberg's comments in "A Faith-ful Jewish Critical Interpretation of the Bible," 211–12. The center had earlier commissioned Nahum M. Sarna's *Understanding Genesis* (New York: Jewish Theological Seminary of America and McGraw-Hill, 1966) for the essentially the same purpose.

5. Other commitments prevented Greenberg from writing a second volume covering the rest of Exodus. Readers will find valuable comments on the rest of the book in his articles "Exodus, Book of," in *Encyclopaedia Judaica*, ed. C. Roth and G. Wigoder (Jerusalem: Keter, 1971) 6:1050–67, and "Šᵉmot, Sefer (Vᵉʾelle) Šᵉmot," in *EM* 8:97–112.

6. The term is used in the sense of editor, but not in the sense of deleting sensitive information as it is frequently used today.

essentially described the same events and phenomena in different and often contradictory ways. The primary clue that led to this hypothesis was the presence in the Torah of various inconsistencies and redundancies, such as the different accounts of creation in Genesis 1 and Genesis 2, the different number of animals Noah is told to take on the ark, seemingly random variations in the names used for God, and redundant accounts of God revealing his name to Moses. These phenomena seem most convincingly explained by the hypothesis that they represent the work of different authors.

The documents posited by this hypothesis are usually referred to as "sources"—meaning written sources—and are known by the abbreviations J, E, P and D (since J and E were combined early, the composite of those two is called JE).[7] In splicing these documents together, the redactor(s) either placed the varying accounts of each episode, in full, one after the other (such as the two accounts of creation in Genesis 1 and 2) or broke them down into smaller components and wove the components from each source together so as to form a single running narrative of the same episode (such as the account of the flood in Gen 6:5—9:17).

Greenberg found this hypothesis convincing, but believed that scholarship has not completed its task until it goes on to ask how all the earlier components, with all of their inconsistencies and redundancies, cohere in the final product, how they work together to communicate the message of the Torah as a whole.[8] Hence the term "holistic," which Greenberg defined, quoting Webster's dictionary, as a method "emphasizing the organic or functional relation between parts and wholes."[9] This focus

---

7. Greenberg refers to JE as "tradition complex A" and to P as "tradition complex B" (see below, 84–86). Apart from a few possible exceptions, Deuteronomy does not figure in Exodus.

8. Greenberg emphasized the importance of the final version since it "is the only historically attested datum," since the earlier sources, being scholarly constructs, are only hypothetical. "[I]t alone has had demonstrable effects; it alone is the undoubted product of Israelite creativity" (*Understanding Exodus*, 4). Greenberg's concern with how the components of composite documents function together in the final product was already evident in his earlier study of Biblical law. See his remarks in "Some Postulates of Biblical Criminal Law," in *Yehezkel Kaufmann Jubilee Volume*, ed. M. Haran (Jerusalem: Magnes, 1960) 26–27.

9. See Greenberg, "The Vision of Jerusalem in Ezekiel 8-11: A Holistic Interpretation," in *The Divine Helmsman: Studies in God's Control of Human Events Presented to Lou H. Silberman*, ed. J. L. Crenshaw and S. Sandmel (New York: Ktav, 1980) 143–64. Greenberg's choice of the term "holistic" was likely inspired by Meir Weiss' method of "Total-Interpretation" (see his comment there, p. 164 n. 7). Unlike his conclusions

dictated the structure of the commentary: rather than a standard verse-by-verse, chapter-by chapter, presentation, Greenberg divided Exodus into literary units determined by the contours of the narrative and, for each unit, discussed (1) "the movement of the story" (2) its "themes and structure," and (3) "the redactional process" by which these were created.

Greenberg's discussion of the process by which each section of Exodus was redacted and how the final product coheres was the most original part of *Understanding Exodus*. A fine example of his method is his study of the narrative in Exodus 3–11, from the burning bush episode through the ninth of the ten plagues. One of the focal points of his analysis is the recognition that the revelation of God's name to Moses in Exod 6:2–8 seems redundant after the same information was already narrated in 3:13–15. Modern source criticism, as Greenberg explains, has shown that these two passages are essentially variant accounts of the same event, the former from the JE source and the latter from the Priestly source, or P. Greenberg goes on to ask why the redactor chose to include both versions, and why he placed the second one exactly where he did, right after the failure of Moses' first meeting with Pharaoh. Focusing on the key words and phrases in the narrative, particularly God's name YHWH ("the Lord" in English) and the phrase "know that I am YHWH," he shows that the redactor very effectively turned the second (P) revelation of God's name from a mere doublet of the first revelation into a rejoinder to both Pharaoh and Moses who, each in his own way, had challenged God's power, capacity and authority—all that is implied by his name: Pharaoh by contemptuously declaring that he does not "know YHWH" and Moses by complaining that speaking to Pharaoh in God's name had made things worse. At the same time, the redactor turned the second revelation into an introduction to the plague story, which revolves around the theme of God's revelation of his name—who he is, his power, his authority—to Pharaoh, to the Egyptians, and to the entire world.

In analyzing the plague narrative itself Greenberg shows how the ten-plague structure was also built out of the two earlier sources, in each

---

regarding Exodus, Greenberg found previous critical analysis of Ezekiel unpersuasive. In his view, careful attention to Ezekiel's style and logic show "a consistent trend of thought expressed in a distinctive style," and indicate that the book was composed by Ezekiel himself and is not a patchwork of original prophecies and numerous additions from later generations. See his commentary, *Ezekiel 1–20* and *Ezekiel 21–37*, Anchor Bible 22, 22A (Garden City, NY: Doubleday, 1983, 1997). His dissatisfaction with critical disintegration of Ezekiel was an important reason for his deciding to write about that book.

of which there were only seven plagues, some identical in both sources and some different. Building on an insight first mentioned by Rashbam and elaborated on by Abarbanel and Cassuto, Greenberg shows that in the present form of the narrative the first nine plagues are arranged in a remarkable symmetrical structure of three triads, in each of which the first, second and third plagues have matching characteristics. In addition, it was the passages from P that saw the plagues as demonstrations of God's power; those from JE conceived of them as punishment. By fusing the two sources the redactor gave the narrative an added dimension: a sense of the multi-valence of events. Such enrichment of the values of the narrative, Greenberg concluded, is characteristic of the redactor's work throughout the Pentateuch.

In ferreting out the redactor's methods Greenberg concluded that the redactor sought to string the variants together in a temporal sequence that would create "a single, reasonably effective narrative out of them. At times we suspect he may have regarded the result as a restoration of the true complexity of the event—a complexity dissolved into its elements among the various traditions he received . . ."[10] In addition, the redactor sometimes ordered the variants in such a way as to achieve a dramatic effect or convey a theological message.[11]

Assessing the results of his analysis of these and other sections of Exodus, Greenberg observed that source criticism provided a valuable stimulus for inquiry that uncovered a grand structure in the present form of the narrative, and that this analysis enables us to appreciate the redactor not as a "second-class mind," as critical scholars had sometimes described him, but as a creative artist who skillfully deployed what tradition gave him and endowed the text with a deeper and richer meaning.

At the same time, Greenberg—ever-conscious of his own methodology and its limits—observed that:

> Such a study, it need hardly be said, is speculative, necessarily bridging over ignorance with hypotheses that cannot be controlled. One may demand that the results be plausible and

---

10. Below, 157.

11. Ibid., 55, 96, 155. See also the observations of R. E. Friedman, who speaks of the redactor being motivated sometimes by "mechanical" considerations (he does not mean the term pejoratively) and sometimes by literary and theological ones. See his "Sacred History and Theology: The Redaction of the Torah," in *The Creation of Sacred Literature: Composition and Redaction of the Biblical Text*, ed. R. E. Friedman (Berkeley: University of California Press, 1981) 25–34.

internally consistent; their probability will depend upon the strength of the evidence, the care with which alternatives have been weighed, on how well-grounded and few the assumptions are.[12]

Although the study of the redactor's work was a focal point of *Understanding Exodus*, the book is filled with deep insights into many other dimensions of Exodus, not the least of which is the psychology of its characters. Here, for example, is Greenberg's summary of Pharaoh's behavior, a summary marked by Greenberg's own insights into human psychology:

> In this dramatic evolution of Pharaoh's reactions, there is a consistency of principle—the core of his intransigence—namely, the maintenance of his sovereignty. That is the crux of the matter; that is the offense to the Godhead's kingship; that is what cannot coexist with God's authority. Thus the opposition of Pharaoh is the archetypal opposition of human power, of human authority to the claims of God. Under pressure it will show flexibility and accommodation, even reversing itself—first by crying for help, then by confessing guilt and making concessions. But after all its retreats, it clings to its last redoubt, a core of self-assertiveness and independence, to surrender which would mean the end of its claim to ultimate, self-sufficient power. Here it resists, careless of the cost, unto death.

Another important feature of *Understanding Exodus* is the way that Greenberg—quite unlike any critical scholar who preceded him—drew on the insights of traditional Jewish commentators. Critically sifting Talmudic-Midrashic works and the medieval commentators, he found a myriad of pertinent interpretations that helped to clarify not only individual passages but also the redactor's achievements. As he explained: "since premodern exegetes shared our interest in the text as a whole, we can profitably have recourse to them. At the very least, their assumption of the integrity of the text has heuristic value for us."

When Greenberg began his work on Exodus he noted that scholarship had begun to show interest in the design of composite creations. But to the best of my knowledge no scholar who had expressed an interest in design had actually given more than a brief nod to source criticism. None

---

12. *Understanding Exodus*, 51. See also Greenberg's methodological remarks in "The Thematic Unity of Exodus III–XI," in *Fourth World Congress of Jewish Studies* (Jerusalem: World Union of Jewish Studies, 1967) 1:151–54.

had engaged in both types of investigation, detailed source criticism and analysis of design, as did Greenberg. In the decades that followed, this changed, and a positive appreciation of redactors' contributions has become a prominent feature of biblical scholarship. Robert Alter, a prominent exponent of the literary analysis of the Bible, has written of the "composite artistry" of the Bible: "even if the text is really composite in origin, I think we have seen ample evidence of how brilliantly it has been woven into a complex artistic whole."[13] Richard Elliott Friedman, author of the well-known *Who Wrote the Bible?*, explains how the redactor's combination of sources "produced something that was more than the sum of the pieces. The story was now richer, with new interpretive possibilities . . . The mixing of the sources into one text enriched the interpretive possibilities of the Bible for all time."[14] The Pontifical Biblical Commission expressed its appreciation of "Redaction Criticism"[15] as the final stage (following source- and other types of criticism) in a critical analysis of the Biblical text:

> Finally, redaction criticism studies the modifications that these texts have undergone before being fixed in their final state, [and] it also analyzes this final stage, trying as far as possible to identify the tendencies particularly characteristic of this concluding process . . . While the preceding steps have sought to explain the text by tracing its origin and development within a diachronic perspective, this last step concludes with a study that is synchronic: At this point the text is explained as it stands, on the basis of the mutual relationships between its diverse elements,

---

13. Alter, *The Art of Biblical Narrative: A Literary Approach to the Bible* (New York: Basic Books, 1981) 20, 131–54. See also his *The Five Books of Moses* (New York: Norton, 2004) xv–xvi.

14. Friedman, *Who Wrote the Bible?* (New York: Harper & Row, 1987) 234–45. See also his "Sacred History and Theology," cited above.

15. The term is essentially equivalent to "holistic method." Redaction criticism studies "the way the writers of the materials, as we now have them, selected, combined, and arranged already existing materials to express special concerns and emphases" and employed "structural and thematic patterns . . . to create a finely crafted, aesthetic final product." See H. J. Flanders Jr. et al., eds., *People of the Covenant* (New York: Oxford University Press, 1996) 34; M. Brettler and A. Berlin, "The Modern Study of the Bible," in Brettler and Berlin, eds., *The Jewish Study Bible* (New York: Oxford University Press, 2003) 2088; M. E. Biddle, "Redaction Criticism, Hebrew Bible," in J. H. Hayes, ed., *Dictionary of Biblical Interpretation* (Nashville: Abingdon, 1999) 2:373–76.

and with an eye to its character as a message communicated by the author to his contemporaries.[16]

⸙

Moshe Greenberg's *Understanding Exodus* remains a model of careful and simultaneous engagement with both source analysis and the coherence of the final version of a biblical book and its message, and a model, as well, of an original and clearly articulated scholarly methodology. Its republication is a welcome gift for students, teachers, and scholars alike.

—Jeffrey H. Tigay

---

16. "The Interpretation of the Bible in the Church," Presented by the Pontifical Biblical Commission to Pope John Paul II on April 23, 1993 (as published in *Origins*, January 6, 1994; online: http://catholic-resources.org/ChurchDocs/PBC_Interp-FullText.htm). The document included a preface by then Cardinal Joseph Ratzinger (later Pope Benedict XVI). The statement continues as follows: "At this point one is in a position to consider the demands of the text from the point of view of action and life . . . [I]t is the text in its final stage, rather than in its earlier editions, which is the expression of the word of God." In its religious appreciation of the final, redacted document the Pontifical Institute statement has a predecessor in an often-quoted letter by the Jewish theologian Franz Rosenzweig (1886–1929):
> Whoever he was and whatever material he had at his disposal, [the Redactor] is our Teacher, his theology is our Teaching. For example: even if criticism should be right and it were true that Genesis 1 and 2 really stemmed from distinct authors . . . even then, what we must know about creation is not to be got out of one of the two chapters alone, but only out of taking them together and harmonized—and from the harmonization precisely of their apparent contradictions from which critical analysis starts: namely the "cosmological" creation leading to man of the first chapter and the "anthropological" creation beginning with man of the second. Only this . . . is the Teaching.

See Martin Buber and Franz Rosenzweig, *Scripture and Translation*, trans. Lawrence Rosenwald with Everett Fox (Bloomington: Indiana University Press, 1994) 22–23.

Preface to the Second Edition

Moshe Greenberg's *Understanding Exodus* was first published in 1969. This new edition incorporates clarifications he made during the years 2005–2009. After Prof. Greenberg's death in 2010, conversations with Mrs. Evelyn Greenberg about publishing the revised edition led to my joining her in the project. I was very happy with the opportunity to help make this pioneering book available to a new generation of readers. Mrs. Greenberg was a constant source of information and helpful advice about her husband's intentions and preferences. Her contributions were indispensable.

For the present edition, indexes have been added, as well as an appendix, "Questions for Uncovering the Message of a Biblical Text," which is a translation of a guide that Prof. Greenberg prepared for his students at the Hebrew University. The new subtitle, "A Holistic Commentary to Exodus 1–11," is based on his later writing about his approach. Editorial changes include revisions to the abbreviations, bibliography and footnotes, including citation of translations of certain scholarly works that were available only in Hebrew or German when the book was first published.

A serendipitous meeting with Dr. K.C. Hanson, Editor-in-Chief, led to Wipf & Stock's acceptance of this revised edition for publication. Sincere thanks to him and the entire staff of Wipf & Stock for all their expert work.

—Jeffrey H. Tigay

Acknowledgments

Aiming to compose a commentary on Exodus that is neither as exhaustive spiritually as Benno Jacob's, nor as thoroughgoingly critical as August Dillmann's, but has literary-critical purposes of its own, I have sought and received comment and advice from various people, thanks to whom this work is less diffuse, erratic, and unpolished than it would have been otherwise.

Drafts of the first part were read and annotated by Edwin M. Good of Stanford University and Brevard S. Childs of Yale. What I have cited of theirs is attributed to them; but I wish to acknowledge here my debt to them for what cannot be specifically attributed: for encouragement given at the initial stages of the work.

Haim Blanc of the Hebrew University gave later portions the kind of friendly, critical hearing that any author would covet. Sara Groll (Hebrew University) responded graciously to queries on Egyptological matters—though responsibility for the present formulation is mine alone.

Golda Werman of Jerusalem markedly improved the style and clarity of the parts of the manuscript she was good enough to read.

This work was begun in 1965 at the invitation of Seymour Fox, then Associate Dean of the Teachers Institute, the Jewish Theological Seminary of America, and Executive Chairman of its Melton Research Center. Other obligations kept me from completing it as soon as I had wished. What is presented here is Part I of a work still in progress. As I proceed, my thought on the material is likely to undergo change. In spite of its provisional state, at the urging of Louis Newman, the Center's Director, I have launched it on its public career in the hope that it will be of use even so, and that reaction to it will be helpful toward improving its final shape.

Moshe Greenberg
Jerusalem
Nisan, 5729—March 1969

Abbreviations

Abarbanel	Don Isaac Abarbanel, exegete, Spain, 1437–1508
ANEP	*The Ancient Near East in Pictures.* Edited by James B. Pritchard
ANET	*Ancient Near Eastern Texts Relating to the Old Testament.* Edited by James B. Pritchard
Ant.	Josephus, *Antiquities of the Jews*
BA	*Biblical Archaeologist*
Bahya	R. Bahya ben ʾAšer, exegete, Spain, 1255–1340
BDB	F. Brown, S. R. Driver, C. A. Briggs, *A Hebrew and English Lexicon of the Old Testament*
BH³	R. Kittel and P. Kahle, editors, *Biblia Hebraica*, 3rd ed.
BSh	R. Yosef Bᵉkor Šor, exegete, France, 12th century
BZAW	Beiheft zur Zeitschrift für die alttestamentliche Wissenschaft
EM	*ʾEnṣiqlopedia Miqraʾit*, 1–5. Jerusalem, 1950–1968
Gk	Greek "Septuagint" translation of the Torah
Hizquni	R. Ḥizqia ben Manoah, exegete, 13c.
IDB	*Interpreter's Dictionary of the Bible*, 4 vols., edited by George Arthur Buttrick
IE	R. Abraham ibn Ezra, exegete, Spain, 1089–1164
JBL	*Journal of Biblical Literature*
JNES	*Journal of Near Eastern Studies*

Kimhi	R. David Kimḥi, grammarian and exegete, Provence, 1160?–1235?
Letteris	Meir Halevy Letteris, editor, *Sefer Torah Nᵉbiʾim Ukᵉtubim*
Maharal	Judah Loew ben Bezalel, talmudist, author of supercommentary *Gur ʾArye* to Rashi, Prague, ca. 1525–1609
Maharzu	R. Ze'ev Wolf Einhorn, commentator on Midrash Rabba, Eastern Europe, d. 1862
Maimonides, Code	Moses Maimonides (philosopher and codifier, Spain, North Africa and Egypt, 1135–1204), *Mišne Tora*
Malbim	R. Meir Leibush ben Yᵉḥiel Michael, exegete, Eastern Europe, 1809–1879
Maʾor	Nethanel b. Isaiah (14th century), *Sefer Maʾor ha-ʾªfelah*, ed. by Y. Kafaḥ (Qafiḥ), Jerusalem, 1957
Meiri	R. Menaḥem b. Solomon Meʾiri, commentator on the Talmud, Provence, 1249–1316
Mek.	*Mᵉkilta dᵉRabbi Yišmaʿʾel*, ed. J. Z. Lauterbach, Philadelphia, 1933–35
Mek. deRashbi	*Mᵉkilta dᵉR. Šimʿon bar Yoḥay*, ed. J. N. Epstein and Ezra Zion Melamed. Jerusalem, 5715 [1965]
Meṣudat David	Part of a two-tiered commentary (*Mᵉṣudat David* and *Mᵉṣudat Ṣiyon*) on the Prophets and the Writings by R. David and R. Yᵉḥiel Hillel Altschuler, E. Europe, 18th century
Mey.	"Peruš R. Mᵉyuḥas ʿal Šᵉmot," ed. A.W. Greenup, *Ha-Ṣofe Lᵉḥokmat Yisraʾel* 13, pp. 1–81, 121–82, Budapest, 1929
MGWJ	*Monatsschrift für Geschichte und Wissenschaft des Judentums*
MHG	*Midrash Haggadol, Exodus*, ed. M. Margulies, Jerusalem, 5716 [1956]
MT	Masoretic text
NJPS	*The Torah: The Five Books of Moses, A New Translation*, 2nd ed., Philadelphia, 1967

Noth, *UG*	Martin Noth, *Überlieferungsgeschichte des Pentateuch*, Stuttgart, 1948
Onk.	*Targum Onkelos*
OTS	*Oudtestamentische Studiën*
Pal. Targs.	Palestinian Targums, i.e. Targum *"Jonathan"* and Targum *"Yᵉrušalmi"* (the "Fragment Targum")
Pir. deRab. El.	*Pirqe dᵉRabbi Eliʿezer*
Qafiḥ	Y. Qafiḥ, *Peruše Rabbenu Saʿadya Gaʾon ʿal ha-Torah*
R.	Rabbi
Ralbag	R. Levi ben Geršom (Gersonides), exegete, France, 1288–1344
Ramban	R. Moše ben Naḥman (Nachmanides), exegete, Spain, 1194–1270
Ran	Rabbenu Nissim b. Reuben Gerondi, Talmudist, Spain, 14th century
Rashbam	R. Šᵉmuel ben Meir, exegete, France, 1080–1158
Rashi	R. Šᵉlomo Yiṣhaqi, exegete, France, 1040–1105
RB	*Revue Biblique*
RI	Yehezkel Kaufmann, *The Religion of Israel*
RSV	Revised Standard Version of the Bible
Saadya	Saʿadya Gaʾon (Saadya ben Joseph), grammarian, exegete, translator, philosopher, Iraq, 882–942 (see Qafiḥ)
Saadya, *ʾᵉmunot wᵉDeʿot*	Saadya's philosophical treatise (*"The Book of Beliefs and Opinions"*)
Sam.	Samaritan Pentateuch
Shadal	Šᵉmuel David Luzzatto, exegete, translator and philosopher, Italy, 1800–1865
ShR	*Šᵉmot Rabba*
ST	*Sekel Tob*, midrash and commentary, Menaḥem ben Šᵉlomo, Italy, 12th century
Tanḥuma	*Midrash Tanḥuma* on the Torah

Targs.	Targums
TJ	*Targum Jonathan*
Tosefot Yom Tov	Commentary on the Mishna by Yom Tov Lipmann Heller, E. Europe, 1579–1654
TY	*Targum Yᵉrušalmi*
VT	*Vetus Testamentum*
ZAW	*Zeitschrift für die alttestamentliche Wissenschaft*

Purpose and Method

This work is an attempt to understand the book of Exodus.

The conception of a book posited here is: an organization of literary units meant to convey a complex ideational message. Articulation into subunits and organization into a coherent whole are the essential characteristics.

By ideational message we do not mean the mind of the author—his ideology, his worldview, or even his intention, but only what is found in the components of the book and implied by the manner of their disposition. While extrinsic information may bear on the message (as when textual corruption is remediable through knowledge of early writing), and the ideology or historical background of the author may offer clues to the meaning of elements in the book, the primary object of understanding is the book's own message, and that must be gathered in the final analysis from the book itself. The relevance of extrinsic information can be tested by its ability to illuminate the inner coherence of the book's elements; whatever helps to explain why a given item is as it is or where it is in the book is a contribution to understanding.

Every literary work reflects its author's ordering of a segment of thought or experience. The ideational message is the coherence of that segment. Even if the components of the work are not entirely the creation of the author, even if they have been no more than collected and arranged by him, it is still valid to speak of the book's message.

Understanding a book means, then, understanding its message through grasping the coherence of its elements. Theoretically this can be divided into steps: first, grasping the internal coherence of the subunits, then the interrelation of the sub-units making up the coherence of the whole. But in reality the "small" and "large" coherence constantly interact and are often inseparable.

Is Exodus a book in the usual sense—a self-contained narrative with a beginning and an end presenting a defined segment of experience?[1] Obviously it is not entirely so. Exodus is one of the "fifths" (ḥomeš, pl. ḥomašim [popularly, ḥumaš, pl. ḥumašim]) of the Torah; it continues a narrative started in Genesis and introduces persons and themes that will be found in Leviticus and beyond.

The beginning and the end of the book indicate that it was designed as a distinct literary unit. Exodus 1:1 does not pick up where Gen 50:26 left off. The first verses of Exodus recapitulate the main event of the last chapters of Genesis: the descent of Jacob's family to, and their settlement in, Egypt. Into the recapitulation the true start of the new narrative has been interwoven (Exod 1:6–7). This manner of opening the narrative means that an author (or a creative redactor) regarded the events about to be narrated as making a sufficiently important break with the past to merit a new start. He therefore provided them with a prologue signifying a new literary unit.

In the same way, the last verses of Exodus are not a natural sequel to what precedes them. The proper continuation of 40:35 ("Moses could not enter the Tent, etc.") is Lev 1:1 ("The Lord called to Moses and spoke to him from the Tent, etc."; cf. IE). Exodus 40:36–38, describing how the indwelling cloud of the Lord guided Israel in their journeys, anticipate Num 9:15–23. Chronologically they are out of place, since the journeying did not begin until after the inauguration of the Tabernacle (Leviticus 8–9). A formative hand is again in evidence, rounding off the account of the tent with a glance ahead to the fulfillment of its purpose (cf. Exod 25:8; 29:43, 45).

The book thus has an epilogue marking its conclusion no less definitely than the prologue marks its beginning.

To these indications that the present book of Exodus was designed as a distinct literary unit within the larger framework of the Pentateuch must be added the balance of its parts. The book falls into halves: chapters

---

1. Modern scholarship regards the material of Exodus as stemming from various tradition-complexes. That does not militate against considering Exodus a book in the usual sense. Historical narratives composed of sources interwoven with or without editorial comment may certainly constitute a coherent literary entity (cf. P. Angel's biography of Lincoln, or M. Hadas's history of Rome). Modern analysis of the Pentateuch assumes a redactor to whom the present amalgam is due, and it cannot be gainsaid that a coherent message has resulted from his work. The question is, then, whether there is justification for regarding Exodus as a work in itself, apart from the Pentateuch to which it (and its analyzed tradition-complexes) belong.

1–19 relating the preparations for the covenant joining God and Israel, chapters 20–40 relating the establishing of the covenant. The central chapters 19–20 describe the climax of the affair—the direct contact between God and all Israel whereby all "saw their king."[2]

These circumstances justify the surmise that the design of the book is as old as its present form. Inquiry into the lineaments of this design is therefore in order, as well as an expectation of a higher level of coherence than might be present in a merely artificial segment of a larger work. Whether that surmise and expectation are ultimately justified must await the results of inquiry.

The Masoretic text of the book of Exodus is the text-form of our study. That is not because of a dogmatic assurance of the impeccability of that text-form, but because (1) the received Hebrew is the best witness to the lost originals[3] and (2) because the study of the received Hebrew is aided and enriched by the greatest number of explications, extensive records of which remain from Mishnaic times onward. Part of our task will be to criticize alternative interpretations of a given passage.

We first resort to philology: lexical aids to clarify verbal obscurities, grammatical aids to explain the use of words in sentences.

Since the best is not always the latest, an effort will be made to exploit more fully than usual premodern sources of information.[4] To understand the coherence of sentences and paragraphs, and the unifying themes that bind literary units, the results of premodern study are at least as valuable as modern efforts.

Modern exegetes are inclined to devote attention to matters other than the message of the present text. Ever since the discovery of the composite nature of the Pentateuch in the seventeenth century, scholarship has focused on the elaboration of the findings and historical implications of the source analysis. Attention has been diverted from the textual entity transmitted by tradition to its newly analyzed, hypothetically reconstructed elements. This is sometimes justified on the ground

---

2. *Mek.* at 19:9 end.

3. While the Gk attests to an earlier text-form, it is neither in the original language nor itself free from corruption; its ultimate relation to the original where it diverges from the MT is still unclear. Samaritan and Qumran fragments offer some variant Hebrew readings that will be noted when they substantially affect the understanding of a passage. On the history of the received text see Cross, *Ancient Library of Qumran*, 161–94.

4. For our purposes a work is premodern if its viewpoint is uncolored by the systematic biblical and philological criticism that arose in the seventeenth century.

that the elements reflect higher, pristine levels of spiritual power; that the compilation of elements into the traditional, received form is the work of a second-class mind.[5] But the received text is the only historically attested datum; it alone has had demonstrable effects; it alone is the undoubted product of Israelite creativity.

True, there are strong indications that the text is composite, but there is also evidence that the composition was thoughtful and expressive of a viewpoint that merits consideration in its own right. The hypothetical reconstruction of the primary components of our text is a legitimate, indeed an inevitable, exercise of historical-philological imagination. But preoccupation with such exercise to the virtual exclusion of other interests is unjustifiable.

Paying due attention to the work of composition, our effort will be directed primarily toward understanding how the redactor (or a contemporary) might have grasped the text in its wholeness. And since premodern exegetes shared our interest in the text as a whole, we can profitably have recourse to them. At the very least, their assumption of the integrity of the text has heuristic value for us.[6]

Resort to these exegetes seriously complicates our task, and not merely by adding much more data to be processed. For the view taken of the message of the text by the best exegetes often turns out to be as varied as the number of exegetes considered. Private or temporally conditioned notions have been imported that can only annoy, when they do not frustrate, the seeker after the plain meaning. The question may therefore be legitimately raised whether the premoderns are truly helpful toward achieving our goal.

Were the text not frequently elliptical, the juxtaposition of its elements not often surprising, its play on sound and numbers not often missed by the modern ear, consideration of premodern exegesis would indeed be merely tedious. But the text in fact is regularly elliptical, omitting motives and syntactical connections. Since the modern reader has no assurance that his supplied connection is apt, coming as he does from

---

5. Fohrer, *Überlieferung und Geschichte des Exodus*, 5; cf. Winnett: "What makes ... great literature is ... some gifted mind which fuses and transforms ... diverse elements into an ordered and organic whole ... All we know of the [redactors] is strongly against [the] assumption [that they had such minds]" (13).

6. Contrasting positions on this issue are taken by Noth (*Exodus*, 18) and Cassuto (*Šᵉmot*, vii [ET = *Exodus*, 1]); see also Greenberg, "Thematic Unity," 151; and McCarthy, "Moses' Dealings," 336–37.

a radically different context—since sometimes no connection at all comes to his mind—the suggestions of early exegetes, of different cultural settings, as to possibilities of coherence are welcome even when not decisive.

It is the same with the juxtaposition of apparently unrelated materials. Modern scholars tend to view inconsequence as a normal result of the redactor's limitations. They are thus prone to interpret as flaws what are in fact the workings of an established principle of ancient composition: linkage through associational, rather than chronological or topical, considerations. But even if one should recognize this principle, occasions arise when, with all the good will in the world, the links between pieces are obscure. Here again the premoderns may be consulted with profit. They are steeped in associative thinking and suggest connections that would never have occurred to a modern reader.

Finally, the flood of verbiage to which we are subjected has so impaired our sensitivity to the use of words that we have trouble reading the works of a less voluble age and clime, when talk was briefer and more charged with meaning, when culture was more homogeneous and speech could therefore be more allusive. Premoderns cherished word plays and heard them everywhere. They were familiar with symbolically numbered repetitions and did not have to be nudged, as does the modern reader, to find them in the sacred text. In these respects premodern exegetes were closer to the ancient modes of expression than we; hence reading them is a freshening experience.

On the other hand, consideration of early exegesis complicates judgment on the message of the text by introducing more possibilities of interpretation than the modern reader is able to handle. He will reject some possibilities out of hand as alien importations, often based on later religious, philosophical, or scientific issues. He will find others that remain, after every effort to decide between them, as competing candidates for the plain sense. Sometimes he will be forced to conclude that the text is irreducibly, perhaps intentionally, ambiguous. At the very least, his appreciation of the latent and manifest meanings of the text will be heightened.

When all aids have been exhausted, difficulties will remain—not merely lexical, but problems of coherence, apparent flaws in design. The assumption of textual integrity made by all premodern exegetes ceases to have heuristic value in these circumstances. An awkward juncture, a break in continuity, inconsistency, duplication—these signal to us a discontinuity of the textual fabric; heterogeneous materials have been joined together. The assumption of integrity led premoderns to strained and fanciful interpretations of these phenomena. The modern hypothesis that they arose out of the combination of diverse elements, while not in itself illuminating the meaning, accounts for the difficulty in a reasonable way.

But we cannot be content with this accounting for the flaw, because if it is visible to us it must also have been visible to the ancients. Precisely the assumption that the flaw arose from the work of composition forces on us the question: What gain flowed from the flawed text that made its production worthwhile to the ancients? We shall try in each case to suggest an answer, aware that it can hardly be more than tentative.

These general considerations dictate the form of our exposition.

We shall begin with a discussion of the larger coherence of Exodus as an element in the Torah book. Then we shall proceed to our main task, the detailed literary study. We shall analyze, one by one, the literary units of the book. The material will be divided and subdivided on the basis of pauses in the action of the story, changes in literary genres, or formal indicators. Each subdivision will be paraphrased to set forth the action of the story in narrative passages and the associative links in non-narrative passages. Items meriting discussion will be taken up in notes whose exclusive purpose is to contribute to understanding the line of thought. Historical and philological information is strictly subordinated to that purpose.

The material of the subdivisions will then be surveyed as a whole, and the themes and structure of the larger unit they constitute will be explicated. Justification of the proposed divisions of the material will be made, and the means whereby they are given form and unity will be indicated.

Finally, the work of the redactor will be discussed. Our point of departure is the question: What did the redactor mean by putting the material together as he did? We shall try to distinguish the work of the final redactor from earlier stages of combination of the material. Our chief clues will be evidence that heterogeneous materials have been joined together; our chief interest, the values arising out of the redactorial work. Even during this most speculative part of our inquiry, the focus will remain on the message and meaning of the text.

Exodus in the Context of Torah

What role was the Torah designed to play in the life of Israel?

The following passage offers a convenient point of departure for an answer:

> When, in time to come, your son asks you, "What are these injunctions, laws and rules which the Lord our God has enjoined upon you?" you shall say to your son, "We were slaves to Pharaoh in Egypt and the Lord freed us from Egypt with a mighty hand. The Lord wrought before our eyes marvelous and destructive signs and portents in Egypt, against Pharaoh and all his household; and us he freed from there, that he might take us and give us the land that he had promised on oath to our fathers. Then the Lord commanded us to observe all these laws, to revere the Lord our God for our lasting good and for our survival, as is now the case. It will therefore be to our merit before the Lord our God to observe faithfully this whole Instruction, as he has commanded us." (Deut. 6:20–25)

The main themes of the father's reply are: (1) the wonderful liberation from Egypt, preliminary to the fulfillment of the promise of land made to the patriarchs; (2) the subsequent giving of the laws, whose observance is a meritorious reverencing of their giver. The two are implicitly related: what God did for Israel authorized him to lay down the law for them. When, faithful to his oath, he delivered them from slavery, he became their king, and as such, was entitled to their obedience. Thus the answer to the child's question takes the form of a history lesson. Israel's religiosity is its response to the will of him who granted it freedom and life as an independent people, a response compounded of awe in the presence of such a mighty God, gratitude for his attention to Israel's need, and loyalty to him who kept faith with men. That the laws were inherently wise and righteous was recognized; acknowledgment of their intrinsic value is put into the mouth of gentiles "who on hearing of all these Laws will say,

'Surely, that great nation is a wise and discerning people.' For . . . What great nation has laws and rules as perfect as all this teaching that I set before you this day?" (Deut 4:6, 8). But the motive urged here for observing God's law is that obedience is the proper response of those who have been saved and sustained by him.[1]

It is also said that the observance of the laws is "for our lasting good and for our survival." Obedience is beneficial—either because God's favor will be gained or because the laws are inherently good, it is not said which. In any case, since God is a compassionate king, as his care of Israel has demonstrated, it is understood that his will toward men will be for their well-being. This understanding too is based on the redemption from Egypt, in which God impressed on Israel for all time his faithful and benign nature. God's authority to command, and Israel's obligation to obey, both spring from historical experience rather than from abstract reflection on the intrinsic worth of the laws.[2]

Both main themes of the reply, as well as its time-horizon, correspond to what is found in the Torah book as a whole. The time range of Genesis to Deuteronomy extends from the promise to the fathers to the verge of its fulfillment in the Conquest. The themes that run through the Torah are the promise to the fathers, the liberation from Egypt and the giving of the Covenant laws. Hence the child's questions discover the motive of the composition of the entire Torah. The Torah is the rationale, in its most extended and detailed form of Israel's peculiar way of life—its values, its religious behavior and customs, its attitudes toward God and man. And the Torah consists of two chief parts corresponding to the father's reply: a narrative of God's acts for Israel, and the stipulations of his Covenant with them.

Since Israel's peculiar way of life was the due response to God's redemptive acts, it was crucial that generations that did not themselves witness these acts, or experience the signs and wonders, be made to feel something of their impact. Children of succeeding ages must be able to say, with their fathers "It is because of what the Lord did for me when I

---

1. Similar historical rationales for observances are given for the first-fruit offering (Deut 26:3–10), the firstborn offering (Exod 13:11–16), and, in Ps 105:45, for the law as a whole.

2. IE to Deut 6:20: "The meaning of the child's question is, Why must we alone among men bear this yoke? You answer that God redeemed us from the house of bondage and since he worked this good for us we are obliged to revere him. We know that he has done good to us in the past, and he will do so in the future, and preserve us, for his commandments are life for all who possess them."

went free from Egypt" (Exod 13:8). The recurrent festivals of Israel were dedicated to celebrate the redemptive events. The spring festival, the combination of Passover and Unleavened Bread (Exod 12:14ff.; 13:5ff.), readily lent itself to the purpose, as the anniversary of the Exodus. The autumn festival is so dedicated in the formulation of Lev 23:43.[3] Other rites too, such as the offering and redemption of first fruits and firstborn, were turned into memorials to the Exodus. These religious occasions were doubtless interpreted to the participants by means of liturgies that recited the redemptive history in précis, drawn from the fuller narrative traditions.[4]

To the preservation of these fuller traditions the literary efforts of Israel were dedicated. References to writing in the Torah are all connected with the recording of God's benefactions or messages to Israel, or reflections thereon: the miraculous victory over Amalek (Exod 17:14); the event and content of the Sinaitic Covenant, including the Decalogue (Exod 24:4; 34:27–28); the list of stations on the wilderness journey (Num 33:2); the admonitory song of Moses (Deut. 31:22); and, most extensively, the last edifying words of Moses (Deut 31:9). The written scroll of Torah served as a testimony (Deut 31:26), a lasting witness that could far outlive the persons whose words it bore, and communicate to generations the testimony of those who saw. The care taken to preserve these words through centuries of war and other disasters until they could be assembled in their standard, maximal form in the Torah bespeaks their vital importance to the community. A people whose distinctive way of life, whose very reason for being, was accounted for by events in its past must necessarily give the preservation of the literary witnesses to those events first place in its order of priorities.

Israel's absorbing concern over its reason for being—which made the Torah so cherished a treasure—is unprecedented in antiquity. No Near Eastern analogues to a national literature like that of the Torah are available. Whether the literatures of the Arameans, the Moabites, or the Edomites once contained similar material is unknown. But the considerable literary remains of Egypt, Babylonia, the Hittites and Ugarit offer no parallels to the message of, and the national function served by, the Torah.

Why should Israel have felt this concern so acutely?

3. The first-fruits festival (as opposed to the individual first-fruit gift in Deuteronomy 26) cannot be shown to have been so transformed before postbiblical times.

4. Such a précis is, e.g., the recitation of the farmer in Deuteronomy 26.

Perhaps owing to its consciousness of being a late-born people, of having come onto the stage only after all its neighbors had already assumed their historical roles. Biblical traditions concerning the beginnings of nations (e.g., Genesis 10) conspicuously fail to list Israel among the primary descendants of Noah's sons—though Egypt, Canaan, and Assyria appear there. Ammon, Moab, and Edom were nations dwelling in their lands when Israel was still seeking its patrimony. Kings ruled Edom before any king reigned in Israel. In order to acquire its homeland Israel had to dispossess the nations living in Canaan.

Being born into a world full of nations made the existence of Israel problematic from the start; it was anything but natural and self-explanatory. In order to justify itself, this late-born and rootless people looked to the Torah of its God. That alone gave it a reason for being and a warrant of survival.

Just because such a reason and warrant were needed from the beginning, the assertion that traditions embodying them were indited and transmitted from earliest times is credible. And the persistence of the need is why Israel clung to them, in spite of occasional lapses, through the ages.

The scope of the Torah was determined by its role of providing the reason for Israel's national existence. Since that reason was observance of the Covenant, the accounts giving the antecedents of the Covenant (Genesis) and the circumstances of its establishment (Exodus–Deuteronomy), together with the detail of its terms (Exodus–Deuteronomy), constitute the Torah.

The Covenant was mediated through Moses, and this mediation extended to the end of his life (cf. the second Covenant ceremony with the children of the Exodus generation in Deut 29:9ff.).[5] Hence the Torah ends with the death of Moses. Nothing new with regard to the fundamental conditions of Israel's national existence arose after Moses' death. Israelite history thereafter was understood as the consequence of the arrangement that God made with Israel through the agency of Moses.

---

5. "Moses probably performed another Covenant ceremony with them, similar to the one he had performed at Sinai, with a whole-offering, and a sprinkling of half its blood on the altar and half on the people. But there was no need to repeat the story of it . . ." (Ramban). It is true that Joshua and king Josiah also mediated covenants with the people (Joshua 24; 2 Kings 23), but unlike Moses, they did not reveal any new content; the mediation of Moses disclosed to Israel its reason for being, that of his successors only reaffirmed it.

Now there is a remarkable gap between the promises made to the Patriarchs and the fulfillment at the time of Moses' death. The Israelites had indeed proliferated and become a great nation, but they had not yet come into possession of their land. The history recounted in the Torah cries to be supplemented by the account of the Conquest of Canaan, and the bond between the Torah and the book of Joshua was recognized from early times.

> Said R. Ada son of R. Hanina: "Had Israel not sinned they would have had as holy scripture only the Torah and the book of Joshua, in which the division of the land is made." (*Nedarim* 22b)

Critics speak of the Hexateuch—the Torah plus the book of Joshua—as presenting a continuous interweaving of Israelite traditions concerning beginnings. Yet the Hexateuch is a product of critical theorizing, while the Pentateuch alone is a historical entity—at least as early as the Samaritan schism. The constitution of Israel, the Torah, ends without telling the story of the Conquest. This is a fact of the first importance; it signifies the absolute character of the Covenantal obligation in contrast to the conditioned character of the possession of the land. The point deserves elaboration.

The events on which God's claim on Israel is based are the Exodus, what preceded it in Egypt and what followed it in the wilderness. By virtue of his freeing them, Israel became his people and he their God (Exod 6:7; Hos 12:10; 13:4; Ps 114:1–2); he invited them to accept his Covenant on the basis of his mighty acts on their behalf prior to Sinai (Exod 19:4ff.); his authority to command the Decalogue flows from his liberating them (20:2);[6] the liberation was a sufficient precondition for God's dwelling amidst Israel in the wilderness (in the tabernacle, 29:46); apostasy violates a relation established between God and Israel at the Exodus (Deut 13:6).[7]

---

6. "Why didn't the Torah begin with the Decalogue? A parable will explain it: A man entered a country and said, 'Make me your king.' The people replied, 'What have you ever done for us that we should make you our king?' So he built them walls, made them water-works, fought wars on their behalf. Then he said to them, 'Make me your king,' and they replied, 'Yes indeed!' Thus God liberated Israel from Egypt, divided the sea for them, gave them manna from heaven, provided them with a water supply, provisioned them with quail, fought Amalek on their behalf, then said to them, 'Make me your king,' whereupon they replied, 'Yes indeed'" (*Mek., Yitro*, 5).

7. J. Wijngaards ("הוציא and העלה") has discerned the prominence of the theme of God the Liberator in the legislative parts of the Pentateuch. Without reference to

Thus, the obligation to recognize God's sovereignty and accept his Covenant laws arises out of the relationship established between God and Israel at the Exodus. In spite of the connection of liberation with landgiving in God's promise (e.g., Exod 3:8, 17; 6:6-8; Deut 6:23), the two are separated with respect to the onset of the Covenant obligations. The Covenant became binding on Israel before they took possession of their land.

To be sure, many stipulations of the law are explicitly contingent on Israel's settlement in Canaan (e.g., Exod 23:10ff.; Lev 19:23). Yet fundamental obligations take effect immediately; e.g., the exclusive allegiance to God (Exod 32:8), the Sabbath law (Num 15:32ff.), the Passover rite (Num 9:4ff.), rules of clean and unclean (e.g., Lev 13:46), the restriction of slaughter to the sanctuary precinct (Lev 17:3ff.), and so forth. Even the stipulations that come into effect on land settlement derive their obligatoriness from the Covenant concluded at, and in effect from, Sinai. If the landtaking be delayed a year, twenty years, or forty years, nothing in the mutual bond of God and Israel is affected. The operativeness of the Covenant laws did not depend on Israel's entrance into the land.

The distinction between the two comes out very clearly in the warnings with which Leviticus (26) and Deuteronomy (28) conclude. The warnings assume that Israel's obligation to keep the Covenant is absolute, having set in when the Covenant was made. What is conditional is Israel's future well-being. If Israel will obey God, they will live securely in their land; otherwise they will perish and be exiled from it.

The Torah thus ends with Moses' death because by that juncture it has related all that is needed to provide the rationale for Israel's way of life. Since that way consisted of a life bound by God's Covenant, it need tell only those events on which the Covenant obligation rested. The story of the conquest could be left out since settlement of the land was not such an event.

The idea that the Covenant obligation took effect prior to and independently of the landtaking had fateful consequences. Thanks to it, when the kingdom of Judah fell, the Judean exiles were able to conceive of the Covenant's validity even when they were no longer in their land. It was a bold and unprecedented thought, but it had its roots in the Torah itself. Just as the obligation was independent of the landtaking before Israel came to their land, so it could be again after they had been exiled from it. And just as keeping the Covenant was a condition of possession of the

---

the landgiving, the liberation from Egypt is a sufficient ground for the stipulations of the Covenant.

land before it was conquered, so now it was conceived to be a condition of its repossession.

There is thus an integral relation between the exclusion of the book of Joshua from the Torah and the Covenant's surviving the Exile, between the idea that the Covenant took effect even before Israel took their land and the decision made by the exiles still to be bound by the Covenant even after they had been expelled from it.

After the description given in Genesis of Israel's antecedents and the promises made to the patriarchs, the book of Exodus (Gk *Exodos* "departure" [scil., from Egypt]; from Hebrew (*homeš*) *yᵉṣiʾat miṣrayim* "[the fifth concerning] the departure from Egypt") relates the fulfillment of the promises in three great divisions:

(1) **The historical preparation for the Covenant**: How God redeemed Israel from slavery, and thus showed his faithfulness, his care and his wonderful might.

(2) **The Covenant made**: How God established his Covenant with Israel, and gave them a rule to make them his kingdom of priests, a holy nation.

(3) **The sovereign's residence**: How God ordained a sanctuary for himself amidst his consecrated people, so that he might dwell among them to care for them and guide them.

The narration of these events takes the following course: After the Israelites had increased and been enslaved by the Egyptians (1–2), God appeared to Moses in the burning bush and sent him to lead Israel out of Egypt (3–4). Pharaoh's refusal to release Israel gave occasion for a display of God's might, in the plagues and on the sea (5–15). God continued to protect and provide for his people as he led them to Sinai (16–18). There he offered them the terms of his Covenant, revealing himself to their sight in a spectacular theophany. Since they could not bear the direct confrontation, he thereafter spoke to them through Moses, and through him concluded the Covenant (19–24). Then God showed Moses the plan of his tent-sanctuary, in which he would dwell among Israel (25–31). But, while Moses tarried with the Lord, the anxious people rashly forced on Aaron the invention of a spurious guarantee of a divine presence in their midst, the golden calf. This breach of the Covenant would have caused their destruction, had not Moses warded off God's wrath and persuaded him to renew the Covenant (32–34). After God was reconciled Moses had the tabernacle built. When it was erected the fiery Majesty of God appeared on it and remained thenceforth with Israel in all their wanderings (35–40).

It is possible to epitomize the entire story of Exodus in the movement of the fiery manifestation of the divine presence. At first the fire burned momentarily in a bush on the sacred mountain, as God announced his plan to redeem Israel; later it appeared for months in the sight of all Israel as God descended on the mountain to conclude his Covenant with the redeemed; finally it rested permanently on the tent-sanctuary, as God's presence settled there. The book thus recounts the stages in the descent of the divine presence to take up its abode for the first time among one of the peoples of the earth.

I. The Prologue
(1:1–2:25)

How the Israelites Became Enslaved (1:1-22)

The Movement of the Story

a. **1:1-7.** Though the family of Israel numbered only seventy souls when it came down to Egypt, it later increased prodigiously.

(1) The story opens with a brief recapitulation of Gen 46:8-27.

Verse 1 = Gen 46:8, with changes in 1b making the sons of Jacob the sole subjects ("with Jacob" replacing "Jacob and his descendants") and allowing for the omission of the detailed lists of the sons of the twelve (through the summary "each coming with his household").

The order of the twelve differs too: in Exodus the sons of the wives (Leah, Rachel) come first—excepting Joseph—followed by the sons of the concubines (Bilhah, Zilpah):[1] in Genesis 46 the order is the sons of Leah and her maid Zilpah, followed by the sons of Rachel and her maid Bilhah.

Neither is the same as the order of birth given in Genesis 29-30, or of the blessing in Genesis 49 (sons of Leah, of the concubines alternately, of Rachel). Different again is that of 1 Chr 2:1.

Since the order of naming seems to have been significant (cf. Gen 48:20), such variation suggests that whatever significance may have inhered originally in the ranking of the twelve had become blurred by the time the traditions were fixed. "All these were the tribes of Israel, twelve in number" (Gen 49:28) and all enjoyed equal status.[2] The position of

---

1. So too at Gen 35:22b-26.
2. As the saying of R. Levi: "Why is the order of the tribes' names not everywhere the same, but now this one is given priority now that one? To prevent one's saying, 'The sons of the full wives rank first and those of the concubines last,' and thus to indicate

Joseph in 5b after the total in 5a (contrast Gen 46:26–27) may be due to the desire too keep references to Joseph there and in verse 6 close to one another.[3]

Our passage is evidently based on the Genesis 46 genealogy, which the author reshaped to provide an introduction to the bondage theme. "Because he wished to state the fact that 'the Israelites were fertile and prolific,' etc., he had to recapitulate and say that when they came to Egypt they numbered only seventy, but after that generation they were fertile and prolific, and a new king arose who schemed to cut their number, but his schemes came to nothing" (Rashbam). The true sequel to Gen 50:26 sets in only in verse 6.

(2) The language of Gen 47:27b (*wayyipru wayyirbu m^e'od*) did not go far enough for our narrator. Expressions of Israel's fertility in verse 7 exceed those in God's blessings to primeval man (*p^{e}ru ur^{e}bu umil'u 'et ha'areṣ*) [Gen 1:28; 9:1] or *širṣu ba'areṣ ur^{e}bu bah* [Gen 9:7]) by two: *waya'aṣ^{e}mu* and *bim^e'od m^e'od* (see below). Outside of our passage and Gen 9:1 (the command to Noah and his family to replenish the desolate earth) the verb *šaraṣ* is used only of the swarming of subhuman creatures; it denotes exuberant animal proliferation. The midrash is within the spirit of the verse when it comments hyperbolically, "Each and every woman gave birth to sextuplets [in accord with the number of expressions of fertility in the verse] ... Some say: Sixty at each birth, and don't wonder at it, for the scorpion, a swarming creature, spawns sixty at once. R. Nathan said: 'The land was filled with them'—like a canebrake (cf. Ezekiel's allegory [16:7]: 'I made you myriad like the growth of the field')."

b. 1:8–14. Alarmed over the increase of the Israelites, a new Pharaoh, who recognized no obligation to Joseph, organized the Israelites into work gangs and set them to work in his building projects. He hoped thereby to check their increase, yet they went on multiplying to the horror of the Egyptians. The Egyptians heaped labor upon the Israelites, field-work as well as construction, driving them ruthlessly and embittering their lives.

(1) *'Am* is used of Israelites for the first time in verse 9. The phrase *'am b^{e}ne yisra'el* bridges the literal sense of *b^{e}ne yisra'el* used heretofore ("children of Israel/Jacob") and the folk-designation to be used hereafter ("Israelites"). To underscore the new usage, the associated verbs and

---

that none were more important than others" (*ShR* 1.6).

3. So *ST*. Gk obviates the awkwardness by placing 5b before 5a.

adjectives in verses 9–12 are in the singular. Pharaoh's concern is thus clarified: "He said to his ʿam, 'Look, the Israelite ʿam,' etc.; two ʿammim cannot abide side by side in one land." Cf. Deut 4:34, "Or has any god ventured to go and take for himself one nation from the midst of another" (goy miqereb goy).

(2) Rab wᵉʿaṣum mimmennu. NJPS, "much too numerous for us," and RSV, "too many and too mighty for us," take into consideration the fact that Israel could not have actually outnumbered the Egyptians;[4] Malbim adds that to render "greater and more numerous than us" makes verse 10 "lest they multiply" unintelligible; they have already multiplied!) Similar considerations seem to have dictated a like rendering by NJPS at Gen 26:16 [Abimelek to Isaac], "You have become far too big for us (ʿaṣamta mimmennu mᵉʾod; but RSV, "you are much mightier than we"), and Num 22:6 [Balak about Israel], "they are too numerous for me" (ʿaṣum hu mimmenni; RSV, "they are too mighty for me"). But the expression and its variants are everywhere else rendered (even by NJPS) as straight comparatives: "much larger than" (Deut 7:1), "far more numerous than" (Num 14:12; Deut 9:14), "greater and more populous than" (Deut 4:38; 9:1). In the light of the emphasis put in verse 6 on Israel's proliferation it is natural for Pharaoh (and, in Num 22:6, for Balak) to say that Israel outnumbered his own people. Even NJPS concedes in its rendering of the Samaritan version of 5:5 (see note there) that Samaritan's rabbim . . . meʿam haʾareṣ must mean "more numerous than the native population." Our phrase may be a hyperbole on hostile lips,[5] but Ps 105:24 does not seem to have regarded it so, for it states as its own view that "the Lord made his people very fruitful, and made them more numerous than their foes." Pharaoh will be alarmed that the Israelites already outnumber the Egyptians; lest they get any more numerous (pen yirbe) he proposes to put them to hard labor.[6]

(3) Pharaoh is opposed to Israel's "going up from the land" (ʿala min haʾareṣ, i.e., emigrating. The expression is the normal Hebrew for leaving Egypt (Gen 13:1; and Exod 12:38; 13:18; Num 14:13; Judg 11:13;

---

4. Ehrlich, Mikra; Ehrlich, Randglossen.
5. Cassuto, Šᵉmot (ET = Exodus).
6. The author (let alone Pharaoh) may well have represented Israel as more numerous than the Egyptians; the midrash, at any rate, does not boggle at making the Israelite population at this time an astronomical sum (Mek. at 13:18 waḥᵃmušim). We have no idea what the author's notion of Egypt's population was, nor have we any knowledge of Moab's population on the basis of which we might judge Balak's statement.

19:30—all with reference to the Exodus), and corresponds exactly to the native Egyptian phrase.[7] It is used here as one of the themes of the story.

Exit from Egypt appears always to have been regarded as a difficulty—understandably so in view of the strong guard set by Egyptians to control movement on their eastern frontier.[8] Several biblical passages depict control of personal movement as a characteristic of Egyptian state authority (Gen 47:21; cf. the idiom of 41:44).

Not for nothing, then, did Jacob fear emigrating to Egypt, and the ground of his fear comes out clearly from the language of God's reassurance (Gen 46:4) "I will go down with you to Egypt, and I will bring you up again."[9]

That viceroy Joseph had to beg permission to "go up" and bury his father in Canaan was perhaps due to his heavy responsibility in the Egyptian administration (Gen 50:5–6). Still, the text seems to go beyond what is due in telling us that the mourning family left little ones, flocks and herds behind when they made the journey to Canaan. Why bother to tell us that?" Abarbanel asks shrewdly, "Should little ones, flocks and herds have gone to bury and lament Jacob?" And he answers, "Pharaoh was concerned that the family would remain in the land of Canaan because of what he saw of the old man's longing for it in life and death. I surmise that Jacob's family would indeed have liked to do what their father did, but Pharaoh and the Egyptians would not let them, for they already contemplated holding on to them. Therefore, in order to allay the Egyptians' suspicions that they intended to flee, they left their women [sic!], little ones and livestock in Goshen as a pledge of their return" [compare Exod 10:10, 24]. In this respect, then, the Egyptian bondage had begun during Joseph's own lifetime.

For the rest of Joseph's family, leaving Egypt at will was out of the question. That would seem to be clearly implied in Joseph's adjuration to his family to remember to "bring up" his bones when, in some future time, God takes note of them and "brings them up from this land" (Gen 50:24–25). At Joseph's death, it appeared that only an act of God would enable the family to leave Egypt. If Pharaoh had any claim over

---

7. *ANET*, 258 n. 3.

8. Ibid., 258–59; cf. the "wall-of-the-Ruler," 446a, 19a.

9. N.B.: To get down to Egypt safely Jacob needs God's company (*'ered 'immᵉka*, not *'oridᵉka* ["I will bring you down"]; to come up again he must rely on God wholly (*'aʿalᵉka gam 'alo*, not *'eʿᵉle 'immᵉka* ["I will come up with you"]). Jacob fears that Egypt is a trap.

HOW THE ISRAELITES BECAME ENSLAVED (1:1–22)

the Israelites other than the mere fact of their residence in his land, it is not stated.

It may be relevant that already in Joseph's time Pharaoh had asked that Jacob's sons serve as royal herdsmen (Gen 47:6). Whatever special favor they may have enjoyed ended as the memory of Joseph faded; only their status as aliens under royal authority remained.

Our story assumes that Pharaoh claimed absolute authority over all in his domain. For the Israelites to win their freedom to "go up from the land" would not have been so much a loss to Egypt's economy—for the people were not yet enslaved, whatever Gen 47:6 implies—as a blow to that authority. What Pharaoh wants, we now learn, is not to be rid of the Israelites—as we might have supposed from his first statement (verse 9)—but to keep them in his power as subjects, to do with them as he sees fit. Such power-hunger cannot bear the thought of a loss of objects to control. That is implied by the apparently uncalled-for reference to the persons and property left behind by Joseph's family when they went abroad. That is expressed by a later Pharaoh's refusal even to hear of Israel's making a three-day's journey into the wilderness to worship its God. That is the reason for this Pharaoh's alarm at the thought that these Israelites might break away from his control.

"It would be bad for us," paraphrases Rashbam, "to lose our subjects and get to be called a truncated kingdom" (*malkuta qᵉtiʿa*).[10] The outcome of the drama is thus foreshadowed in its opening lines. Israel will "go up from the land"; a greater might than Pharaoh will come to their rescue and "bring them up from that land" *lᵉhaʿaloto min haʾareṣ ha-hi*; 3:8).

(4) Pharaoh's cunning is revealed in the way he resolved his contradictory attitude toward the Israelites. He would turn their numbers to good use by putting them to huge work projects—whose drain on their energies could be counted on to abate their increase (see ahead).

---

10. The paradoxical ending of verse 10 has long been a crux. Exegetes have sought to get around it by assuming a euphemism (for "and we shall [have to] go up from the land" [ShR; Rashi]; cf. Saadya: "They will chase us out of the land") or a special sense (NJPS 1962: "gain ascendancy over the country"—following M. Lambert, "Notes exégétiques," 300, and Ehrlich, *Mikra*, and Ehrlich, *Randglossen*, who compare Hos 2:2, itself a crux). But "going up from Egypt" is thematic to the whole account of the Egyptian sojourn; it is unlikely that just here it should bear an entirely anomalous meaning. And the paradox in Pharaoh's attitude toward Israel is an essential motif of the story which will reach extreme expression in the self-defeating decree of verse 22, below.

Building the store-cities (NJPS: garrison cities)[11] of Pithom and Raamses is evidently to be understood as an enterprise of the first magnitude, and is meant to indicate the great toil of the Hebrews, as well as to testify indirectly to their number.

The latter city is usually identified with Egyptian Per-Ramses ("The house of Ramses"), the splendid new residence city of the kings of the 19th dynasty, built by and named after Ramses II (1304–1237). It was in the northeast delta, near the land of Goshen where the Israelites lived.[12]

Pithom is probably identical with Egyptian Per-Atum ("the house [= temple] of [the god] Atum"), after which the town Tjeku was named, located in the same area.[13]

The motive behind the specification of these cities is even more vividly realized in the amplification found in Josephus:

> They ordered [the Israelites] to divide the river into numerous canals, to build ramparts for the cities and dikes to hold the waters of the river and to prevent them from forming marshes . . .; And with the rearing of pyramid after pyramid they exhausted our race, which was thus apprenticed to all manner of crafts and became inured to toil . . . It was indeed a contest between them, the Egyptians striving to kill off the Israelites with drudgery, and these ever to show themselves superior to their tasks." (*Ant.* 2.9.1)

Both Josephus and Exodus make reference to what their readers presumably knew as imposing products of Egyptian forced labor.[14] Josephus alone wrests some grim consolation from the enslavement by averring it had a tempering and training effect on the victims.

---

11. I.e., fortified cities where supplies were stored, chiefly for military purposes; cf. 1 Kgs 9:19; 2 Chr 17:12, 32:28; Mazar, *EM*, 5:165ff.

12. See Helck, "Ṯkw und die Ramses Stadt," 46–47. Two poetical compositions celebrating the glories of the new capital are found in *ANET*, 470–71.

13. *ANET*, 259. Helck, "Tkw und die Ramses Stadt." Whether or not the reader knew anything about these cities—Per-Ramses was referred to as Tanis (Heb. ṣoʿan) after the 12th c. BCE—he could gather from Gen 47:23–26 that Pharaoh required great depots for storage of his tax income.

14. The tendency to modernize the narrative, visible in Josephus's substituting dikes, canals, and pyramids for the by then meaningless town names, already appears in Gk's appendage to the town names: "and On, which is Heliopolis." Retention of the two names alone in the Hebrew, long after they could have signified anything concrete to the reader, attests to the conservatism of the Hebrew text tradition.

HOW THE ISRAELITES BECAME ENSLAVED (1:1-22)

(5) The relation of verses 13–14 to the preceding is not altogether clear. Unlike verses 9–10 and 15–16, no new royal decision is related; hence the impression that 13–14 may be no more than a summary of the preceding measures. On the other hand, expressions of bondage are intensified: derivatives of ʿabad "work, slave," occur five times, twice qualified by bᵉparek "ruthlessly"; and in addition to construction ("mortar and bricks") the people are said to have been put to "all kinds of field labor" (agriculture, irrigation; Deut 11:10).[15] Perhaps we are to infer that, the oppression having so far failed to achieve the intended result, its administrators intensified it on their own, latitude to do so having been included in Pharaoh's original charge to impress the Hebrews.

(6) "They embittered their lives" is a unique expression whose meaning the midrash embellishes in a constructive way:

> Four things are said to embitter: childlessness—as it is said [of Hannah], 'She was bitterly distressed' (1 Sam 1:10); loss of children—as it is said [of the Shunammite], 'Let her alone, for she is in bitter distress' (2 Kgs 4:27); heartbreak—as it is said, 'The heart knows its own bitterness' (Prov 14:10); and grave illness—as it is said [by Job], 'He will not let me catch my breath, but fills me with bitterness' (Job 9:18). Thus the Egyptians enslaved Israel and brought every bane upon them. (*MHG*)

No passage being found where labor itself is called "bitter," the midrash applies the reference to its effects—the effects cited being suitable enough to the context of the story.

The effect aimed at by ruthlessly driving the Israelites is aptly described by Shadal: "Their vitality would be sapped so as to check their reproducing, and what children would be born would not be so strong and healthy." The midrash arrives at the same result by another route: "He ordered the taskmasters to drive them to complete their daily quota[16] so as not to let them sleep at home—aiming to cut down their birth rate . . . The taskmasters said: 'If you go back home to sleep, by the time we call you out, an hour or two of daylight will have passed, so you will not

---

15. According to Bakir (*Slavery*, 3–4) field labor must have been regarded by the Egyptians as very hard work. A scribe's pupil is threatened: "I shall cause thee to be a field-laborer"; a report of the flight of field laborers "before the face of the stablemaster Neferḥotpe, as he beat them," ends with a lament over the abandoned fields of Pharaoh, "for there is no one to till them."

16. The theme derives from 5:13.

be able to complete your quota! ... As a result, they had to sleep in the field" (ShR 1.12).[17]

c. **1:15–22.** Pharaoh now ordered the midwives who served the Hebrew women so to manage things that all male infants should die at birth. But the midwives, being God-fearing, disobeyed, and when Pharaoh called them to account, displayed a shrewdness in their answer to the king that matched his own. Having failed to secure the cooperation of the midwives, Pharaoh then called upon all his people to lend a hand in the destruction of the male infants.

(1) Tradition does not speak with one voice concerning the ethnic affiliation of the midwives. The common view that they were themselves Hebrews is not the oldest, and the arguments against it are weighty. Gk renders *lam^eyall^edot ha'ibriyyot* "to the midwives of the Hebrew women." Josephus (*Ant.* 2.9.2) relates: "The king ... ordered ... that the labours of Hebrew women should be observed and watch kept for their delivery by the Egyptian midwives: for this office was, by his order, to be performed by women who, as compatriots of the king, were not likely to transgress his will." Abarbanel argues: "They were not Hebrews but Egyptians, for how could he trust Hebrew women to put their own children to death! They were Egyptian women who delivered the Hebrews (*m^eyall^edot 'et ha'ibriyyot*)"—an argument that is supported by the language of verse 16 *b^eyalledken 'et ha-'ibriyyot*. Ehrlich adds that Pharaoh's command "to *all* his people" in verse 22 implies that heretofore his murderous order had gone out only to some of them—namely the Egyptians who midwived the Hebrews.[18] Accordingly, the received vocalization implies an elliptical construction: *lam^eyall^edot 'et ha'ibriyyot* "to those midwiving the Hebrew women" (Shadal compares *ha'adam ha'okel habboser* [Jer 31:29]). But it is likely that this vocalization reflects the later view that the midwives were really Hebrews (the midrash identifies them with Jochebed and Miriam), while that presupposed by the Gk and Josephus was *lim^eyall^edot* "to the midwives of." The context favors their being Egyptian.[19]

The Semitic-sounding names of the midwives[20] are not a fatal obstacle to this view. The Egyptian maid Hagar also has a name with a Semitic

---

17. Parallels in the Nazi treatment of enslaved populations are described in W. L. Shirer, *The Rise and Fall of the Third Reich*, 947, 950, 965–66; Lord Russell, *The Scourge of the Swastika*, 140–41.

18. Ehrlich, *Randglossen*; Ehrlich, *Mikra*.

19. So too Beer; Rudolph, *Elohist*, 3 n. 3.

20. Shifra, apparently from the root *š-p-r* "beauty"; Puah, of obscure derivation

ring,[21] not to speak of "Bithya daughter of Pharaoh" (1 Chr 4:18).[22] During the New Kingdom period there were in fact many Egyptianized Semites in Egypt, especially among the menial and slave classes.[23]

(2) ʿIbri is used here as it is commonly in the early literature when (but not whenever) other nationals speak of Israelites (or their ancestors), or when (but not whenever) the author treats of Israelites (or their ancestors) in relation to other nationals. The first occurrences are in the patriarchal narratives, where ʿibri is the only gentilic available to set off the patriarchs from other peoples (Gen 14:13—note how the chapter teems with gentilics; Gen 43:32—contrast of ʿibrim-miṣrim, as in our passages, of ʿibriyyot-miṣriyyot). Through the bondage narrative this usage is continued: Exod 2:6, 7, 11, 13; 3:18. It is found again in the accounts of the Philistine–Israelite wars in 1 Samuel 4, 13–14, 29. (On the use of ʿibri in the slave laws, see Exodus 21.)

Opinions to the contrary notwithstanding, ʿibri is used exclusively as a gentilic, never as a class designation; it is not inherently pejorative (see its uses in Genesis and Jonah 1:9) nor does it include more than the Israelites (and their ancestors): that YHWH is called "God of the ʿibrim" (Exod 5:3; in 5:1, "God of Israel") is decisive. After the founding of the Davidic monarchy the term is found only in Jonah, being otherwise replaced by such locutions as yisraʾel or ʾiš yisraʾel (for the plural) or mib-bᵉne yisraʾel (2 Sam 15:13; 21:2; 1 Kgs 9:20). It is thus evidently an archaic term that served in pre-Davidic times to designate Israel as one ethnic group vis-à-vis others. No extrabiblical attestation of the word is known; its origin and etymology are obscure.[24]

---

connected by the midrash with p-ʿ-y "moan, bleat" [Isa 41:24]) but perhaps the same as "Paghat" daughter of the Ugaritic epic hero Danel (ANET, 153–55). Cf. Albright, "Northwest-Semitic Names," 229.

21. Compare Arabic hajara "forsake, retire."

22. A hebraized analogue of the Canaanite name Bint-Anat, one of Ramses II's daughters.

23. Cf. the Egyptian-named soldiers with Semitic-named fathers at the time of Merneptah (ANET, 258d).

24. Traditional etymologies operate with bᵉne ʿEber of Gen 10:21 (=Eberite) or ʿeber hannahar of Josh 24:2, 3 (thus ʿibri = "trans-fluvian"). These are unconvincing and misleading: IE spends much effort in his comment to Exod 21:2 to refute the misconception promoted by these etymologies that ʿibri is a broad designation covering, e.g., the descendants of Ishmael, Keturah, and Esau as well as Israel. That West-Semitic gentilics may be based on the name of a distant ancestor, with intervening generations not being given that gentilic is argued by A. Malamat, "King Lists," 167–68; cf. also the "Rechabites," so named after an ancestor of their founder (Jer 35:6).

A connection of ʿ*ibri* with ʿ*apiru* (cuneiform spelling: *ḫapiru*)—the name (itself of obscure origin) of a polyethnic class of unprivileged, uprooted refugees widespread over the Near East during most of the second millennium BCE—has often been suggested. Present knowledge makes such a connection no more than a possibility. However, nothing known about the ʿ*apiru* has a clear bearing on the biblical Hebrews/Israelites; attempts to explain the terms and the respective groups by reference to each other have repeatedly proven to be misleading. It is true that among the Asiatics taken captive by Egyptian kings of the New Kingdom and put to work in labor gangs ʿ*apiru* are found,[25] but these appear in Egypt far later than the latest date proposed for the Exodus (as late as Ramses III, 1195–1164), nor is there anything in common between them and the Israelites other than their slave status. But this status in the case of the ʿ*apiru* is derived from their capture in war, in contrast to what is told about the Israelites.[26]

In our passage the term ʿ*ibriyyot* is no more a social designation than is ʿ*ibrim* in Gen 43:32, nor does it embrace any group other or broader than the Israelites of the preceding passage. We have to do with the gentilic familiar from the patriarchal stories, used, in accord with the early convention, when foreigners speak of Israelites.

(3) The condemnation of male infants seems either self-defeating or inadequate. If Pharaoh wanted to exploit Israel's manpower, the decree was self-defeating; if he wanted simply to reduce the Israelite population, he should have condemned the females,[27] or at least included the females.

Pharaoh's aim can be surmised by imagining that his plan had succeeded: Israel would have been gradually reduced entirely to females (the subject sex [Gen 3:16b]). Insurrection would have been impossible, the people would have been dissolved, leaving to Egypt their women-power and reproductive capacity. It would have been an ideal fulfillment of Pharaoh's purpose to keep Israel under heel (see above), though, to be sure, with the sacrifice of their working capacity. Similar war measures were

---

25. ANET, 247, 261.

26. On the ʿ*a/ḫapiru* problem and the relation to the Hebrews, see Greenberg, *The Ḥab/piru*.

27. "Said the Holy One, blessed be He, to him, 'Villain, a fool proposed this plan to you! You should have destroyed the females, for without females where would the men take wives from? A woman cannot take two husbands, but a man can take ten, or even a hundred wives!'" (*ShR*).

taken against captive populations: Gen 34:25; Num 31:7; Deut 20:13–14; Judg 21:11; 1 Kgs 11:15.[28]

To make this decree comprehensible to later ages, a motif of classical hero legends was grafted on to the Moses' birth-tale in postbiblical times; namely, the danger to the infant hero from a prophecy of his greatness told to his future rival (cf. the Cyrus legend in Herodotus; the Oedipus legend). Its earliest Jewish form is found in Josephus (*Ant.* 2.9.2.):

> One of the sacred scribes—persons with considerable skill in accurately predicting the future—announced to the king that there would be born to the Israelites at that time one who would abase the sovereignty of the Egyptians and exalt the Israelites were he reared to manhood, and would surpass all men in virtue and win everlasting renown. Alarmed thereat, the king, on this sage's advice, ordered that every male child born to the Israelites should be destroyed by being cast into the river . . .

The story was taken up and embellished in Rabbinic midrash (see *Sotah* 11b; *ShR* 1.18, 24).

---

28. From the contradiction between Pharaoh's decree against the male infants and his use of Israel's manpower it has been argued that the two motifs cannot originally have been united in one story. "Murder of boys and corvée are irreconcilable opposites. A king who needs many slaves for his building projects must have as a primary object the maintenance of his human material. He must lay particular stress on a high reproduction rate; the thought of doing away with the children of his slaves could never occur to him" (Gressmann, *Mose*, 3). Such a king would be reasonable, and Pharaoh, as depicted, is not. But to conclude from that that he is a literary hybrid is hasty; it is to ignore abundant evidence of the reconcilability of opposites in policies motivated by contradictory purposes. To take modern examples: Nazi Germany exploited the manpower of conquered East Europe in its war industry, yet it also aimed at diminishing the number of its prolific "undesirables." The result was such careless maintenance as led to a life-expectancy of three months in the forced labor factories—highly detrimental to the German war effort. Soviet Russia is systematically obstructing Jewish cultural activity, being intent on obliterating Jewish distinctiveness. At the same time it is suspicious of Jews, and so compels even the assimilated to identify themselves officially as Jews—thus keeping alive their Jewish consciousness.

The inconsistency of Pharaoh's attitude toward the Israelites is displayed in the paradox contained in his opening statement, 1:10: Israel is more than Egypt can stomach, yet they must not be allowed to get away. That this should have culminated in a self-defeating policy is an entirely natural outcome.

There is indeed room to doubt the homogeneity of Moses' birth story (of which Pharaoh's decree is a necessary part) with the rest of the bondage narrative, but not on account of Pharaoh's unreason (see below, p. 54).

(4) The virtue of the midwives, for which their names were immortalized,²⁹ is ascribed to their being God-fearing, that is, religious—standing in awe of the divine and therefore conducting themselves morally. Pagans are so described when it is desired to stress their goodness: Gen 42:18 (Joseph speaking as an Egyptian); wicked pagans, on the contrary, are said to lack God-fearing: Gen 20:11 (Abram's apprehensions concerning the Philistines); Deut 25:18 (the Amalekites). Value is thus recognized in the pagan religion, and moral alertness not made to depend on knowledge of Israel's God and his Torah.³⁰

God rewarded the midwives with *battim*, "households," by which an enduring progeny is meant. Cf. 2 Sam 7:11–12, but especially Ruth 4:11 in which Rachel and Leah, "the two of whom built up the house (i.e. established the family) of Israel" are invoked in the marriage blessing to Boaz and Ruth. The midwives' reward thus corresponds to their good deeds.³¹

(5) From the danger to the infant Moses (2:3) it seems that the Egyptians carried out Pharaoh's decree. Together with verses 8–14 this establishes the guilt of the people at large, to which the goodness of the midwives, and later of Pharaoh's daughter, serves as a foil. The plagues that will strike the whole population are thus justified. "The people were guilty along with Pharaoh. At the start he took counsel with them (1:9); had they not been wicked, they could have tried to avert the harm from his wrath; but they kept silent. More, they accepted his proposal with alacrity and set (n.b. the plural in 1:11 *wayyasimu*) taskmasters over Israel. We note that the midwives, weak as they were, could have avoided executing Pharaoh's command and escaped punishment. How much more easily could the people at large have annulled Pharaoh's decrees, or at least mitigated them" (Shadal at 9:27).

Themes and Structure

a. How the Israelites came to be enslaved is thus told in three brief passages (consisting of 7, 7, and 8 verses respectively). The first passage ends

---

29. As it is said (Ps 112:6): "The righteous shall be held in everlasting remembrance."

30. "Love of his own people does not prevent the narrator from doing justice to the Egyptians. He lauds the Godfearing of the midwives and bestows on them the highest honor at his disposal by gratefully transmitting their names to posterity. In so doing he gives beautiful testimony to his own piety" (Gressmann, *Mose*, 16).

31. Cassuto, *Šᵉmot* (ET = *Exodus*).

HOW THE ISRAELITES BECAME ENSLAVED (1:1–22)

clearly with verse 7, as is recognized by the Masoretic *parasha*. The second comes to a less decisive ending. While verse 15 plainly begins a new passage, the story line beginning with verse 8 is rounded off with verse 12; verses 13–14 do not seem at first blush to add new movement to the story. Do they recapitulate the preceding or tell a new stage of oppression? The third passage is the most composite. The midwives story ends in verse 20, with verse 21 an enlargement upon 20a. Verse 22 climaxes the story up to this point, at the same time setting the scene for the next episode. That verse 22 marks a break is again recognized by the *parasha*.

The place of the problematic verses 13–14 may be illuminated by studying the interrelation of theme and structure in the chapter.

b. The simplest literary device for indicating a theme is repetition; if repetition occurs regularly—say, in the same location in a series of units—the dominance of the theme is assured.

Throughout our chapter elements of verse 7 keep recurring:

Passage a (1–7)	7 *paru wayyišr^eṣu*	*wayyirbu*	*wayya'aṣ^emu*	*bim^e'od m^e'od*
Passage b (8–12 [13–14])	9	*rab*	*w^e'aṣum*	
	10	*pen yirbe*		
	12 *ken yipros* (*para* + *šaraṣ*)	*ken yirbe*		
Passage c (15–20 [21–22])	20	*wayyireb*	*wayya'aṣ^emu*	*m^e'od*

These elements not only recur in each of the three passages, they occur most fully at the end of each story movement, the two fullest recurrences taken together (in verses 12 and 20) suggesting, refrain-like, the whole of the first occurrence. After having been stated in full in verse 7, the proliferation formula, pivoting around the verb *raba*, echoes through the chapter as its binding theme.

c. The tension of the story is provided by the Egyptians' alarm at Israel's increase, which spurs them to ever more drastic countermeasures, each of whose failures is signaled by an echo of the proliferation formula.

First the Israelites are made to construct cities; nonetheless, and in defiance of nature itself, they go on increasing. To Pharaoh's *pen yirbe* events counter *ken yirbe wᵉken yiproṣ*. Dread seizes the Egyptians; something uncanny is here at work.

The next clear reaction is Pharaoh's secret scheme to do away with the male infants. That runs aground when the midwives fail to cooperate; Israel goes on increasing exuberantly.

So Pharaoh openly enlists the cooperation of his whole people in the genocide (verse 22). That this verse is not followed by the proliferation refrain gives it its transitional character. The action forms the climax of the chapter, but the story line hangs in suspense. There is a feeling that the old theme is done and a new one about to break upon the scene.[32]

d. How do verses 13–14 fit into this structure?

Following the concluding formula of verse 12, 13 ought to relate a new countermeasure to Israel's increase. But since countermeasures are otherwise initiated by Pharaoh, and since the next concluding formula does not appear until verse 20, verses 13–14 do not have the form of a countermeasure in itself. On the other hand, they do not merely summarize what has gone before, for, as we noted above, several new emphases are made here: the Israelites "slave" and are driven "ruthlessly," not only at construction but in field work too. A heightening of oppression is suggested.

Perhaps we are to take verses 13–14 and 15–21 as two aspects of the second stage of countermeasures: an overt aspect, not involving a new policy, but only an intensification of the old one (and hence not issuing from the highest instance); and alongside it, a covert aspect, initiated by the king himself, the new scheme of child-murder.[33] This interpretation recognizes the Janus-faced quality of verses 13–14: as a public measure taken to check Israel's growth they belong with what has gone before; but coming after the concluding formula of verse 12, they ask to be regarded as a new stage of countermeasures. Sam. attaches these verses to what precedes and makes a break after 14; the Masoretes declined to sunder verses 13–14 from either adjoining passage: NJPS sunders them from both. No expedient does full justice to the literary situation.

e. Verse 21 is an enlargement upon 20a, spelling out the reward in kind—and precisely in the terms of the story's theme (E. M. Good)—that

---

32. "But note that the new element is precisely the birth of Moses—a new direction of the proliferation theme" (E. M. Good).

33. "The two oppressions do not seem simply chronologically linked; there is a sense in which one is painted with the large brush, the second with the small" (B. S. Childs).

the just God meted out to the midwives who feared him. This is the only activity ascribed to God in the chapter. Notably, God does not figure here as the protector of Israel, but as the undefined divinity that even pious pagans acknowledge and believe to be the guardian of right and justice.

The fact is that in the main theme of the chapter—Israel's increase—God does not figure at all. That tale unfolds from a wholly mundane standpoint; only that which is visible is narrated—an uncanny biological productivity made dreadful by its defiance of nature and its immunity to all measures taken to curtail it. It is not even said that Israel cried to God for help in their agony. God seems absent from Israel's life.[34]

To be sure, even without directly ascribing the events to God the text gives the clearest indications that his hand is behind them. These indications lie in the proliferation formula, whose antecedents must now be looked into.

f. The first and fullest statement of the proliferation formula in verse 7 incorporates all the expressions of fecundity found in the blessings to the first human pair and to Noah—and more. The added elements—ʿaṣam, bimeʾod meʾod, and we may now add verse 12's paraṣ (telescoping para and šaraṣ of verse 7)—show the more immediate antecedents of our formula to be the promises made by God to the patriarchs.

The covenant with the patriarchs includes two promises: their descendants will become a populous nation; they will be given the land of Canaan to live in. The terms of the first promise are of present interest to us. Genesis 17 has God saying to Abraham *weʾarbe ʾoteka bimeʾod meʾod* (verse 2; cf. 22:17), *wehipreti ʾoteka bimeʾod meʾod* (verse 6; cf. analogous

---

34. It need hardly be said that Pharaoh and the Egyptians at large have no inkling of what is behind Israel's increase. They are wholly ignorant of the divine purpose in history—with an ignorance that only the sustained blows of the ten plagues will penetrate for a brief time. Even the midwives' Godfearing extends no further than an awareness of good and evil; it is not because they realize that God is behind Israel's increase that they disobey Pharaoh.

To this characteristically biblical conception of the godless ignorance of the pagan, rabbinic conceptions offer an interesting contrast. The midrash makes Pharaoh aware of his true adversary: "'Let us, then, deal shrewdly with them' (1:10): It is not written '(Let us deal shrewdly) with them' (*lahem*) but 'with him' (*lo*). Said R. Hama bar Hanina, 'He meant: Let us deal shrewdly with the God of these people.'..." namely, by finding a way to avoid his vengeance (*ShR*).

Another midrash interprets *mimmennu* of the preceding verse as "(great and numerous) from—or due to—him (God)" (*ST*). For the rabbis, the pagan was the man who knew God and defied him—a reflex of the sophistication of the Roman-Hellenistic world.

blessings to Isaac [26:4] and Jacob [28:3; 35:11; 48:4]). In 18:18 God foresees that Abraham is to father a nation *gadol wᵉʿaṣum*. And Jacob's first blessing from God includes the promise *uparaṣta* (28:14).

What we have, then, in Exodus 1, is the fulfillment of these promises, a fulfillment not only to the letter (that is the sense of taking up every single term of the promises) but beyond it, in the manner of the exuberant fecundity called for in primeval times to fill an empty earth (conveyed by *šaraṣ, malᵉʾa ha-ʾareṣ*). The proliferation formula thus binds not merely the individual passages of Exodus 1, but Exodus to Genesis. God is carrying out the first part of his covenant with the fathers: their offspring have increased enough to constitute a people. (The huge size of Israel is necessary in view of the expectation that they were to go directly from Egypt to occupy Canaan, the land of "seven nations.") But this has plunged them into a sea of troubles, for the land of their sojourning can no longer bear them. The time must soon come when God will fulfill his second covenant promise.

g. It is a feature of the introductory section that the hand of God does not appear directly on the scene. He has set events in motion through his covenant promise, but in spite of Israel's affliction—perhaps as a reflex of Israel's spiritual condition (see below)—he remains out of sight. Hence the large role played by human motives in the introductory section. The visible motives of events are the alarm of the Egyptians, Pharaoh's cunning, the midwives' piety, and finally the desperation that drives the Egyptians to genocide. All this will work an effect the very opposite of that intended by Egypt. All unknowingly, men collaborate with God in the execution of his purposes.

The Life of Moses before His Call (2:1-25)

The Movement of the Story

a. 2:1-10. A baby born to Levite parents during the time of Pharaoh's decree was put into a box by his mother shortly after his birth, and committed to his fate in the Nile's canebrake. He was discovered there by Pharaoh's daughter, recovered for his mother by a ruse of his sister, and eventually returned as a boy to Pharaoh's daughter. She named him Moses and adopted him as a son.

(1) The story is very spare and focuses exclusively on getting Moses to a safe haven in the custody of Pharaoh's daughter. Moses is the only

THE LIFE OF MOSES BEFORE HIS CALL (2:1–25)   31

character named, and that only at the very end; the anonymous rest are identified by their relationship to already known characters. Details and motives cry to be supplied. Some are given elsewhere in the Bible, others have been variously furnished by later readers.

Moses' parents are identified in 6:20 as Amram son of Kehat son of Levi, and Jochebed, Amram's aunt—that is, Levi's daughter (Num 26:59). As the sister of his father, Jochebed would have been prohibited to Amram by Lev 20:19. Thus the parentage of Moses continues the inbreeding characteristic of Abraham (Sarah was his half-sister, Gen 20:12), Isaac (Rebekah was the daughter of his cousin, Gen 22:22–23), and Jacob (who married the two daughters of his second cousin). In Moses' case it is particularly close, giving Moses descent from the sacerdotal tribe on both sides.[35] This is not chronologically implausible: if Kehat were born early and Jochebed late in Levi's life, Amram, son of Kehat, could have been Jochebed's contemporary. A difficulty arises when trying to harmonize the 430 year length of the Egyptian sojourn as given in 12:40 with the few generations between the descent into Egypt by Levi and the Exodus under his great-grandson. More on this at 12:40.

The impression given by *wayyelek ʾiš* (verse 1) is that the marriage occurred after Pharaoh's murderous decree.[36] That the child was the first issue of the marriage is the natural inference from verse 2; the danger to his life means that he was born when the decree was in force. But if the marriage came after the decree and the infant Moses was its first issue, whence came the sister of verse 4? Something has been omitted. The problem is compounded by the genealogies of 6:20 and Num 26:59 that make Aaron Moses' older brother[37]—older by three years according to Exod 7:7.

---

35. Rabbinic opinion was that the Noachide rules of incest, far less stringent than those of later Israel, excluded only relatives through the mother. Thus Abraham was allowed to marry his half-sister on his father's side, and Amram allowed to marry his aunt, who—it is supposed—was only a half-sister of his father (the two being children of Levi from different wives) (*ST* at 6:20).

36. Since *waw*-consecutive usually implies succession; an indication that the marriage had been before the decree would have been *wᵉʾiš halak* "Now a man had gone, etc." (cf., e.g., Gen 31:33b–34). But since *waw*-consecutive sometimes occurs when there is no idea of succession (Joüon, *Grammaire*, 324 [ET = Joüon, *Grammar*, 393]) the marriage may have occurred before the decree, the birth of the child after.

37. Num 26:59 ranks Miriam last, probably because she is a female. But IE finds in that ranking a way out of the difficulty of our passage: Miriam was born after Moses, hence the *ʾaḥot* of our passage cannot be his "sister" but some other female relative.

These omissions, it may be said, result from the intense focus of the story, the narrator ignoring everything but the adventures of the infant. Elsewhere, in the intrusive genealogy of 6:14ff., and the detail of Num 26:59–60 the omissions are remedied. But can the opening lines of this narrative be construed to allow for previous births to the couple? Various attempts have been made to do so. That of the midrash keeps to the apparent order of events by interpreting the marriage of verse 1 as a remarriage of the couple to one another: "Amram was the chief man of his age. After Pharaoh decreed [to drown male infants he thought, 'We labor for nothing,' and immediately divorced his wife; thereupon the rest all followed suit. His daughter then said to him, 'Your decree is harsher than Pharaoh's: Pharaoh's struck at the boys only, while yours strikes at boys and girls alike.' He immediately took back his wife, whereupon the rest all followed suit" (*ShR*). According to this, Miriam (and Aaron) were the issue of Amram's first marriage to Jochebed, well before the decree.

Less colorful is the assumption that the marriage alluded to in verse 1 occurred some time before the decree. Then, skipping the births of any previous children because of their irrelevance, the story takes up the birth of Moses in verse 2. Such a telescoping is pointed out by IE in 2 Sam 12:24–25. Bathsheba seems to have borne Solomon directly after the death of her child, yet 1 Chr 3:5 (cf. 2 Sam 5:14) has Bathsheba bearing three children before Solomon. We must assume that the narrator focused on what was relevant to his purpose—the naming by God of a child who symbolized David's return to grace—ignoring intervening events that were not germane.

While either expedient will smooth over the inconsistency of the narration, one wonders whether the formulation of the first three verses of our story really allows them. Not only are essential facts omitted that will have to be supplied later; barely any room is left for them at all. All the same, it must be admitted that the absence of genealogical detail has made for a vivid, quick-moving tale. The roughness must have been mitigated (as it still is today) by the familiarity of readers with all the necessary details.

(2) After three months the child could no longer be hid presumably because as he grew his crying became louder. This implicit motive is enlarged upon by the midrash: "The Egyptians used to visit every house in which they reckoned a child was born. They brought with them an Egyptian baby whom they made cry, so that, hearing it, the Israelite baby would cry too" (*ShR*).

The mother's motives in adopting the method she used to try and save her baby are not spelled out; Abarbanel supplies them with sympathetic imagination:

> First, because to keep the child at home was certain death, while in setting him out there was a possibility of his being saved: one couldn't be sure whether he was an Egyptian or Hebrew, and because of the doubt he might not be killed . . .
>
> Second, she placed the box near the bank to make it accessible to passersby, in the hope that God would be gracious to the child and some kind soul would come along and find it—as indeed happened.
>
> Third, if the child was to die after all, it would not die in her presence. A like thing is said of Hagar. She left the child under one of the bushes, and went and sat down at a distance, a bowshot away; for she thought: "Let me not look on as the child dies" (Gen 21:16) . . .
>
> We can also surmise a fourth reason: The good woman figured shrewdly that perhaps her son was fated to be thrown into the Nile. She therefore contrived to have him thrown into it in this fashion, so as to satisfy his destiny and assuage God's anger . . .

This last surmise, playing on the congruence of Pharaoh's decree with the disposition of the child, comes close to the interpretation given to this act in the hero-prophecy legend mentioned above. Abarbanel does in fact allude to a passage from *ShR*'s version of the legend. "Moses was cast into the Nile to make the astrologers think that Israel's savior had already been thrown into the Nile, so that from that day on they'd call off the search for him. Indeed from that day on (say the Rabbis) the decree was annulled, for they divined that Israel's savior had already been attacked by water." That is how the midrash accounts for the strange disappearance of the infant-killing motif after this episode. It is almost as though the decree was designed to get Moses into the custody of Pharaoh's daughter.

Verses 2–3 dwell on the measures taken by the mother and sister to see to the child's well-being. The caulking of the reed-box, the placing of the child in the box, its placement among the reeds near the shore, the sister's vigil—all are set forth at a length that contrasts with the terseness of the narrative up to this point. The teller has gone out of his way to indicate that there was no intention to abandon the child to his fate.[38]

---

38. Jacob, "The Childhood," 247; Cogan, "A Technical Term," 134.

That local color is present here is suggested by the numerous mythical references to the concealment among papyrus reeds of the infant Horus to protect him from his persecutor, Seth. A late Egyptian text reads, "Seth went searching for Horus, still a child, in his hiding-place (lit. "nest") in Chemmis [the Delta marshland], after his mother [Isis] had hidden him in a papyrus thicket and [her sister] Nephthys had spread her mat (?) over him." The same text tells a bit later that the infant was in a "reed-boat."[39]

(3) The handmaidens—the court companions of the princess—are mentioned as a realistic touch: the princess never went abroad unescorted ("It is not the wont of the daughter of a king to be alone" [ShR]). But when she bathed, only her slave-girl accompanied her into the water; her companions stayed on the bank of the river to guard her privacy.[40] This worked for the good of the baby. The handmaidens would have been far less ready to disobey the king's order, and had they gotten to the child first, his rescue might not have gone so smoothly. As it happened, the decision to save him was reached without their having a say in the matter. (The midrash has them deprecating the rescue, but contrives to spare the princess the embarrassing necessity of answering them.)

The good deeds of the midwives and the princess are differently motivated in accord with their different stations. For the midwives to disobey the king required more than pity; it needed fear of God to override fear of the king. The princess, who did not stand in the same terror of her father and whose risk was less, could be sufficiently moved by pity alone.

Saadya observes how the princess serves as a foil to her father: "Pharaoh was cruel in the extreme—'Every boy that is born you shall throw into the Nile'—while 'She took pity on it.' He was wickedly unjust in the highest degree, while she was scrupulously fair—'I will pay your wages'" (paraphrased by R. Abraham son of Maimonides, in Qafiḥ, 49 n. 4).

(4) How could the princess tell that it was a Hebrew child? "She took the situation into account, reckoning that it was to save the child or to avoid seeing it die that his parents left him there. And why should any Egyptian have to do such a thing?[41] Some say [=the midrash] that she saw

---

39. Helck, "Ṯkw und die Ramses Stadt," 48; the text cited is Pap. Jumilhac (J. Vandier, ed.) vi, 10ff. On the comparison with cast-away infant legends, see Excursus.

40. McNeile, *Exodus*, 3.

41. BSh glosses 2:6, "This must be a Hebrew child" by "[one of those] cast into the Nile," implying that what these Hebrew parents did for their child was being done by others too in a desperate attempt to evade the worst consequences of Pharaoh's decree. Cf. above, on 2:3.

that the child was circumcised, but that would require her undressing the child and examining him for this—all needless assumptions" (Ramban). Whether or not Egyptians were uncircumcised is unclear; the evidence is contradictory (see, e.g., Jer 9:24–25 [and perhaps Ezek 32:32] in conflict with the evidence of Egyptian texts and pictorial representations of circumcision[42] and Herodotus, who reports them practicing it). Perhaps, too, the dress of the infant identified it, or its features and skin color (cf. the markedly darker color of the Egyptians in the Beni-Hasan picture of an Asiatic caravan).[43]

(5) The quick assent—indeed it appears to be a preference—of the princess to engage a Hebrew wet nurse bespeaks her compassion. Egyptian antipathy toward the Hebrews, mentioned in Gen 43:32 (cf. 46:34) and now likely to have been aggravated by their slave status, might have entailed careless, if not harsh, treatment of the baby by an Egyptian wet-nurse. By returning the child to Hebrew hands, the princess showed her concern for its welfare.[44]

Later readers, contrariwise, made the antipathy of the baby toward Egyptian women the determining factor. Josephus (*Ant.* 2.9.5) relates: "[The princess] ordered a woman to be brought to suckle the infant. But when instead of taking the breast it spurned it, and then repeated this action with several women, Miriam, who had come upon the scene, apparently without design and from mere curiosity said, 'It is lost labour, my royal lady, to summon to feed the child these women who have no ties of kinship with it. Wert thou now to have one of the Hebrew women fetched, maybe it would take the breast of one of its own race.' [The mother having been fetched] the infant, gleefully as it were, fastened upon the breast, and, by request of the princess, the mother was permanently entrusted with its nurture."

(6) The child "grew" (*wayyigdal*) under its mother's care. That this lasted beyond the nursing period[45] is implied by the absence of an intervening *wayyiggamal* "and was weaned" before the next verb; contrast Gen 21:8. *Wayyigdal* alone can signify an infant's reaching any age from boyhood to early manhood (Gen 25:27; Judg 13:24; 2 Kgs 4:18). Here the

---

42. *ANET*, 326.
43. *ANEP*, 3.
44. Cf. Jacob, "The Childhood," 247.
45. The Egyptian *Instructions of Ani* makes this out to be three years (*ANET*, 420d).

context and *wayyigdal* in the next verse ("When Moses had grown up") indicate boyhood.

Moses' stay with his mother imbued him with an awareness of his Israelite origin—an essential and indispensable element in the development of the story. His stay at the Egyptian court enabled him to grow up free of the crippling physical and spiritual effects of slavery. Later readers supplemented the biblical data on Moses' early years with generous surmises concerning his princely character and his education (Josephus, *Ant.* 2.9.6–10.2; Acts 7:22; *ShR* 1.26). The midrash remarks the irony that "Pharaoh's daughter was busy bringing up the one who was destined to punish her father" (*ShR*).

(7) It has long been realized that the interpretation given in the text of Moses' name is bad grammar. Midrashim made capital of the obvious "error": "The name and its midrash do not agree. He should have been called *mašuy* [passive participle, 'drawn out (of water)'] to accord with the statement, 'I drew him out of the water.' But without realizing it, she prophesied when she named him *moše* [active participle, 'one who draws out (of water)'], for he did draw Israel out of the Sea, as it is said, 'Then he remembered the days of old, of him who drew his people out (*moše* ʿ*ammo*); where is he who brought them up from the Sea?'" (Isa 63:11; see *ST*). Or, again, "He should have been named *mašuy* . . . but she called him *moše*, meaning, 'He drew himself out,' that is, his merit was enough to save him" (*MHG*).

However, the grammatical ineptitude of this interpretation is no greater than that of the name of Samuel (1 Sam 1:20) or Reuben (Gen 29:32) or Cain (4:1). In all such cases the interpretation of the name is a notion suggested by assonance rather than etymology.

As to how an Egyptian princess could give a Hebrew name to the child,[46] IE suggests that either (a) our passage is a translation from Egyptian, in which tongue the name was different; or (b) the princess learned Hebrew, or (c) she consulted with someone who suggested an appropriate Hebrew name. Benno Jacob cites as parallels Pharaoh Necho's renaming Eliakim Jehoiakim and Nebuchadnezzar's renaming Mattaniah Zedekiah (2 Kgs 23:34; 24:17).[47]

---

46. Abarbanel argues ingeniously that it was really Jochebed who named her own child, saying to the princess when she returned him, "I am calling him *moše* because you drew him out of the water." The form *mᵉšitihu* (note the lack of *yod*) is amenable to this construction but the context is not.

47. Jacob, "The Childhood," 252–53.

Ever since Josephus, attempts have been made to explain the name as an Egyptian word (in which case the interpretation will again convey what the *sound* of the name suggested to a Hebrew ear regardless of its true origin).[48] Present scholarship generally regards the name as Egyptian, and for an etymology has settled upon the final element in such names as Ahmosis, Thutmosis, with the initial god-component missing.[49] If Moses is an Egyptian name, it is one of several among the early Levites, some others being Hophni, Phinehas, and Merari.[50]

Whatever the origin of his name, Moses was reared as and taken for an Egyptian (verse 19 below). His feeling that Egypt was his native land is reflected in the interpretation of his son's name (verse 22 below).

b. 2:11-22. One day, after Moses grew to manhood, he went out to observe his kinsmen's toil. Coming upon an Egyptian who was beating a Hebrew to death, Moses stepped in and killed the man—assuming he was not witnessed. Undaunted by the first day's contretemps, Moses made a second excursion to his brothers. This time he found two of *them* fighting, and when he intervened again he was taunted with his killing. Word of Moses' act soon reached Pharaoh, and Moses was forced to flee for his life. He escaped to Midian, where, as a result of rescuing some shepherd-girls from bullying shepherds, he found a home with the local priest, their father.

(1) At the end of verse 11 the repeated *(me)ʾeḥaw* serves only to reflect Moses' subjective feeling. Often the narrator chooses words to reflect the feelings of characters, as was pointed out by Buber and Rosenzweig. Note in the story of Hagar (Gen 21:9ff.) how to Sarah the unwanted child is *ben haʾama*, to Abraham it is *bᵉno*, to God, *ben haʾama* when seconding Sarah, but otherwise the neutral *naʿar*. To Hagar it is always *yeled* (her "bairn"), while to the narrator it is *naʿar*. (In this connection it is worth noting the exceptional use of *naʿar* in verse 6 above; it is perhaps only a narrator's variation, but it has not been put into any of the dialogue, where *yeled* alone is subjectively apt.)

---

48. The currency and seriousness of word plays on names in the ancient Near East, sometimes in disregard even of language boundaries, are nicely illustrated by the Sumero-Akkadian puns on the name of the chief god Marduk; see *ANET*, 62b and n. 35; 69c and n. 112. On biblical name plays (including "Moses") see G. R. Driver, "Playing on Words," 124-25.

49. Griffiths, "The Egyptian Derivation."

50. Albright, *Yahweh and the Gods of Canaan*, 165.

(2) When the object of *ra'a* is introduced by *b^e*, emotional involvement is implied (BDB s.v. *r-'-h*, 8.a [907–8]). In Gen 21:16 it is grief, in 29:32, sympathy; here Rashi glosses, "He lent his eyes and heart to grieve over them." The midrash takes the cue and proceeds to detail practical measures that Moses took to alleviate their misery.

(3) Moses' killing of the Egyptian was a deliberate act—note Moses' caution[51]—of rescue from imminent death: *hikka* must be the same in verses 11 and 12 and implies that the Egyptian was giving the Hebrew a murderous beating. "The story intends to display Moses' sense of justice; it can hardly have represented Moses as punishing ordinary blows with a fatal beating."[52]

Undeterred by the mishap, Moses sallied forth a second time. The repeated *wayyeṣe* "he went forth" (verse 13) suggests the concern Moses felt for his kinsmen, a concern that overcame any apprehensions he might have had over the consequences such visits might bring upon him.[53]

(4) The taunt of the Hebrew foreshadows the truculence and perverse ingratitude that Moses will experience from this people decades later. The taunter's "as you did to the Egyptian" betrays his knowledge of Moses' kinship with him, which emboldened him to show such insolence to one whose station should otherwise have struck terror into him. The midrash amplifies aptly: "Why, you're nothing but the son of Jochebed! By what right are you called the son of [princess] Bithya? And you dare to try and lord it over us: We'll inform on you about what you did to that Egyptian!" (*ShR*). In accord with midrashic policy—"R. Shimon bar Yohay said, 'Whatever you can lay at the door of the wicked, do!'" (*MHG*)—the Hebrews here are identified as Dathan and Abiram. The poetic truth of the identification emerges from comparison with Num 16:13b.

(5) The end of verse 15 is awkward, with *wayyešeb* used differently in the two last clauses.[54] The first clause states that Moses "settled in the

---

51. The one other occurrence of "and he saw that there was no man" is Isa. 59:16, where God is said to act on his own because no one else was about when the time to redeem Israel came. *ShR* is probably right in taking the Isaiah passage as an interpretation of the Exodus phrase justifying Moses on the ground that he acted only when he saw that "there was no one else" who would perform the rescue. (Maharzu at *Wayyiqra Rabba* 32.4 finds here the basis of Hillel's maxim, "Where there are no men, try to be a man" [*Abot* 2.5; cited by Jacob, "The Childhood," 257].)

52. Gressmann, *Mose*, 18 n. 3.

53. Cf. Noth, *Exodus*; and *ShR*.

54. It is true that in verses 10 and 11 *wayyigdal* is likewise used in different senses: "grew" and "grew up." But there, the two verbs are in different verses, and,

land of Midian," anticipating the outcome of what follows. The events leading to that outcome start with the next clause, "He sat down beside a well." The Gk version spells it out with a third, inserted clause: ". . . and settled in the land of Midian. [*He came to the land of Midian*] and sat down beside a well." Anticipations of this kind are not unprecedented; cf. Gen 37:21, "He [Reuben] rescued him from their clutches;"[55] and Gen 42:20, "they did accordingly."

(6) The scene at the well recalls the episode with Rebekah in Genesis 24, and even more strongly Jacob's encounter with the shepherd-girl Rachel, his wife to be (29:2ff.—Jacob too watered her flock). Two significant differences are that Moses rescues the girls from bullies, and his good deed appears to be wholly disinterested. For in contrast to Jacob's situation, he was not in search of a wife, nor did he meet one girl, an eligible relative, at the well. The interest of the story lies elsewhere than in telling how Moses found a wife (see ahead).

The girls say that Moses drew water for them (verse 19), while the previous narrative has them drawing the water (verse 16) and Moses only watering the flock (verse 17). But there is no necessary contradiction between what the girls and the narrative say Moses did.[56] Moses may well have drawn more water for the flock, to see to it that they were never so well watered as on that day; or the other flocks may have consumed some of the water drawn by the girls, so that Moses had to replenish the troughs.[57] The narrator omitted this detail in verse 17, reserving it for the girls to reveal. Such omissions, to be supplied later in a dramatically more effective context, regularly occur. Compare, e.g., Gen 42:21 with 37:24 (no notice there of Joseph's anguished supplication), or 43:7 with 42:9ff. (no notice there of Joseph's questioning the brothers about their family,

---

more important, in different episodes. Moreover, the two senses are nicely consequent on one another, the second denoting "growth" from the point reached in the earlier "growth" period. In verse 15, on the other hand, the two heterogeneous verbs crowd one another as though referring to a single event, and there is no consequential relation between the events signified by them.

55. NJPS, "he tried to save him" (so Shadal) is unnecessary in view of its own recognition of anticipation in Gen 42:20. In our passage NJPS again disallows the usage by rendering *wayyešeb bᵉʾereṣ Midyan* "He arrived in the land of Midian" (so too Saadya:) relegating the literal—and unavoidable—"sat" or "settled" to a note.

56. As Ehrlich (*Randglossen*) and Gressmann (*Mose*, 16 n. 7) believe.

57. IE suggests that the girls may have gratefully credited Moses with what they themselves did; alternatively, that what they had first drawn was not enough for all their flock.

though 44:19–20—spoken to Joseph's face—validates it); 50:16 may be another such instance (contrary to the notion [*Bᵉreshit Rabba*; Rashi] that the brothers fabricated Jacob's deathbed admonition to Joseph).[58]

(7) The identity of Moses' father-in-law, the priest of Midian, is a longstanding problem. Verse 18 would seem to make him Reuel, but 4:18 and chapter 18 call him Jether/Jethro. Numbers 10:29 names one "Hobab son of Reuel Moses' father-in-law," of whom we hear again in Judg 4:11. A common expedient is to identify Jether/Jethro with Hobab, making Reuel his father. In our passage then, "father"="grandfather," and "daughter"="granddaughter" (IE; Rashi at Num 10:29; this usage is attested elsewhere [Gen 29:5ff.; 32:6; 2 Sam 19:25]). Since having more than one name was not unheard of in biblical times[59] this solution is possible. But it is a desperate expedient, and rather than adopt it, modern scholars prefer to view the ancient tradition as divided on the name of Moses' father-in-law.[60]

However, tradition speaks with one voice of his having been a Midianite priest.[61] Was this a factor in preparing Moses for his calling? Jethro confessed YHWH after the Exodus as the greatest of gods, and sacrificed to him; he gave Moses good advice on judicial and administrative matters (ch. 18). So far, then, did Moses find a kindred soul and mentor in his father-in-law. Did he also teach Moses something of the God whom he was to encounter while shepherding his flocks? Some scholars regard Jethro and his tribe, the Kenites, as the first worshipers of YHWH. Moses is supposed to have learned from his Kenite relatives both the name of the God and the location of his holy mountain—close by Midianite territory (as it is supposed). The combinations supporting this theory are quite speculative, the data few, so that it is far from persuasive;[62] but a strange counterpart to the theory is found in Jewish midrash.

The following considerations go into the midrashic depiction of Jethro: First, though a Midianite (= pagan) priest, he was quick to confess

---

58. A Gk ms. (B) does add "and drew water for them" after "he rescued them" of verse 17, probably reflecting a Heb. text that added these words to obviate the difficulty.

59. De Vaux, *Israel*, 45–46.

60. Noth, *Exodus*; Driver, *Exodus*.

61. Later readers were unhappy over the fact; *Onk.* and *Mek.* (at 18:1) render *kohen* "a chief" following an apologetic device of the Chronicler, who turned David's sons from *kohᵃnim* "priests" (2 Sam 8:18) to *rišonim* "chief officials" (1 Chr 18:17).

62. See Meek, *Hebrew Origins*, 93ff., who deprecates the theory, and Kaufmann's rebuttal of it in *Religion of Israel*, 242ff.

Israel's God (18:10–11); second, his daughters were treated with an insolence out of keeping with his station; third, in spite of the constant abuse they suffered (inferred from his surprise at their early return [2:18]) he did not hire others to shepherd his flock. The midrash accounts for all of this by the following romance: "Jethro was an idolatrous priest at first, but when he realized that there was nothing to idolatry, he rejected it and considered turning to God even before Moses came. So he summoned his townsmen and said to them, 'All along I have been your priest; now I am old, choose a new priest for yourselves.' He moved all the trappings of idolatry out of his house and handed them over to them. Thereupon they ostracized him, forbidding anyone to work for him or tend his flock. So when he asked shepherds to work in his flock and they refused, he had to put his own daughters to work." The ostracism explains, too, why the shepherds behaved so churlishly to his daughters (*ShR*). This notion of Jethro's spontaneous abnegation of idolatry explained to later readers how Moses could "consent to stay with the man."

A further, piquant detail is supplied in *TJ*: "One day Moses entered Jethro's garden . . . and saw there a rod created on the eve of the first Sabbath, on which the tetragram was inscribed, and by which he was to perform miracles . . . [No one had ever been able to budge it from its place (Abarbanel at verses 20–21), but] Moses at once lifted it. That is why he consented to stay with the man and Jethro gave him his daughter." Abarbanel regards the legend—perhaps not improperly—as an allegory: Moses found in Jethro a tree of life-giving knowledge and having acquired the knowledge, Moses was prepared to become a prophet. An odd analogue to the Kenite theory.

(8) The interpretation of "Gershom"—grammatically as inept as that of Moses (its base is *g-r-š* rather than *gur*)—indicates that Moses not only looked, but felt himself an Egyptian. Home for him meant Egypt, and Midian was "a foreign land." Without the long exile in Midian he would not have experienced even a semblance of the alienness that was his people's lot in Egypt.

c. 2:23–25. During the many years that Moses stayed with Jethro, the Pharaoh under whom he had grown up and who had sought his life, died. The Israelites in the meanwhile continued to labor without respite. They cried out because of their labor, and their cry reached God. Mindful of his covenant, God took note of the people's distress and considered what he must do.

(1) The death of the king who sought Moses' life was a precondition of Moses' return to Egypt. It is referred to again in 4:19. Gk recognizes the interrelationship of the two passages by repeating this death notice just before 4:19.

The rest of 23–25 relates another precondition of Moses' return: God's decision to take note of the people's plight. Notwithstanding all sorts of guesses as to the interrelation of the two parts of verse 23,[63] it appears that there is no causal connection between them. Rashbam glosses the passage thus:

> *After a long time*: After Moses killed the Egyptian and Pharaoh sought to put him to death, so that he had to flee from him, and had now reached eighty years of age (7:7) . . . *the king of Egypt died*, the king who sought to put him to death. All the while *the Israelites had been groaning*[64] until God took note of their distress. *Now Moses was tending the flock* (3:1) when God . . . ordered him back to Egypt; but Moses was unwilling for he was afraid until God said to him, 'All the men who were seeking your life have died' (4:19), referring to Pharaoh. The text tells us now that *the king of Egypt died* to prepare the reader for God's statement later. A similar anticipation is *Now Ham was the father of Canaan* (Gen 9:18).[65]

But in fact it is enough to account for the death notice here that God could not commission Moses at the burning bush to return to Egypt before his persecutor's death (BSh; cf. Hizquni, Cassuto, and IE at 4:19).

That not even messengers of God were expected to risk death unnecessarily, is a point nicely made in 1 Sam 16:1–3, where God himself supplies Samuel with a ruse to put off Saul's suspicion as he goes to anoint David. On that passage Kimhi remarks: "Though God performs miracles

---

63. E.g., "[Israel's groaning] indicates that the new king was crueler than the old one" (IE, short commentary on Exodus)—a suggestion proven specious by comparison of the deeds of the two; no act of the new Pharaoh related in ch. 5 and its sequel matches the cruelty of the old one's condemnation of the male infants to death.

64. That Israel's groaning was not a consequence of the king's death would, admittedly, have been far clearer had verse 23a begun *ub*ᵉ*ne yisra'el ne'enḥu wayyiz'aqu*—indicating that their groaning was going on *at the time* of the king's death. Cf. the sequence of tenses in 1:6–7: the Israelites' proliferation was going on already at the time of the death of Joseph and his generation (Gen 47:27). This exegesis takes *wayye'anᵉḥu* as an instance of *waw-consecutive* that does not imply succession (see above, p. 31 n. 36, on *wayyelek* of verse 1 and Num 1:48, where *wayᵉdabber* is pluperfect; also below on 11:9).

65. Another such is the reference to Absalom's abundant hair in 2 Sam 14:26.

on behalf of those who fear him, as a rule they follow the course of nature ... [By this ruse] God showed [Samuel] that it is not proper for a man to take some dangerous course and rely on miracles, for it has been commanded, 'You must not put the Lord your God to the test'" (Deut 6:16).

(2) The Israelites are not said to have cried out to God (let alone YHWH), but to have cried out, and their cry reached God (contrast Deut 26:7). The language of the Sodom story (Gen 18:20–21; cf. 19:13) is almost identical, and there can be no question there of calling to YHWH; the oppressed of Sodom did not know YHWH that they might call upon him. Regardless of whom they invoked, God heard their outcry as the judge of the world; as in the Nineveh of the book of Jonah, God acts as the guardian of universal justice. It is no condition of the deity's maintenance of his creatures that they recognize him; "Man and beast you save, O Lord" (Ps 36:7).

Our text leaves it entirely obscure to what divinity, if any, the cry of Israel was directed, saying only that their cry (like that of Sodom's victims) reached God and moved him to action. The only clue given in our story to the nature of Israelite religion at the time refers to the faith of Moses' family. At the bush, God identifies himself to Moses as "the God of your father, the God of Abraham, the God of Isaac, and the God of Jacob" (3:6; cf. 18:4). The ancestral God was known at least in Moses' family; but we hear nothing of his worship in Israel at large before Moses,[66] and only Moses is said to have revealed his name to the people.

From 8:21 it emerges that before Moses' confrontation with Pharaoh, the king had never allowed the people to sacrifice to their God in Egypt; and from verse 22, that even if he had they could not have done so without offending the Egyptians. The absence of God in the story up to this point has been noted above. It is as though religion were paralyzed through the years of bondage. From the theocentric standpoint, at any rate, it was a time when God "hid his face" from Israel (Ramban's formulation).[67]

---

66. *ST* on 5:3, "'Let us go ... a distance of three days ... to sacrifice to the Lord our God': They said, 'From the time our ancestors left Canaan we have not offered him a single sacrifice ...'"

67. The early Jewish liturgy alludes to Israel in Egypt as having been "forgotten." One of the special prayers of the fast-day liturgy invoked "him who answered our fathers on the Reed Sea ... Blessed are you, O Lord, who remembers what has been forgotten" (Mishnah, *Taanit* 2.4). On the formulation of the benediction pseudo-Rashi comments: "Because Israel were forgotten [Meiri, with more tact, 'presumed themselves forgotten'] in Egypt for many years till they lost hope of being redeemed, but

Later biblical texts expressly charge Israel in Egypt with idolatry, indeed with a veritable addiction to the idols of Egypt (Ezek 20:7–8; cf. Josh 24:14). These passages, together with the allusion to the covenant in verse 24 as a motive of God's arousal, were decisive for the midrashic view of the people's religious state:

> Israel was so wicked it did not deserve to be saved; redemption came only because of the merit of the patriarchs . . . "God saw the Israelites and God knew"—[He] knew that he must redeem them for the sake of his reputation, for the sake of the covenant that he made with the patriarchs. That is what is meant by "He remembered his covenant with Abraham" etc.; as Ezekiel (20:9) says in his name, "I did it for the sake of my reputation [not that Israel deserved it]!" (*ShR*)[68]

(3) When God is said in verse 24 to have remembered his covenant with the patriarchs, the reference is to its second part, the promise of a land for their descendants. (Its first part, the promise to make them numerous, had already been fulfilled.) God's delay in fulfilling it is accounted for in Gen 15:13–16: Abram's offspring will be enslaved 400 years in a foreign land; only afterward will they be brought back to occupy the land, "for the [measure of the] Amorite's iniquity [i.e., the amount of sin God decided to tolerate before dooming them] will not be filled until then." "Now," writes Rashbam, "the 400 year term . . . was about to expire."

That is, to be sure, only a partial explanation of the delay. It accounts for the stay in execution, but not for Israel's enslavement in the meanwhile. Nowhere in the Bible is that accounted for; not even those passages that accuse Israel in Egypt of idolatry offer that as a justification for the enslavement. The liberation from Egypt was the great fountainhead of meaning; the enslavement was at best its morally opaque premise.

Early biblical historiography does not give moral reasons for every calamity. The famines in the age of the patriarchs are not motivated (cf. Ruth 1:6). Not every defeat of Israel has a retributive aspect (e.g., Judg

---

God remembered and redeemed them, as it is written (Exod 6:5); 'I have remembered my covenant'" (Pseudo-Rashi ad loc. at *Taanit* 15a).

68. Ramban makes God's compassion the determining factor; "At first he hid his face from them, abandoning them to spoliation, but now 'God heard their groaning . . .' The text heaps up grounds for their redemption—'God heard their groaning, remembered his covenant, saw, took thought' . . . —because, despite the expiration of the [400 year] term they were unworthy of redemption . . .; only their anguished cries moved him in compassion to accept their prayer." This indeed is the sole motive of God's action set forth at the burning bush (see below).

THE LIFE OF MOSES BEFORE HIS CALL (2:1–25)   45

20:18–26; 1 Samuel 4). A disaster may—routinely it seems—be ascribed to God's wrath, without any reason offered for that wrath (1 Sam 24:1). The attempt systematically to explain misfortune as retributive is made only in the latest historical writings—e.g., Chronicles and the midrash.[69] Our text accepts large parts of experience as unaccountable givens—if their effects at least can be incorporated into larger, meaningful wholes.[70]

(4) *Wayyeda'* (verse 25) standing without an object has a fellow in the Sodom story (Gen 18:21); the meaning is "consider, take thought of what to do."[71] Onkelos paraphrases aptly, "God determined to redeem them."

The four clauses of verses 24–25 are in ascending parallelism. In each verse a verb of sensation is followed by one of mental activity, the first of each parallel pair a grade beneath the second in intensity: "heard" / "saw" (cf. Job 42:5: "remembered" / "took thought (of what to do)." The increasing vagueness of the objects in verse 25—with the last verb entirely lacking an express object—similarly heightens the reader's anticipation. What will happen next? God's arousal issues directly from the revelation at the bush.

Themes and Structure

a. The life of Moses before his call is told in two roughly equal passages of 10 and 12 verses respectively (2:1–10; 11–22). The events of the first passage, ending with his adoption by the princess, are consecutive, continuity being broken slightly only in verse 10.

"Some time" has passed before the story resumes in verse 11. Moses has grown up. Events seem to run consecutively again through verse 22, where a *parasha* marks the end of the passage.

---

69. Cf., e.g., the reason for Josiah's untimely death in 2 Kgs 23:26–27 and 2 Chr 35:22.

70. See below on 4:24–26. Various meanings were later wrested out of the bondage: On the one hand it served to purge Israel of sin (Rashi at Deut 4:20; Kimhi and Meṣudat David more clearly at Jer 11:4—all taking "iron furnace" to refer to the purging of dross from metals [Isa 48:10]; its plain sense—a symbol of excruciating suffering [Shadal at Deuteronomy]—underlies Akiba's fancy that Israelite children were burned in furnaces [cited by Hizquni in Deuteronomy]). On the other hand, the length of the bondage bespoke great sin: 2:22b–25 shows that only by dint of his covenant promise did God finally act.

71. Rashi at Genesis passage; Ehrlich (*Mikra*) and Shadal here; NJPS "take not(ic)e."

A third, brief passage serves as both the climax of the whole introductory section and a Prologue to the next movement of the story. The scene shifts back from Midian to Egypt to apprize us of what has been happening in the meanwhile on the main stage of action from which Moses has fled. Verse 25 is followed by another shift in the scene and a *parasha* break.

b. Moses' advent in the story serves as a response to Pharaoh's last and most drastic measure; it is therefore fitting that the narrative of his early life in 2:1–22 begin and end with a birth notice—an echo of the proliferation formula of verse 7. Thus the pattern: repressive measure—frustrating response is carried to its conclusion. Noteworthy too is the balanced ending of the main passages: verse 10 and verse 22 each concludes with a name-giving.

The themes of each passage are underscored by repeated words. In the first passage *yeled* "child" is repeated seven times; in the second, *'iš* "man," is repeated seven times again (though not always referring to Moses).

The third passage revolves around two poles: (a) first come three terms of anguish (*nᵉʾenaḥ, zaʿaq, šawʿa*), then (b) four clauses in which God's notice is expressed. The two are interlocked by the mention of God in the *šawʿa* clause on the one hand, and a fourth term of anguish (*naʾᵃqa*) as the object of the first of (b)'s clauses. The iterative effect of *wayyišmaʿ ʾᵉlohim, wayyizkor ʾᵉlohim, wayyar ʾᵉlohim, wayyedaʿ ʾᵉlohim* is that of a tolling bell.

c. While in the first passage the child Moses is necessarily the passive object of tender womanly regard, in the second he appears as the active subject of various, even violent deeds. Taken together, the three episodes of his early manhood provide a pointed characterization of the future champion of Israel.

On his first sally out of the court to witness his people's misery he comes to the defense of a kinsman against an Egyptian. Moved to visit them again, he intervenes in a quarrel between two of his kinsmen. Later, he champions the cause of helpless Midianite girls. The scale of disinterestedness rises: he not only defends his wronged kin against outsiders, he defends one wronged Israelite against another; he intervenes not only when the wronged are Israelites, but when they are total strangers. The misfortune he suffered through his zeal for justice does not dampen that zeal; it burns on and impels him to side with the victims of injustice even when he is a fugitive in a foreign land. Wherever he is he cannot

THE LIFE OF MOSES BEFORE HIS CALL (2:1–25)

remain aloof from his environment; the wrongs he sees compel him to take action.[72]

The significance of the choice of details out of Moses' early life was not lost on later readers.

> "Even from the acts of a youth it is known whether his deeds will be pure and right" (Prov 20:11 [so taken by the midrash]): Though Moses lived in the royal palace ... he felt the anguish of his kinsmen, thus exemplifying Hillel's teaching, "Do not separate yourself from the community." (*ST*)

> These three episodes ... follow the account of Moses' upbringing in the king's palace not because they actually were the immediate sequel, but to display the excellence of Moses' character. He grew up in Pharaoh's royal palace, in a position to learn the methods of government and the ways of leadership—matters that would embolden him and enlarge his spirit. As a result, he could hold his own with the bravest, and was afraid of no one. Nor could he brook the sight of evil, either in Egypt or in Midian where he was a stranger and a fugitive. All this indicates that Moses was by nature righteous, just, and largehearted—having a character worthy of prophecy [we should say, of a champion of the oppressed] and truly qualifying one for the office. (Abarbanel)

d. The last brief passage resumes the bondage story of 1:8–14 to prepare the ground for a turning point. Two changes have occurred enabling the process of redemption to be set in motion. The Pharaoh who was after Moses' life has died; now Moses may safely go back to Egypt. Of greater moment is the stirring on high. The cry that has gone up from the Israelites through the long years of oppression has finally reached heaven: God has taken notice. The four solemn clauses with which the passage ends toll the good tidings: the time of God's action has at last arrived.

---

72. "The episode with Jethro's daughters proves Moses' virtue: he defended not only his own, but championed the cause of the wronged among mankind at large" (Malbim); cf. also Ahad Haʿam, "Moses," 314–16.

The Prologue: General Considerations

The Preliminary Nature of Chapters 1-2

What justifies our combining chapters 1 and 2 and setting them apart from what follows?[73]

The preliminary nature of the material in these chapters is indicated first by the briefness of the passages into which it is divided, and their episodic character. The narrative skims along, touching only on highlights, until it comes to rest on the main event that begins at the burning bush. The two chapters are parceled into no less than six passages, each clearly marked by a change in characters or a leap in time. To be sure, the pieces lengthen—from 7 to 8 to 10 to 12 verses[74]—as Moses comes into focus, while the time span covered shortens. (Chapter 1 covers the events of four generations, chapter 2 of two-thirds of Moses' life.) But this hardly lessens the contrast between them and what follows. That the principal interest of the story begins in chapter 3 is evident alone from the unbroken stretch of narrative that sets in at 3:1 and extends with no more than breathings to 4:17. Moreover, within these thirty-nine verses there is strict unity of time, place, and characters. The rest of the book of Exodus covers the events of little more than one year from the time of the burning bush revelation. But a single character of any consequence remains to be introduced after chapter 2—Aaron, who only once is anything more than Moses' alter ego.

Chapters 1 and 2 are, then, a Prologue to the main narrative, introducing its theme and chief characters. This is done in three steps: the theme is sounded; it is gradually deflected into a diversion; then it is resumed and rounded off suspensefully.

---

73. This is by no means a generally accepted division of the material. Driver, *Introduction*, 22, combines the two chapters as the first unit of the book; McNeile, *Exodus*, xii, makes the unit end at 2:22; Cassuto (*Šᵉmot* [ET = *Exodus*]) takes each chapter as a separate unit, and connects 2:23-25 with 3:1ff.; Noth (*Exodus*) divides thus: 1:1-22; 2:1-10; 2:11—4:23; Fohrer (*Überlieferung*) 1:1—2:10; 2:11—4:31.

74. The final three-verse passage of chapter 2 is a bridge, more self-contained than 1:22, to what follows. As the herald of the revelation at the bush, it might justifiably have been joined to the next unit (so the Sam. paragraphing; cf. Rashi, Rashbam [cited above, p. 42], Ramban; see also preceding note). That I have not done so is due to my conception of the story line as set forth below. Note that the division of both Jews (*parasha, sidra*) and Christians (chapter) makes a break after 2:25.

First the people of Israel come into being, and a domineering Pharaoh is sketched. His oppression of the people produces the crisis that demands resolution. That is the first statement of the theme.

For the resolution, two factors are needed: a human agent and the divine initiative. And so the diversion begins. With the theme gradually receding into the background, the story goes on to unfold the circumstances of Moses' birth—the midwives episode flowing into the birth story—Moses' manhood in Egypt (where the bondage theme comes momentarily into the foreground), his flight, and his settlement in Midian. The human agent has been introduced, but his very zeal on behalf of his brethren has been his undoing.

The Prologue ends with a return to the theme—the unchanged, unresolved crisis in Egypt. But now a second, decisive factor emerges: the deity has bestirred itself. With God, the suffering people, and the Egyptian oppressor on stage, and Moses in the wings, all the elements of the drama are present. The play can begin.

Two Progressions

a. Worked into the threefold movement of the Prologue are two progressions that enhance the climactic effect of the narrative. There is, first, a progression of initiatives. Throughout chapter 1 Israel is a passive mass, a collective, teeming victim. All the initiatives lie with the Egyptians, even the defense of Israel. Only in chapter 2 do individual Israelites come into view, and as actors, not merely victims. Absent until the very end of chapter 2 is the God of the Fathers. His will underlies all the events related in the two chapters, but he does not appear until the end, on the threshold of the burning bush story.

b. Within this progression of initiatives (Egypt–Israel–God) is a steady accession of power working on behalf of Israel.

At first Israel has only its fecundity with which to oppose the oppressive government. Israel is a witless matrix, an infinitely fertile womb. The first intelligent countermeasure on its behalf is taken by the non-Israelite midwives. That countermeasure is taken by women, invokes the purported animal vitality of women, and succeeds by womanly wiles. At the next stage, Israelite actors appear, but the weakness of Israel is expressed by those who work on its behalf: a mother and a sister moved by love—note it well! Neither Moses' father or brother plays any part in his preservation. The baby is saved by yet another woman, moved by feminine pity at the sight of his crying.

Here we may observe that the point of these narratives is precisely the contrast between the success of the feeble champions of Israel and the thwarting of their all-powerful opponents. Nothing could express so clearly the providential nature of the events.

A decisive change occurs with Moses' adulthood: a man has finally been born to Israel and the action reflects it. He sallies forth to see what is happening (women are supposed to stay indoors—the lesson of Dinah!), he kills—but he is thwarted; the Egyptian machine is too much for him. So he must flee, but he is not broken. In exile he is still the man; he rescues girls from bullies (the circle is full: he who was saved by women now saves them). He marries and has a son—but he has abandoned the field of action. His zeal has miscarried; the time was not ripe. And then, when the prospect is blackest, the highest instance stirs. The sole force capable of crushing the Egyptian juggernaut awakens at last. The narrative hangs expectantly on the verge of his action,

The Redactional Process

a. Study of the six passages that make up the Prologue has revealed that they are not of one quality. They are not equally smooth or equally homogeneous. Parts look as though they had once existed independently of one another, and parts raise a doubt whether they were originally as they now are.[75] This suggests that some development lies behind the present text; some, if not all, of the individual units may have had a history of their own. Later they were combined into the whole in which we now have them.

The possibilities are too little known and the evidence too meager to do more than guess at the ultimate origin of the material. Analogies from other ancient literatures and modern non-literate cultures, combined with such biblical evidence as exists,[76] indicate that an oral stage preced-

---

75. For homogeneity, contrast 1:1–7 with 1:15–22; for smoothness, the transition between Moses' childhood and manhood (2:10–11) with that between Moses' flight and his Midianite adventure (2:15 end); 1:13–14 appear to be independent; the sudden presence of the sister in Moses' birth story raises doubts. On these and more, see the full discussion below.

76. See further the Excursus. An extensive treatment of the preliterary stage of biblical literature will be found in Eissfeldt, Part One.

ed written literature in Israel. Formulas, cadences, balanced sentences, groupings of ten sayings all argue for a background of oral delivery. But however important that background may be, in the final analysis the received text is the only extant evidence of ancient Hebrew literature and literary art. To the extent that we base our considerations on it, they lie within the scope of public control and discussion. The further we depart from the final deposit of literary development, the more speculative and private must our opinions become.

Though a historian of literature must try to penetrate to its origins, for the exegete, whose interest is the present form of a given text, it is the ultimate and penultimate stages of literary development that are immediately relevant. By the ultimate stage is meant the combination into its present shape of pre-existing entities, with seams and connecting pieces supplied as needed by the combiner. By the penultimate stage is meant the pre-existing entities before their combination, such entities possibly being composite themselves, the products of yet earlier stages of development which are no longer recoverable. To trace these two stages of development is to enter the workroom of the combiner—henceforth to be called the redactor—to see what he had to work with and how he fashioned it. Perhaps the most interesting part of this study is the attempt to discover why the redactor acted as he did, the attempt to enter his mind and lay bare what we can of his ways of thought and mode of literary operation. Since the understanding of Exodus cannot be considered complete until some explanation can be given of its discontinuities, the study of the redactorial process is a part of modern exegesis of the book. It alone enables one to appreciate the extent to which the present text is a creative achievement.

Such a study, it need hardly be said, is speculative, necessarily bridging over ignorance with hypotheses that cannot be controlled. One may demand that the results be plausible and internally consistent; their probability will depend upon the strength of the evidence, the care with which alternatives have been weighed, on how well grounded and few the assumptions are.

b. The block of narrative concerning Moses, called above "the diversion," consists of the three largest and most homogeneous passages of the Prologue (1:15–22; 2:1–10, 11–22).

In the first passage, verse 21 alone gives the appearance of an increment to the text, a footnote, as it were, to the preceding verse.

The second passage, Moses' birth-story, has, as noted above, an internal inconsistency that, while not snagging the reader, yet suggests that the tale is not in its original form. It is an almost inescapable *a priori* that a narrative creation will be coherent, and inorganic strands in it unoriginal. On that basis, the present form of Moses' birth-story must be regarded as at least a step removed from its original state. The return of the child to its mother, in which the sister—the source of the inconsistency—is instrumental (2:4, 7–9), may be a superadded element.

The third passage has one rough spot, the juncture of Moses' flight and his Midianite adventure (in 2:15). Is this a seam joining what were at first separate tales? One tends to doubt that a freely composed narrative of Moses' early manhood would have expressed itself so awkwardly at this point.

It thus appears that in each of these three passages there are signs of at least two stages of development. In every case, however, no serious impairment of the unity of the text has occurred. Perhaps this is because the development took place early, when the material was still fluid enough to absorb the new elements.[77]

c. The three passages containing the theme of the Prologue and encasing the "diversion" (1:1–7, 8–14; 2:23–25) show considerably more disunity.

The first passage is quite heterogeneous, tailored out of various materials to form an introduction to the narrative. The adapted genealogy is followed by a snatch of narrative (verse 6) and what appears to be a deliberately constructed proliferation formula. The routine formula of Gen

---

[77]. The underlying assumption of the argument has been that simplicity and originality correlate. This assumption is bolstered by the impression gained from such narratives as Hagar's expulsion (Gen 21:8–21), the near sacrifice of Isaac (Gen 22:1–14), most episodes of the Joseph story, and many other short pieces. An auxiliary assumption (made at the end) is that earlier stages of tradition were more fluid than later, and that therefore absorptive and integrative capacity may be used as a criterion of age. This assumption rests on the commonly observed behavior of traditional materials, especially of sacred materials.

It is interesting to note how, starting from a diametrically opposed assumption, Erlich arrives at the same judgment of the age of these narratives. Of Moses' birth story he says, "The sudden appearance of the sister, who offers her services unasked, and must thus betray her relationship to Moses, shows the unskilled manner of the early narration. The later author of Genesis would have brought about Moses' return to the care and supervision of his mother in an entirely different manner" (Ehrlich, *Randglossen*, at 2:7]). To my knowledge, Ehrlich never systematically developed his views on the dating of biblical literature, so one cannot readily subject them to examination.

47:27b has been systematically expanded (see above). The whole gives the impression of a piece made to order, rather than an existent element of tradition.

The second passage contains the problematic verses 13–14, whose detached character (they would not be missed if omitted), references to Israel in the plural (contrast verses 8–12), and new terminology (derivatives of ʿabad, the term bᵉparek) speak for a separate provenance. Was there another version of the bondage story, of which this is an excerpt? If so, is there any clue to the provenance of that version or its larger connection?

The term bᵉparek occurs again only in two places in the Bible: Lev 25:43, 46, 53 and Ezek 34:4. Ezekiel and Leviticus are related in that both use the phrase rada bᵉparek. But the Leviticus passage—a series of laws concerning bondage—is more closely related to ours both by the presence of ʿabad derivatives (verses 42, 46) and by its subject: the ban on working an Israelite bondman bᵉparek, "for they are my servants, whom I freed from the land of Egypt" (verse 42; cf. 55).

It seems likely that our Exodus passage belongs to the same body of material as Leviticus 25. As a narrative associated with law it will bear a relation to Leviticus 25 somewhat like the relation of the narrative of Gen 2:1–4 to later Sabbath laws (especially Exod 20:8–11),[78] namely, that of the historical ground of the law. Inclusion of the excerpt here (although it does not substantially advance the story), will thus have served the larger design of the Pentateuch. To sum up: we have in 1:13–14 a passage needed to give the proper overtone to legislation in Leviticus that originally belonged with it as part of a self-contained version of the bondage story.

That this heterogeneous excerpt lent itself to being exegetically construed in its context was doubtless a condition of its incorporation into the narrative. Its literary integration, however, was minimal: all distinctive features were retained, and no attempt was made to work the material into the fabric of the preceding narrative. The piece was simply juxtaposed to what came before, a process that, with its suggestion of crystallized elements, would seem to belong to a later stage of literary development than the almost seamless integration of heterogeneous materials postulated above in section (b).

The last passage of the main theme, 2:23–25, sets in with a difficulty: the notice of the king's death is not connected with the rest of verse 23,

---

78. Cf. Rashbam at Gen 1:1: "This whole account of the six days of creation was placed here by Moses in anticipation of God's reference to the Sabbath at Sinai . . ."

although *wayye'anᵉhu* does sound as if it were a sequel to some preceding statement. The two elements thus appear to be heterogeneous. Now, the twice-repeated *ᶜᵃboda* of verse 23 connects the bulk of the passage with 1:13–14; only here and there has the term been found so far; the other passages use *siblot* instead (1:11; 2:11). What is more, 2:23ab–25 reads well as a sequel to 1:13–14, leading us to assume that it belongs to the other version of the bondage story. The notice of the king's death, on the other hand, corresponds to that of his accession in 1:8 and may be ascribed to the same source. Here again, then, we seem to have juxtaposition rather than integration of heterogeneous elements.

d. What does it mean that the bondage theme is set forth in more composite units than the "diversion" treating of Moses' early life? Presumably that there were more versions of the bondage tale—that is, it was incorporated in more tradition complexes—than the Moses story. As a crucial, if not the crucial, event in Israel's history, the Exodus must have been included in every formulation of early tradition. That would have required telling the story of the bondage, but not necessarily the colorful detail of Moses' early years. And so when the standard form of the tradition was crystallized as we now have it, while few if any variants of the Moses story were available, the bondage theme was to be found in more than one version. Our text-form makes maximal use of the versions, supplementing the one with the other as the need arises.[79]

e. The components of the Prologue may be summarized as follows:

(1) An introductory piece, made to order out of pre-existing elements adapted to their new purpose.

(2) Narratives of the bondage and Moses' early life. The stories about Moses show signs of having undergone some development, but at a time before they reached the redactor. It is manifest that these narratives belong to a larger tradition-complex, extending backward and forward from Exodus. We shall call this tradition-complex A.

(3) Two excerpts of another version of the bondage tale, used to fill out the aforementioned narratives and combined with them at a late

---

79. Further indication that the story of Moses' early life (1:15—2:10) is on a separate footing from the other tradition-elements is the absence of any later reference to the decree against the infants. The narrative of 5:6–23 seems oblivious of it: the heightening of Israel's travail entailed by depriving them of a regular supply of straw seems puny after the murderous decree of 1:22. Nor are Moses' years in Pharaoh's household mentioned again, "not even where one might have expected it, as in the later negotiations with Pharaoh, where 'the old relation to the court might so readily have lent itself to effective use'" (Gressmann, *Mose*, 3 [citing E. Meyer]).

stage. When put together, the two excerpts cohere, but they do not include the beginning of the story—how Israel came to be enslaved. A relationship between this narrative version and legislation in Leviticus can be shown, as well as between it and narratives in Genesis. (See ahead at 6:2ff.) We shall call this narrative-plus-legislation tradition-complex B.[80]

What was the work of the redactor?

It would seem that he must be credited with composing the introductory passage, signaling the start of a new literary unit, not a mere continuation of Genesis. Through the proliferation formula at its end, the expressions of increase that were already present in subsequent passages of the chapter were transformed into a refrain, thus lending both a unity and a rhythm to the movement of the story.

He then strung the narratives in an order that seems to have been determined as much by dramatic effect as by their position in the pre-existing tradition-complexes. He cannot be credited with the values that inhere within the narrative units. But the supplementation[81] of A with engraftings of B is likely to have been his doing. The shape and placement of the final passage of the Prologue, in which we are brought to trembling anticipation of God's appearance in the history, are therefore the redactor's achievement.

The horizon of the redactor was not bound by the book of Exodus. The tradition-complexes at his disposal extended both forward and backward: from materials in Genesis he fashioned the introductory passage; his engrafting of 1:13–14 on to the preceding narrative seems to have been dictated at least in part by the formulation of a law in Leviticus.

His work is an amalgam of freedom of action and fidelity to tradition. On the one hand, he did not scruple to discard that part of B's narrative that he deemed superfluous (its account of how and why the Israelites were enslaved). On the other, he left intact the inconsistency in Moses' birth story that could no more have escaped him than us. And when he fashioned a piece to give a shape to the narrative, he utilized only traditional materials. With the inspiration and building blocks received from tradition he created a structure whose design is his own.

---

80. It is generally supposed that verse 7 (minus *wayyirbu wayyaʿaṣ^emu*) belongs to the same narrative strand as verse 13. Even so, one still misses a nexus—brief as it might be—between the increase and the enslavement, an equivalent to what is told in verses 8–12.

81. Noth stresses R's desire to enrich his product by incorporating all unique elements of his sources (*UG*, 268–69 [ET = *History of Pentateuchal Traditions*, 249–50]).

II. Moses' Commissioning (3:1–7:13)

The Revelation at the Bush (3:1–4:17)

The Movement of the Story

a. **3:1–10.** Moses, tending the flocks of Jethro, drove them on one occasion far abroad in search of pasturage, till he happened upon the mountain of God. There a strange apparition—a bush that burned without being burnt—arrested his attention. Approaching it, he began to hear the voice of his ancestral God telling him of his decision to rescue Israel from Egypt and bring them to the promised land. And Moses was to be his agent in this undertaking.

(1) As a humble shepherd of his father-in-law's flock Moses has reached the station most opposed to what he was and what he will be. How important persons rose unexpectedly from lowly beginnings, thus showing the working of Providence in human affairs, is a favorite biblical theme. Two other men who were "taken from following the flock" to greatness are the first literary prophet, Amos (Amos 7:15), and the ideal king, David. A dramatic representation of David's ascent, skipping (for the sake of contrast) all intermediate stages, is Ps 78:70–72:

> He chose David his servant
>   and took him from the sheepfolds;
> From tending suckling ewes he brought him
>   to shepherd Jacob, his people, Israel, his inheritance.
> With upright heart he tended them,
>   and guided them with skillful hand.

The figures of this passage illustrate the poetic fitness of the shepherd's office as a preparation for leadership. Both divine and human chiefs were regularly figured as shepherds of their people in the ancient Near East, and the people as flocks.[1] Moses himself uses the figure in Num 27:17, "Let not the people of the Lord be like a flock that has no shepherd." The midrash elaborates how Moses' tender care of his flock proved his qualification for leadership.

(2) The precise sense of *'aḥar hammidbar* is not clear. NJPS "into the wilderness" at least conveys something of the implication of the Hebrew that on this occasion Moses ranged farther than usual "after good pasturage" (Targs.), going to the highlands after the lowland grass had dried up or had been consumed. That the vicinity of the mountain of God was grazing-land we hear in 34:3 ("neither shall the flocks and the herds graze at the foot of this mountain"); its abundance may be gauged by its sufficiency to sustain the livestock of the entire camp of Israel for close to a year (cf. Num 10:11).

Pressing into these fertile highlands, presumably at some distance from Midian toward Egypt (4:27; 18:5, 27; Num 10:30) Moses arrived at Mount Horeb. That it was the mountain of God is made out to be as little known to Moses as Bethel's being the "gate of heaven" was to Jacob. Nothing but the wondrous apparition marked the place as sacred to Moses; there was no sanctuary or altar already there. Hence the epithet "mountain of God" has been regarded as anticipatory of later experience (so, e.g., *Onk.*, Rashi).[2] All the same, the language of God in 19:4 ("You have seen how I . . . brought you to me") does suggest that, unbeknown to men, Horeb was in some sense "God's mountain" even before Moses happened upon it.

As in the case of Bethel, the sanctity of Horeb began for Israel with a divine revelation there to an ancient worthy. But there is this difference between the two: Bethel became an important sanctuary-site in later times, while Horeb's sanctity was historical only. Because of its

---

1. See *ANET*, 159c (Lipit-Ishtar), 164c, 165c, 178a (Hammurabi), 289a (Esarhaddon), 368a (Egyptian Sun god), 371d (Ptah), 388a (Shamash); in the Bible, Gen 48:15; Ps 23:1; 80:2 (God); 1 Chr 17:6 (judges); Jer 23:1ff.; Ezek 34:2ff. (chiefs); Mic 7:14; Ps 79:13 (people as flocks).

2. B. S. Childs remarks in this connection: "I wonder whether there is a double perspective reflected in these first verses, which would explain . . . the apparent tensions . . . 2a and 2b do not match. But 2a is a sort of superscription by the author (cf. the parallel in Gen 18:1) while 2b takes up the historical sequence. The 'mountain of God' would then also reflect the author's perspective."

associations, Elijah later fled there for a renewal of his charge (1 Kings 19). As a relic of the notion that it was a seat of God, poets portrayed divine help as coming to Israel from the revelation desert (e.g., Judg 5:4ff.). But in the life of later Israel, the "mountain that God desired for his abode in which his presence dwelled forever" (Ps 68:17) and at which the national temple was erected was Mount Zion; there was no site of worship at Horeb in later times.[3]

It is plain from verse 12b that no distinction between Horeb and Sinai (chs. 19 and 24) was recognized by biblical tradition. Hence IE's notion of a connection between Sinai and s^ene—a rare word found again only in Deut 33:16 in an evident allusion to our passage[4] may have been shared by the early tradition.

(3) Within verses 2–4 the apparition in the bush is described variously. First, "an angel of YHWH appeared to Moses in a blazing fire out of the bush." We then read that Moses was startled, not by any shape in the fire,[5] but by the unburnable quality of the bush; next, that "when YHWH saw that he had turned aside" to get a closer look, "'$elohim$ called to him out of the bush." Was the "angel" other than the fire? Is YHWH other than the "angel" and '$elohim$? To ask these questions is almost to answer them—negatively; how, then, are we to construe the passage?

$Mal'ak$ YHWH here, as everywhere, refers to a visible manifestation of YHWH, essentially indistinguishable from YHWH himself (see the alternation between them in Judg 6:12, 14, 16, 20, 22, 23), except that here the manifestation is not anthropomorphic but fiery.[6] There is,

---

3. The very location of the mountain of revelation was unknown in postbiblical times; see G. E. Wright in *IDB*, s.v. Sinai. On the lack of continuity of Horeb's place in the life of Israel and its historical and literary implications, see Kaufmann, *Religion of Israel*, 242ff.

4. "God is called 'the s^ene-dweller' because he revealed himself to Moses first in it, and dwelled for a length of time upon Mount Sinai, the place of the s^ene, whence he later removed to dwell amidst Israel" (Ramban at Deut 33:16). "[God is so called] because he dwelled on the mountain named after the s^ene, namely Sinai . . ." (Shadal, ibid.).

5. Since, as will be noted below, the burning bush revelation adumbrates the later theophany at Sinai, something may be suggested about the former from Moses' insistence with regard to the latter that "you heard the sound of words, but you saw no image" (Deut 4:12).

6. "The angel took the form of a blazing fire" (*Ma'or*). B. S. Childs makes the luminous suggestion that the *bet* of *b^elabbat* is *bet essentiae* (BDB 88b [7]). The construction will then exactly parallel that in 6:3a (*wa'era . . . b^e'el šadday*) and is to be rendered "appeared . . . as/in the form of a blazing fire."

THE REVELATION AT THE BUSH (3:1—4:17) 59

then, no especial difficulty in the shift from "angel" to YHWH in verses 2 and 4. The shift from YHWH to *'elohim* in verse 4 is strange (the versions obliterate it: the Samaritan Pentateuch reads *'elohim*; Gk, YHWH in both clauses). Since *'elohim* is a general term for all celestial beings, angels included, perhaps it is used here to refer to the *mal'ak* who was in the bush (IE).

Later homilies exploited the sermonic possibilities offered by the lowly thornbush as a revelation-site. The point in context seems to be that a familiar sight in pasture lands, a scrubfire, introduced Moses to the theophany as its strangeness dawned on him ("the bush remained green and was not burnt" [*TY*]). The contrast with the awesomely spectacular later theophany at the same site suggests that this modest form of revelation was chosen out of solicitude for Moses' inexperience; with veterans God did not hesitate to pull out the stops (e.g., 1 Kgs 19:11ff.).

The choice of fire as a divine element (as in Gen 15:17) flows from its manifold God-like characteristics. As burning and fire are used in similes of fury (Esth 1:12) and love (Song 8:6), so the passionate nature of Israel's God ("whose name is Impassioned" [Exod 34:14]) is often expressed in similes of fire (Jer 4:4; Ps 79:5; Zeph 3:8). The destructive power of fire provides an analogy to God's dangerous holiness: in his dangerous aspect God is actually called "a consuming fire" (Deut 4:24; 9:3; cf. Lev 10:2; and 2 Kgs 1:10ff.). Purity (Num 31:23; Mal 3:2) and illumination (cf. Exod 13:21) are further points of comparison. Finally, the mysterious texture of fire—its reality yet insubstantiality, its ability to work at a distance—must have contributed to its aptness as a divine symbol.

In view of the later fiery form of the Sinaitic theophany, the midrash fittingly finds here a preparatory experience. "When he comes to Sinai and beholds those flames he will not be afraid of them" (*ShR*). This is but one of several foreshadowings of the later theophany in the revelation at the bush.

(4) From the fact that Moses retained enough of his wits to answer the call to him, it appears that the voice he heard was far removed from the "voice of YHWH" described, e.g., in Psalm 29; see next section. The second stage of his growing awareness of what he was experiencing was imparted to him in the statement that he was on holy ground. He clearly did not yet realize fully the import of the apparition, for only after God's self-introduction (verse 6) did he cover his face—and his eyes, now still drinking in the marvelous sight.

The urgent call to Moses, who was approaching the bush—urgency is indicated by the repetition of his name (cf. Gen 22:11)—aims at stopping him before he profanes sacred ground with his shoes. Shoes are worn to keep the feet from dirt and harm; as such they are an insult to sacred ground. Moreover, they are liable to touch all sorts of impurity which would profane the holy (Hizquni). Hence "wherever the divine presence reveals itself, wearing shoes is forbidden. So in the case of Joshua (Josh 5:15), and so too in the case of the priests: they served barefoot in the temple" (ShR).[7]

(5) Only when the voice out of the apparition identifies itself does the full awareness break upon Moses that he is in the presence of God, and he covers his face in fear (cf. 1 Kgs 19:13; Isa 6:2). The voice identifies itself as the God of Moses' father, and only afterward as the God of Israel's patriarchs. It is a delicate touch, this self-introduction by association with the family worship, the earliest and most intimate experience Moses would have had of the ancestral God. The midrash enlarges upon the point meanwhile highlighting the motif of gradualness that dominates verses 2–6. "R. Joshua the priest son of Nehemiah said: When God revealed himself to Moses, Moses was a tyro at prophecy. Thought God, 'If I reveal myself to him in a loud voice I'll frighten him; if in a small voice, he'll disdain my mission.' So what did he do? He revealed himself to him in the voice of his father. Moses answered, 'Here I am. What does father want?' God replied, 'I'm not your father, but the God of your father; I approached you tactfully in order not to frighten you'" (ShR).[8]

---

7. Barefootedness was also part of the self-abnegation practiced by mourners along with removal of all amenities of dress and display (see especially Ezek 24:17; also 2 Sam 15:30). Is this idea, too, present here as a humiliation due the presence of God (suggestion of Dr. Naomi Cohen)?

The idea that because barefootedness is a natural state it was proper for contact with the holy (Noth, *Exodus*) seems to be foreign to biblical thought. Adam's feigned horror at appearing naked before God (compared with Moses covering his face in verse 6 by B. Jacob), the concern that priests not expose themselves during their service (Exod 20:26; cf. Michal's taunt of David, 2 Sam 6:20), and the rite of circumcision, speak against a valuation of nakedness and the natural state. By contrast, Sumerian priests did serve their gods naked (*ANEP*, 597, 600, 603, 605).

8. How closely this midrash hews to biblical prototypes emerges from comparison with 1 Sam 3:5–6: the voice that called Samuel was so like that of his guardian, Eli, that Samuel could take it for Eli's.

The point, so fitting the consideration of Moses' inexperience that marks our whole passage, is obliterated by the Samaritan Pentateuch reading "your fathers" (*'aboteka*), as in verse 15.[9]

The threefold repetition of *'elohei* before each of the patriarchs suggests the sameness of the God and the constancy of his concern throughout generations; he who addresses Moses is the same who cared for Abraham, for Isaac, for Jacob. That constancy (it is no more than suggested by the repetition) is now about to benefit their descendants.

(6) In verses 7–8 God tells how he has been moved to act on behalf of Israel, the background of his call to Moses in verse 10. The two verses beginning with *we'atta* (9, 10) are the business or concluding part of the communication. The repetitiveness of verse 9 (going over the substance of verse 7) and its failure to get to the point (the commissioning of Moses, verse 10) can be paralleled in the style of 2 Sam 7:28–29. In the preceding verse, 7:27, David grounds his boldness in praying for a dynasty on God's own promise. Verse 28 opens with *we'atta*, but instead of coming to the point (the prayer) it repeats the aforementioned ground in other words (*wattedabber 'el 'abdeka 'et hattoba hazzot*). Only in verse 29, which again opens with *we'atta*, does David pray that God fulfill his promise.

Both here and there the formal conclusion is a compound whose first element restates the ground. This reflects the importance that the speaker attaches to keeping in the forefront of the hearer's consciousness the ground of his action—in our case, God's sympathetic notice of Israel's misery.

(7) Each of the qualifications of the promised land in verse 8 answers a different purpose. "Good and spacious" is a unique combination (in Deuteronomy "good" alone occurs frequently); it evokes amplitude and freedom of movement in contrast with the shackles of Egyptian slavery (cf. Ps 31:9, where *'oni* [verse 7 above] and *sara* contrast with *merhab*). "A land flowing with milk and honey" is a stereotyped expression of fertility and abundance ordinarily referring to the promised land (e.g., Exod 13:5; Lev 20:24). The attributes of the promised land are such as are required to fill the needs of a vast population now consisting of seven nations.

---

9. BH³ commends this as the probably correct reading. Ramban achieves the same result by interpreting "your fathers" as "each one of your forefathers," comparing 15:2 below, which again he glosses as "God of my fathers." But neither expedient is necessary in view of 2 Kgs 20:5 ("YHWH, God of David, your [Hezekiah's] father"), which shows that "God of your father" may be used of a distant ancestor. The phrase is thus ambiguous.

Only the equivalents of Egypt's paradisiacal circumstances can attract the oppressed Israelites to risk a revolt against their masters.

b. 3:11–12. Moses reacts to God's proposal by protesting his inadequacy for the task. God assures him of support and offers him a sign of his commission:[10] Israel's worship at this mountain after Moses has led them out of Egypt.

(1) Verse 12, with its echoes of the twin clauses of verses 10 and 11[11] must somehow answer to Moses' expression of inadequacy. The difficulty is that it seems to go beyond the matter at hand by introducing a "sign" and referring to Israel's future worship at the mountain of revelation. The integration of these elements into the line of thought is perplexing.[12]

The interpretation of 12a found in ShR (and underlying NJPS), although it leaves 12b outside the train of thought, merits notice. "By this it will be manifest that you act as my agent: I will be with you and whatever you wish I will accomplish."[13] But most modern scholars (see note 12) are inclined to attach the sign to the last clause of the verse, both to keep

---

10. The force of "that it is I who send you" is not entirely clear, but it seems to mean "that you go as my agent." Moses failed to refer to his agency in 11a, speaking instead as though he were on his own. God assures him that he will not be alone and promises him a sign confirming his agent status. Moses can rest assured that all he does has God's backing.

11. Verse 10:   *lᵉka wᵉʾešlaḥᵃka ʾel parʿo*   / *wᵉhoṣe ʾet ʿammi bᵉne Y. mimiṣrayim*
    Verse 11:   ... *ki ʾelek* ...   / *wᵉki ʾoṣi ʾet bᵉne Y. mimiṣrayim*
    Verse 12:   ... *šᵉlaḥtika*   / *bᵉhoṣiʾᵃka ʾet haʿam mimiṣrayim* ...

12. The heart of the problem is the "sign" clause: to what does *zh* refer, backward (as in 1 Sam 14:10) to the preceding clause (so, e.g., ShR; Ehrlich, *Randglossen*; NJPS), forward (as in 1 Sam 2:34; 2 Kgs 19:29 [= Isa 37:30]; 20:9 [= 38:7]; Jer 44:29) to the following clause (so, e.g., Driver, *Exodus*; McNeile, *Exodus*; Cassuto, *Šᵉmot* [ET = *Exodus*]), or perhaps to the burning bush itself (ST, IE, Shadal)? No alternative yields an immediately lucid construction of the whole verse. Noth concludes, accordingly, that something has fallen out. But the structural agreement of the verse with what precedes it (see previous note) indicates that it is original and in order. Perhaps the obscurity results from a certain telescoping of ideas, as is suggested below.

13. Two other attempts (in part mutually exclusive) to account for 12b as discontinuous with 12a follow: "Moses had doubted that he could manage the liberation of Israel from Egypt. To this he receives the reply, 'This very mountain on which you expressed your doubt... will be the scene of lawgiving to the liberated people'" (Ehrlich, *Randglossen*). "[Verse 12b] is a command to memorialize the portent [i.e. the burning bush theophany] ... by consecrating the mountain and worshiping God there—as indeed was done (Exod 24:4–5). The future revelation of the law is not mentioned here, only that which will suffice to encourage Moses to believe that Israel would really be liberated by him [namely, the assurance that he *will* bring the people out of Egypt]" (Shadal).

the sentence together, and because it appears to be the more natural way to read it. It will then follow that for the final "proof" of his commission Moses will have to wait for some future event; "No other sign is given *to Moses* for his encouragement [in contrast to 4:1–9, which seeks to meet the doubts of the people.] His belief in his own divine mission would be justified and strengthened by his return, with the Israelites, to this very same mountain of God."[14]

Verse 12, then, will have God reassuring Moses in two ways. (a) Moses will not be alone, (Moses has been so frightened by verse 10 that he has forgotten verse 8a) for God will be with him; (b) the proof that the God who spoke out of the bush has really made him his agent will be all Israel's worship of him after the Exodus at the selfsame spot. Render: "And this will be the sign for you that it is I [who speak to you out of this bush on this mountain] who send you: when you bring the people out of Egypt you will worship God at this very mountain." The moment will have a private, corroborating meaning to Moses that no one else will share, since only for him will the fulfillment recall its first promise at the same place.[15]

Verse 12b thus assures Moses of success in bringing Israel out of Egypt by taking it for granted in the course of promising him proof of his divine mission through a subsequent event. That is puzzling; we should have expected Moses' second query (11b) to have been answered simply "You shall bring them out, for I will be there at your side to guarantee it," or the like.[16] Why, instead, is reference made to a subsequent event? Moreover, if a confirmatory sign of Moses' mission was needed—as, e.g., in the case of Gideon (Judg 6:14ff.)—it should have appeared then and there—as with Gideon[17]—and not at some indefinite future time.

The fact is, of course, that, unlike Gideon, Moses did not ask for a sign; hence God's proffer of one must have intended more than

14. McNeile, *Exodus*.

15. The objection that the probative value of Israel's worship at the mountain would be vitiated by the fact that Moses himself led the people there (Jacob, *Exodus*, 27) is met by the consideration that not Moses but God led the people in the wilderness (13:17, 18, 21; 17:1; 40:36–37).

16. As God answered Gideon's protestation of inadequacy: "Indeed I will be with you and you shall defeat Midian as though they were but one man!" (Judg 6:16). Habel ("The Form and Significance") notes that the pattern of statements of reassurance in accounts of the call of prophets is that they "repeat in essence the content of the commission."

17. Hence the view (of *ST* and *IE*) that the sign was the burning bush itself.

reassurance (though by taking for granted Moses' success it gives that too). What that "more" can have been may be surmised from the subject it speaks of that appears to go beyond Moses' immediate concern: Israel's future worship at the mountain of revelation. That reference is nothing less than an adumbration of the great theophany to come, the merest suggestion of what God has in store for Israel through an allusion to a single one of its elements (24:4ff.; cf. IE).

From the start, God intended the liberation to be only the precondition of a greater event: making Israel his people, "Serving God" instead of Pharaoh is the goal toward which Israel will march. The element of service, moreover, will prove to be directly related to Moses' immediate task: in verse 18 he will be instructed to approach Pharaoh with a request to let Israel sacrifice to its God in the wilderness—presumably, we may now infer, at the mountain of revelation. The ground for that request is prepared in our verse (cf. Rashbam).

To sum up: In the course of reassuring Moses, God has hinted at something beyond mere liberation of Israel as his ultimate aim. That "something beyond" will indeed confirm Moses' agency—and not only privately—in an as yet undreamed-of way,[18] while for the present it will serve as a basis for negotiating with Pharaoh. Such ulterior motives appear to underlie God's proffer to Moses of an unasked-for sign.[19]

c. 3:13-22. Assuming that he accepts God's commission, Moses now protests he will not know what to answer if requested by the people to name his sender. God puts an answer into his mouth, to which he then appends two speeches, to be made, respectively, to the elders and to Pharaoh. Pharaoh's stubbornness, the unheard-of punishments that will be inflicted upon him, and the final exodus of the people, laden with the goods of Egypt, are then foretold.

(1) Since the speaker has not identified himself more closely than as the "God of the fathers" (verse 6), Moses anticipates embarrassment when and if he should be asked to name him. Why the people should

---

18. Ramban, with an allusion to 19:9.

19. In a seminar on Exodus, G. Kravitz objected that on the above interpretation the sign would be meaningless: instead of heralding and confirming an event that was still to come, it would appear after the event had already materialized—when it was no longer needed (this is admittedly the peculiarity of the sign). Kravitz proposes to regard Moses' mission as a unity consisting of both the Exodus and the landgiving (3:8, 16-17). The confirmatory sign will appear after the Exodus, to be sure, but before the landgiving, of which it will be an assurance.

ask for and Moses not know the name is not explained and can only be conjectured; indeed it is one of the enigmas of the book.

Moses' query affords God the occasion to communicate to him both the tetragram and its meaning. That both were unknown to Moses is plausible, in view of his estrangement from his people. That the meaning, if not the tetragram itself, was unknown to the people too is quite likely, inasmuch as this is the first record of it. Whence it has been argued that Moses anticipated being tested by the people through his knowledge of the name and its meaning: only if he could produce these would he be credited as an emissary of God.[20]

However, the notion of a test, not to speak of the notion of secret knowledge, is not in the text. And so it has been alternatively supposed (Cassuto) that both Moses and the people were ignorant of God's name. Having had no experience of their God during the bitter years of slavery, having indeed ceased practicing his cult—the vehicle of perpetuating his name—it had faded out of memory. Israel in Egypt sank into a barbarous (cf. Ps 79:6) ignorance of its God's name, though it clung to the memory of divine promise to its fathers of an eventual redemption. One claiming to speak in the name of that long-hidden God must reveal his name to enable the people to have access to him once again (for the name's place in the cult, see below). Moses could never hope to enjoy the trust of the people and belief in his message unless he could produce the name of his sender.[21]

But it is possible to explain our passage on a less dramatic assumption. The patriarchal narratives show that God was addressed by various names: *ᵉlohim, ʾel Šadday, ʾel roʾi, ʾel ʿelyon, ʾabir yaʿaqob* and the

---

20. ST (at 3:13) supposes that the tetragram had been transmitted secretly among the elders from generation to generation through the years of the bondage; neither the people at large nor Moses knew it. Moses is told to gather the elders (verse 16) because they would know it and be able to confirm his divine commission. Segal (*Masoret uBiqoret*, 52) supposes that it was not the name—which surely all Israel knew—but the meaning that was secretly transmitted, and knowledge of which certified Moses to the elders as a true emissary of God. Mowinckel ("The Name of the God of Moses") believes the name was commonly known; Moses asked God's name to be assured that it was really the patriarchal God who spoke to him, and was informed of its mysterious meaning to convince the people of the same.

21. This interpretation accords with the evidence that the patriarchs knew the tetragram. However, Israel's ignorance of the name in pre-Mosaic Egypt might also be a continuation of an earlier condition, with Moses not reinstituting, but newly instituting a new name. That is what 6:3 seems to say, in manifest disaccord with data in Genesis; see below.

tetragram. No distinctions are made among these names, though, in the manner of ancient religion, it must be assumed that, at least originally, different aspects of divinity were alluded to by them.[22] Not all of these names might be lastingly valid: *'el ro'i*, for example, was an innovation by Hagar (Gen 16:13), too personal to be used by anyone else (God who sees me). And *'el šadday* (God Almighty) is expressly restricted to the pre-Mosaic divine nomenclature (Exod 6:3). Finally, heretofore no clue had been given as to the proper name of God, the one expressing his essence (of which all the other names were only partial evocations), the one that would make him accessible in his fullness to the call of men.

One bringing a message from the God of the fathers, a message of critical importance, might well be asked, "By what name, in what character do you know him? As what did he now reveal himself to you, by what name can we now call on him to attend to us?" This anxious inquiry (not examination) of the people calls for a singling out by the deity of his eternal proper name. In the event, God goes further and reveals its heartening meaning as well.[23]

The chief link between verses 13ff. and what comes before is the verb *'ehye* (see ahead in text); the cultic implications of verse 15b (*zeker* is "callword"; cf. verb *hizkir*, Ps 20:8; Exod 23:13) evoke verse 12b. Indeed Josephus (*Ant.* 2.12.4) directly relates Moses' query of verse 13 to the cult: "[Moses] also besought [God] ... to tell him how he should be addressed, so that, when sacrificing, he might invoke him by name to be present at the sacred rites." "To invoke YHWH by name" is the indispensable element in every sort of worship (Gen 12:8; 26:25; 1 Kgs 18:24–25; Ps 116:4, 13, 17). The many Psalms that open with a call to YHWH to listen, help, or receive the acclaim of worshipers illustrate the phrase.

(2) God's answer opens with a clause intended to give the key to the name, and continues with two formulations of Moses' communication of it to the people. The name YHWH is taken as the 3rd person form of a verb whose 1st person is *'ehye*.[24] The meaning of the interpretative

---

22. An example of the varied values of the names of a single god is the catalogue of fifty names of Marduk (*ANET*, 69ff.). Cf. also the statement of the god Re: "I am Khepri in the morning, Re at noon, and Atum who is in the evening" (*ANET*, 13).

23. The implications of the name of God in the Bible are set forth in the second part of the article of Jacob, "Mose am Dornbusch."

24. "I shall encode the reason why in verse 15 he replaced the initial *alef* with *yod*: [the following is a cryptogram] He calls himself *'ehye* but we call him *yihye*, YHWH, with *waw* for *yod* as in *howe* (Eccl 2:22, for *hoye* [cf. *hoya*, Exod 9:3])." This explanation of Rashbam's represents correctly the view of the biblical author.

clause, however, is—surely not by accident—vague. Perhaps the simplest way to take it is as expressing the essence of the phrase *'ehye 'immak* (verse 12): "[My name is] *'ehye* (for the ellipse cf. verse 14), for/in that[25] I will be/I am (present)." Thus the phrase *'ehye 'immak*, found time and again in the mouth of the deity (Gen 26:3; 31:3; Exod 4:12, 15; Deut 31:23; Josh 1:5; 3:7; Judg 6:16, etc.) acquires the overtone of a 3rd person statement "*'Ehye* [is] with you" = "YHWH is with you" (Judg 6:12). Verse 14b is transitional to the "3rd person" form of the name, the tetragram (verse 15), and means, "He who calls himself *'Ehye* has sent me to you."[26] The significance of the name is, accordingly, "the present one, he who is there"—a heartening message to those who heretofore felt forsaken by God.

A different, widely accepted view of the meaning of 14a takes its cue from the similar construction in 33:19—likewise in a divine response to Moses' request for a self-revelation: "I will be gracious to whom I will be gracious and show compassion to whom I will show compassion." Such constructions are employed in Hebrew when it is not desired or possible to be explicit.[27] Our phrase will thus mean: "I will be/am what I will be/am"; that is (adapting Driver), "My presence will be as something undefined, something which, as my nature is more and more unfolded by the lessons of history and the teachings of the prophets, will prove to be more than any formula can express." The paraphrase in *MHG* catches the flight from definition that this view takes the name to be: "You wish to know my name? I am named after my acts. As judge of men I am called Elohim; as he who battles the wicked, *Ṣebaot*; as the delayer of punishment, *Shadday*; as the compassionate ruler, *Raḥum*; and similarly the Impassioned,

---

25. *'ašer* has this sense in, e.g., Josh 22:31; Judg 9:17; 1 Sam 15:15; 1 Kgs 3:19; 15:5; Jer 16:13.

26. "The theological character of Yahweh's word of reassurance (*'ehye 'immak*) is ... demonstrated by the subsequent dialogue (v. 13-15), for this word is none other than the very name of God ... The meaning of the name is experienced by Moses in and through his call" (Habel, "The Form and Significance," 304). A possible allusion to this form of the name occurs in Hos. 1:9: "You are not my people nor am I *'Ehye* to you"; and perhaps again in Ps 50:21: "You imagined *'Ehye* to be like you" (hence the infinitive construct). Both verses are, appropriately, utterances of God.

The close relation of the expressions of verse 14 with *'ehye 'immak* was felt by the midrash. The interpretation of 14b in both *ShR* ("I will be with you now as I will be with you in the future") and Onkelos ("I will be with whom I will be;" so cited by Ramban) assume this relation.

27. A full list is in Jacob, *Exodus*, 129 (ET = *Second Book*, 71); cf. e.g., 4:13 ahead; and Deut 1:46; 1 Sam 23:13; 2 Sam 15:20.

the Vengeful, He who makes poor and rich, Judge, Righteous, Loyal, Holy, Trusty, Strong, Great, Mighty, Awesome, and so forth. That is what is meant by, 'I will be what I will be.'"[28]

In this view, 'ehye of 14b is a truncated form of the full clause of 14a—an artificial literary device to serve as a bridge between the two-membered interpretative clause and the tetragram of verse 15.[29]

Verse 15 finally gives the standard "3rd person" form of the name by which God is to be invoked henceforth. YHWH is identified with the God of each of the fathers, intimating that the aspect under which he now appears is that of constancy, of keeping faith with the fathers and their descendants. The solemnity of the moment is indicated by the parallelism at the end of the verse, in which prose passes into poetry (cf. Ps 135:13).

Scholars are still far from agreement on the etymology and the pronunciation of YHWH; indeed it is not even clear that it is ultimately Hebrew. But whatever its origin, its significance is that given to it in the religious life of Israel. That significance is epitomized in the pregnant interpretative phrase that came to Israel through Moses.[30]

---

28. Gressmann (*Mose*, 35) regards God's response as an evasion, and paraphrases it, "I am called what I am called"; cf. Kittel, *Geschichte*, 1:323. Ehrlich (*Randglossen*) too takes it to express God's reluctance to name himself and thus promote the idea that he is one among like beings; the phrase signifies, "my name is not really to the point." But Gressmann's comparison of Gen 32:23-33 (the refusal of the divinity to reveal its name to Jacob) only highlights the contrast with our passage. The name of God is, in fact, revealed here; Gressmann himself finally admits that "[only] seemingly does Jahve avoid his name; in reality he does name himself." So why assume a halfhearted and unsuccessful evasion?

29. Cf. the fanciful explanation of the truncation in *ShR* and Rashi ("One distress at a time is enough!").

30. For discussion and bibliography, see Anderson, "God, Names of." A handy summation of views on the meaning of the interpretative phrase is Lindblom, "Noch einmal die Deutung," who defends the sense "I am he who really is" (cf. Schild, "On Exodus iii 14"; and earlier, Schleiff, "Der Gottesname Jahwe": the phrase takes the name to mean, "he who is incontrovertibly there," in contrast to the unreal idol-gods). As to origin: Schleiff suggested that a pre-Mosaic deity Yah(u)—the short form is preserved in poetic and solemn biblical passages—whose name was merely the demonstrative "one there," was transformed through Moses into an intelligible "verbal" form. Mowinckel, "The Name of the God of Moses," defends a derivation from a primitive invocation *ya huwa* "O He!," in which he is followed by Buber (*Moses*) and Jacob. The conventional pronunciation Yahweh, based partly on the name-element *yahu*, partly on early transliterations into Greek, is attacked and defended in articles by Eerdmans ("The Name Jahu") and Thierry ("The Pronunciation"). On YHW[3] as a place-name in the Edomite Negev, see Grdseloff, "Édôm," 69; Meek, *Hebrew Origins*, 109. A possible pre-Nabatean divinity 'HYW is referred to by Alt, "Der Gott der Väter," 6 n. 1 (ET =

(3) The sacrifice to the Lord about which Moses is to negotiate with Pharaoh is the worship at the mountain alluded to in verse 12b. Without disclosing their full intention Moses and the elders are to test Pharaoh's disposition by asking permission to take a temporary leave to worship their God.

"God instructed [Moses in this deception] to show forth Pharaoh's obduracy and recalcitrance so as to justify his judgments and actions against Egypt. We see that the Israelites asked at first for nothing more than leave to go on a three-days' journey to sacrifice to their God; from their language it was to be inferred that they would return. Yet Pharaoh would not hear of it—how much less would he have countenanced a request to liberate them! Moses was thus instructed to begin by asking for a small thing . . . for thereby Pharaoh's brazenness and obduracy would be exposed" (Abarbanel).

But cannot Pharaoh's refusal spring from a legitimate fear that he might lose his slaves altogether—as comes out from his later demand to leave hostages?

"Had he demanded hostages immediately, he would have been in the clear, but he did not do that till after several plagues. On the contrary in his first reaction he not only failed to demand hostages, he increased the cruelty of his measures, thus revealing his evil mind" (Shadal).

The element of deception, integral to Moses' negotiations with Pharaoh, is a reflex of Israel's weakness. "It can only be regarded as a relic of an old tradition—whether of a ruse by which Israel got permission to leave Egypt, or of a more general tradition about Israel's helplessness there—that left no room for the bold notion that Israel simply presented an outright demand to be emancipated."[31] Here, as elsewhere, the biblical narrator conceives of God as working within the framework of human frailty rather than having his way by recourse to miracle. Thus he counsels an ambush at Ai (Josh 8:2), and a pretext whereby Samuel might avoid endangering his life when he goes to anoint David (1 Sam 16:2–3).[32] Where wicked, superior force must be overcome for a just cause, an effective deception is as much a part of God's arsenal as miracles. A generalized expression of the policy is found in Ps 18:26, "With the crooked you [God] are wily"; Rashi glosses, "with Pharaoh."

"The God of the Fathers," 7 n. 10).

31. Loewenstamm, *Masoret*, 49 (ET = *Evolution*, 114).
32. Compared with our passage by Rashbam.

(4) The synopsis of coming events given Moses in verses 19–22 accords with the policy enunciated in Amos 3:7 "Surely the Lord God does nothing without revealing his secret to his servants the prophets." Such revelations always serve some purpose. In the case of the "prophet" Abraham (Gen 20:7), for example, foreknowledge of the fate of Sodom and Gomorrah was designed to instruct him in the workings of divine justice (Gen 18:17–19).

In our passage, the purpose seems to be to let Moses know in advance that though he will get nowhere with Pharaoh, all is part of the divine plan to make an object lesson of the king for all time. "God foresaw how Pharaoh would increase the burdens of the people from the time Moses brought him his message. In order to keep Moses from misconstruing things, God predicted to him that thus and so would happen, so that he would not come back to God with accusations. All the same he did come back with accusations, illustrating the verse 'For oppression makes the wise man foolish'" ([Eccl. 7:7] ShR; cf. Hizquni).

(5) The spoliation of Egypt (verses 21–22) fulfills the covenant promise of Gen 15:14, "But I will pass judgment on the nation they shall serve, and in the end they shall go free with great wealth." That after all the plagues, the Egyptians will be favorably disposed to the Israelites is only explicable as a divine work (but see exegesis at 11:2).

Whether here too a deception is intended is an old question depending on the meaning of ša'al. "According to many," BDB reports, "here and in 11:2 and 12:35 the verb means 'borrow'; it is, however, not clear that there was any pretext of mere temporary use." Ša'al can also mean "ask for something" with no suggestion of return; so in Judg 8:24 (also with spoil); 1 Sam 1:27; 2:20; 2 Kgs 4:28.

The act is described well by BSh: "Let each woman say to her neighbor, 'We have to leave for a festival; let me have a gold or silver cup, or some other vessel of yours, so that I'm not embarrassed among my friends'—and so for linen and embroidered clothes."

"There was no fraud in God's command. The act was altogether legitimate, since the labor they had provided them with was incalculable, and its wages [which they never received] without measure. Now the Torah lays it down that a man who has slaved for his master seven years should receive a parting bounty, as it is written, 'When you release him, you must not send him out emptyhanded' (Deut 15:13–14 [note the striking similarity between our *ki telekun lo tel^eku reqam* and Deuteronomy *w^eki t^ešall^ehennu . . . lo t^ešall^ehennu reqam*.] How much more so in the case of the Egyptians, for whom the Israelites slaved for 210 years" (Bahya at 11:2). In other words, God saw to it that the emancipated Israelites were treated in accord with the Torah's regulations concerning the obligation of masters to fit out Hebrew freedmen when discharging them. For the stuffs stipulated by the Deuteronomic law, however, gold and silver and clothing, more conveniently borne across the desert, were substituted.[33]

An exquisite touch is the injunction to deck the children with the spoil. The sense is: take enough even to deck out your children, but why mention that? Because the recovery of dignity by the liberated slaves would be signalized by their being able to provide good things for their children. Of even greater moment than their own enrichment was their capacity to assert parental solicitude toward their children, whom they had been unable heretofore to care for properly or save from cruel oppression. For Philo of Alexandria's depiction of the event see his *Life of Moses* 1.25 (§§140–142 [Colson, *Philo*, 349]).

d. 4:1–17. Moses now raises the objection that the people may refuse to believe his claim. Accordingly, he is given three signs to prove that divine power has been put at his disposal. He then protests his lack of eloquence—and is told, sharply now, that God will be with his mouth. Having reached the end of his tether, Moses nakedly pleads that another than he be sent. Angered, God assigns Aaron to be his spokesman and ends the conversation.

(1) Deuteronomy 13:2ff. takes for granted that a prophet will produce miraculous signs to confirm his mission; Hezekiah's request for such a sign from Isaiah (2 Kgs 20:8) shows that what Moses anticipates (and his question as to how to meet it) was perfectly legitimate.[34] Later we read that the signs were performed before the Israelites and led to belief.

The signs are all ominous, exemplifying the dread power that God has just said (3:20) he would exercise against Egypt. (B. Jacob aptly contrasts the benignity of the flowering rod sign, intended to show whom God has chosen to be his priest [Num 17:20].) A harmless staff is transformed into a deadly serpent from which the untried Moses recoils in terror, and Moses' healthy hand becomes leprous—in each of these he is shown how he can control the sign, thus proving he can call upon

---

33. The relation of our passage to Deuteronomy was seen by Hizquni, and developed at length by Jacob, "Gott und Pharaoh," 285–89. See also my remarks in *Jewish Exponent* (Philadelphia), 12 April 1968, 25–26.

34. Nevertheless, his flat contradiction in 4:1 of God's statement in 3:18a is remarkable. "Moses spoke improperly at that juncture," ShR observes.

superhuman powers. The capper, which can only be promised not demonstrated since it involves Nile water, suggests the ability of Moses' God to cut off Egypt's source of life (a herald of the first plague). Note the dramatic structure of 9b: the first clause hangs incomplete so that its verb can be repeated before the idea is ended.

That the snake and leprosy signs seem to threaten Moses is only incidental to their being effected with an absolute minimum of paraphernalia, with only that which Moses normally has on him—his shepherd's staff and his limbs.[35] The implications of this technical simplicity will be pointed out below.

(2) It seems significant for the development of the story that from 4:1 on to the end of the theophany Moses drops the subject of his dealings with Pharaoh and concerns himself wholly with the problem of convincing the Israelites of his mission. The signs are to be performed before the people, to create belief in them; nothing is said of the job of convincing Pharaoh. (Similarly, Aaron is to be Moses' spokesman to the people [verse 15]; Pharaoh is again ignored.) And in fact when, in chap. 5, the encounter with Pharaoh is described, signs to convince him are badly wanted. It thus appears that for the desired development, the immediate concurrence of the people of Israel is as important as the immediate rejection by Pharaoh. Everything is done to convince the former, nothing to convince the latter. Israel at least must be in the clear and deserving of salvation; as to Pharaoh, the more prominent his evil becomes, the more solidly his fate is justified.

(3) Moses' objection that he is not eloquent has in view the large part that advocacy and negotiation are to play in his mission. The accusatory or complaining overtone in Moses' statement that his ineloquence persists even "now that you have spoken to your servant" provokes a sharp retort from God, a reminder that the implanting or denying of faculties belongs to him. Moses' fluency has been and will be just what God intends it to be. If he is not ready of speech, it is easily enough remedied: God will instruct him in what to say on the spot. The implication that lies

---

35. Since the midrash regards Moses' continued hesitation after God's assurances as improper ("God had said to him, 'They will listen to you' (3:18) and he says, 'What if they do not listen to me'!" [ShR]) it regards the two signs that adversely affect Moses as evidences of God's displeasure, and gives even the water-blood sign an interpretation threatening to Moses (ibid.). But the legitimacy of Moses' question has been indicated above, and since the portents were designed to be ominous as well as technically simple—i.e., requiring no extraordinary equipment—the appearance of adversely affecting Moses was unavoidable, though inessential.

just beneath the surface of the text, that God's choice of a slow-tongued man to be his messenger was deliberate, is made explicit in the midrashic paraphrase of verse 11: "If you are not fluent do not worry; I am the creator of mouths . . . and if I want you to be fluent you shall be. [Why, then, have I not chosen a fluent man?] because I prefer to work a miracle through you at the time you speak—that you will say the right thing due to my being with your mouth" (ShR).[36]

(4) In persisting to demur (verse 13) Moses passes the bounds of legitimate humility (of which quality he was a paragon, Num 12:3). He now appears as though lacking faith in God's capacity to stand by him; but negotiations have gone too far for him to turn back. And so "'The Lord grew angry with Moses', saying to him: 'All you wanted was to find out about my name and speak with me all this while? You should have said at once, 'Make someone else your agent'! After all our dealings you reject my proposal this way!" (ST).

A certain callousness might also be charged to Moses: "My children are in distress and you are at ease, and I want to bring them out of Egypt and you say 'Make someone else your agent'!" (MHG). Yet God meets him halfway: if he is unwilling to speak publicly, his brother Aaron will not be. The right word, however, will still depend on divine instruction; the promise to be with Moses' mouth is now extended to cover both Moses and Aaron. Thus the co-opting of Aaron is done only to appease Moses, not that God's original plan was wanting. It is not Aaron's fluency that will carry the day, but the word of God mediated to him through Moses (cf. Malbim).

(5) That Aaron's epithet "the Levite" is somehow connected with his future priesthood[37] was perceived as early as the midrash (ShR). That is to say, it refers to office rather than tribal affiliation; it can do so owing to the eventual dedication of the entire tribe of Levi to clerical service (32:29; Deut 10:8; in Mal 2:4, 8, "Levi" equals "priests" of verse 1). The Levite's role, particularly the Levite-priest's, was to be teacher and mediator to the people of God's revelation to Moses: "To teach the people of Israel all the statutes which the Lord has spoken to them through Moses" (Lev 10:11; cf. Deut 24:8; 33:10; 2 Chr 17:8–9; Neh 8:7–8). That role, we now hear,

---

36. The citation from Theodoret in McNeile, *Exodus*, to the effect that God picked a slow-tongued man for his minister in order to make a greater display of his power, says the same.

37. Cf. Noth, *UG*, 197 (ET = *History of Pentateuchal Traditions*, 218); Kahana's comment comes close to my own; cf. Kittel, *Geschichte*, 1:308 n. 1.

derives from and is grounded in the relationship to Moses of the father of the levitical caste: "[Aaron] shall speak for you to the people and he shall be a mouth for you . . ." It is as an archetypal teacher of revelation that Aaron is here styled "the Levite," and that more for the benefit of the hearer (who could immediately perceive the reference to the later role) than for Moses.

(6) The plural "sign" of verse 17 is strange, since only one sign has been spoken of so far in which the staff is to be used. Evidently the later use of the staff in connection with the plagues and the crossing of the sea, etc. is reflected in this reading.

Themes and Structure

a. The burning bush story is the most elaborate account in the Bible of the commissioning by God of a messenger. In length, it is exceeded only by the account of Ezekiel's call (Ezek 1:1—3:15), but the bulk of that is taken up with a description of the divine vehicle. Elements of Moses' call are found elsewhere: Gideon was told "I will be with you" and encouraged by signs (Judg 6:16, 36–40); young Samuel was called by a repetition of his name (1 Sam 3:4–10) and only gradually realized what was happening; Jeremiah pleaded that he did not know how to speak (Jer 1:6–9); Ezekiel's attention was arrested by a marvelous daytime vision in which fire played a prominent part (Ezekiel 1). Moses' commissioning alone contains all of these and more. It is thus the fullest statement we have of the conditions of God's call and his relation to his messenger. Moreover, such statements as Num 12:7 and Deut 18:18 and 34:10 show that Moses was considered the ideal and archetype of God's messengers. The story of his call bears a corresponding significance.

b. The commissioning of messengers in general is described in a fairly standard way. The sender addresses the messenger(s) with "So shall you say to so and so: so says (the sender):" (Gen 32:5; 45:9; 1 Kgs 22:27; abridged in 1 Sam 11:9; 18:25; 25:6). A dictated speech follows, which the messenger is expected to produce verbatim (2 Kgs 9:17–18).[38] The form of the commissioning is naturally a monologue, the messenger not being

---

38. While biblical narrative does not commonly repeat the message as the messenger delivers it (cf. below at 10:3–6 on the plague-narrative speeches), such repetition is frequently found in extrabiblical ancient Near Eastern material: see, e.g., *ANET*, 64–65 (Babylonian); 122bc (Hittite); 130, 137, 146bc (Ugaritic).

THE REVELATION AT THE BUSH (3:1—4:17) 75

expected to respond, but only to listen attentively so that he might be a faithful mouthpiece of his sender.

Exceptional is the exchange between Abraham and his servant over the acquisition of a bride for Isaac (Gen 24:5ff., 39–40): the servant asks for instructions in the event of a difficulty and Abraham gives them. The situation differs from a standard commissioning in that the servant goes not as a mere messenger but as a representative of his sender. His higher status and independence are reflected in his participation in the shaping of the mission.[39] Even here, however, there is no question of the servant's balking at Abraham's charge.

Accounts of the call of God's agents follow a pattern more like that of Abraham's charge to his servant than of standard messenger-commissionings.[40] But they go well beyond that pattern with respect to the self-will shown by the called in the course of his dialogue with God. The extent of the difference is most sharply etched in the account of Moses' call.

The primary characteristic of the burning bush narrative is that it is a dialogue of negotiation. After the setting has been described and Moses comes to know who his interlocutor is (3:1–5):

1. God declares his purpose to rescue Israel through Moses (verses 7–10). There follows:

2. Moses' first difficulty: his inadequacy for the task (verse 11);

3. God's response: "I will be with you," prediction of the future worship of the people at the mountain of God (verse 12);

4. Moses' second difficulty: his ignorance of God's name (verse 13);

5. God's response: revelation of the name, speeches to be made to Israel's elders and Pharaoh, prediction of happy ending (verses 14–22);

6. Moses' third difficulty: the people's incredulity (4:1);

7. God's response: three signs (verses 2–9);

8. Moses' fourth difficulty: his lack of eloquence (verse 10);

9. God's response: "I will be with your mouth" (verses 11–12);

---

39. The servant's high standing is stressed in verse 2 (in an expression strikingly like that used of Moses in Num 12:7); his plenipotentiary status, in verse 10.

40. As has been argued by Habel ("The Form and Significance"), who finds five elements common to the first two: a. introductory word; b. commission; c. objection; d. reassurance (in which the initial charge is repeated); e. a sign.

10. Moses' plea to be replaced (verse 13);

11. God's anger and his concession of a spokesman to Moses (verses 14–17).

c. The dialogue of negotiation initiated by God expresses perfectly the basic character of Israel's God as "anthropotropic" (i.e. turned toward man), as concerned with, accessible to, and considerate of men.[41]

While the idea that man is under divine care and guidance is shared by all ancient Near Eastern religions, the regard in which the biblical God holds man is without parallel. There is a rabbinic dictum to the effect that "the Holy One, blessed be He, does not tyrannize over man"; this dictum is concretized in the dialogue between them.[42]

After Abraham (Genesis 15; 17:15–21; 18:23–33), Moses is the next person with whom God repeatedly initiates dialogues. He neither disregards nor overwhelms Moses with his acts and commands:[43] he does not require his self-effacement. Those who are brought close to him retain their integrity even in moments of closest contact. They are not merely passive recipients, but active, even opposing respondents. There is true address and response, genuine give and take. The human partner has a say in shaping the direction and outcome of the events.

The first condition of such dialogue is God's willingness to adjust himself to the capacities of men, to take into consideration and make concessions to human frailty. Such divine forbearance is evident throughout our story. A prevailing theme is Moses' diffidence and timidity. He hides his face in fright when he learns what the apparition is, he recoils from the serpent, he will not speak in public. God is correspondingly considerate: he leads Moses gradually, with a care not to overwhelm him, from the familiar scrub fire, to the strange unburnableness of the bush,

---

41. The subject is developed and a vocabulary for it created in Heschel, *The Prophets*, 439ff.

42. God is, of course, depicted at times as issuing peremptory orders in monologue (Gen 3:3–19; 12:1–3; 22:2; and elsewhere). It is in the dialogues, however, that God's affectability is exhibited in its most patent form—to the point of his even changing his mind in response to human arguments. The significance of God's readiness to adjust himself to his human partners can be properly gauged only when it is kept in mind that from the time of Moses, at any rate, the presence of God strikes terror into those who are aware of it.

43. In the light of the dialogues, the monologues take on a different hue. Abraham could have retorted to God's peremptory command in Gen 12:1ff. and 22:2—as, say, Ezekiel did in Ezek 4:13ff. The very fact that he did not exhibits his absolute trust in God.

to the awesome heart of the theophany. Thus assured of God's benevolence, Moses is not frightened into silence, but can carry on a reasoned dialogue with him (contrast God's purpose in the later terrifying public theophany, Exod 20:20; Deut 4:36). God allows Moses to talk out all his doubts, and provides him with one assurance after another. He forewarns him of the initially discouraging course of events. And even when he is at last provoked to anger, he makes a concession to Moses' weakness so that the ultimate shape of Moses' mission is not what God had intended but owes something to Moses' choice.[44]

Even more striking is the assumption of God's forbearance that underlies Moses' strong language in Exod 5:22–23. But its fullest expression will come when God abandons his plans to destroy Israel in the face of Moses' intercession (Exod 32:14; Num 14:20). A readiness, in principle, to do the like is evident already in the dialogue with Abraham in Genesis 18, but it was Moses' intercession that provided the model for prophets in subsequent ages. In time, it became the duty of the prophet to expostulate with God on behalf of Israel until pardon was obtained (1 Sam 12:23; Ezek 22:30; cf. Ps 106:23). In this way, God made room for men to share with him the determination of their destiny.[45]

A condescension that disposes God to negotiate and compromise with men emerges from the dialogue at the bush. Later readers, made

---

[44]. The midrash underscores this astounding forebearance in the following remonstrance put in God's mouth: "Moses! When at first I revealed myself to you in the bush, you hid your face from me ... Since when have you been given license to speak to me like a human slave who is entitled to talk back to his master? ... By rights, you should be done away with at once, but what can I do? I am compassionate and faithful" (*MHG*).

It is noteworthy how Moses' diffidence vanishes later. At first afraid to look at the divine apparition, he will later ask boldly, "Oh let me behold your presence!" (33:18), and be singled out of all prophets for "beholding the likeness of the Lord" (Num 12:8). He who was at a loss to deal with an incredulous people until armed with a few petty signs, will later face a popular uprising and spontaneously call upon God to create an unheard of prodigy to crush it (Num 16:30). He who is not "a man of words (d^ebarim)" will, at the end of his life, make some of the finest orations (d^ebarim) in the whole of scripture (Deuteronomy). The midrash perceived some of these contrasts, and depicted them characteristically in terms of merit and reward: "God said to Moses: 'By your life! Because you did me honor I will do you honor in the sight of all Israel.' In return for 'He was afraid' (3:6), 'they were afraid to come near him' (34:30); 'because you would not look at the apparition', 'he beheld the likeness of the Lord' (Num 12:8); 'because you hid your face', 'all Israel saw that the skin of Moses' face was radiant'" (34:30). Compare too what is remarked below on 5:22–23; 8:5.

[45]. But not necessarily or always, of course, as Jer 15:1ff. shows.

accustomed by the Bible to such condescension, took it as a matter of course. "Rabbi Elazar Ben ʿArak said, 'How is it that God left the highest heaven to speak with Moses in a thornbush when he might have spoken to him from mountain heights or the cedars of Lebanon? . . . God made his presence lowly and adopted an earthly mode of speech so as not to give room for mankind to say, Just because he is God, and master of the world, he acted high and mighty! That is also why he kept Moses six days'" (according to a fanciful interpretation of 4:10 [see Rashi ad loc. and *Wayyiqra Rabba* 11.6])—when he could have simply given his order and brooked no retort: but, in consideration of mankind's opinion, he bore with Moses all that while (*Mek. deRashbi*).

d. Moses, the first messenger of God in Israel, is the archetype of the later judges and prophets who throughout Israel's history evidenced God's concern for, and government of his people. The diffidence that marked Moses' reaction to God's call is paralleled in the commissioning stories of other messengers of God (e.g., Gideon, Jeremiah). It points to the essential nature of their role: they are not naturally endowed with courage, strength, or ability. The key to their office is the verb *šalaḥ* "to send," occurring frequently in our passage (3:10, 12,[46] 13, 14, 15, cf. 4:13) and henceforth recurring in the calls of saviors and prophets through the ages (Judg 6:11, 14; 1 Sam 12:8, 11; 15:1; 16:1; 1 Kgs 14:6; Isa 6:8; Jer 1:7; Ezek 2:3, 4; 3:5, 6, etc.). The words and acts of these "men of God" were not their own, did not redound to their glory or establish their power, but stemmed from and reflected the power of God who sent them.

That is the point of the insistence that, with or without Aaron, the public pronouncements of Moses would be supplied by God (4:12, 15). This is made concrete in 3:14–17, where, having begun by dictating Moses' answer regarding the divine name with the message formula "*ko tomar ʾel/lᵉ-*," God proceeds himself to reformulate the content of verses 6–10 as Moses must report it to Israel: YHWH is inserted before the God-of-the-fathers formula; "Your father" replaces "thy father"; the *paqod paqadti* clause[47] epitomizes verses 7, 9, and so forth.

---

46. Note how God's *lᵉka wᵉʾešlaḥᵃka* in verse 10 is distributed in the next two verses: Moses retains only *halak* in verse 11, overlooking his agent status, while God, contrariwise, mentions only *šalaḥ* in verse 12—the assurance of Moses' success lying precisely in his being merely an agent.

47. The language is doubtless intended to recall Joseph's parting admonition (Gen 50:24–25). This is fancied by the midrash to have been transmitted down to the time of Moses, so that Moses' speech would serve as a password to his people (*ShR* 5.13).

Another evidence of the mere agency of the messenger is the nature of the signs he is equipped with to prove his mission. Abarbanel felt that Moses' miracles were worked with an ordinary shepherd's staff for deliberate contrast with magic. "Just because Egypt's magicians worked strange and extraordinary things through sleight of hand and trickery[48] God directed Moses to what he had in his hand. He did not send him to some out-of-the-way object, but to the staff that he happened to have with him." It is true enough that Egyptian magic was fond of bizarre combinations of substances.[49] Yet, since magic may equally be used to transform simple objects, the contrast here must be sought rather in the complete absence of technique, even of speech, in the transformation. We shall read later that Egyptian magicians, too, transformed staffs into serpents, but they did so "with their spells" (7:11, 22).[50] In contrast, Moses is neither instructed in magical arts or spells, nor endowed with magical powers; indeed, he does not utter a word when performing the signs. Their occurrence, then, reflects not on him but on the God in whose name he comes and whose authority he professes to represent. It is the same with all the succeeding messengers of God. The wonders they perform are designed to signify not their own powers, but that it is God, "who alone works great wonders" (Ps 136:4), who has sent them.[51]

The Exodus story contains a density of wonders greater than anywhere else in the Bible. Kaufmann plausibly takes this to reflect the genuine Egyptian background for these traditions—ancient Egypt having been notoriously ridden with magic.[52] The motif will then be the nullity of pagan "science" in the face of the will of God; cf. Isa 44:25, and the comments below on 7:8—9:15.

But long before, the Ran had remarked the coincidence of the plethora of miracles and the Egyptian setting, supposing that it was hardly accidental. Why, he asks, should Moses have been thick-tongued? For this reason, he answers, "Since the revelation and acceptance of the Torah was an event of the greatest moment for humanity, it was important that the participants be clear as to its divine origin . . . Hence, great miracles

---

48. Unlike the Bible, this 15th-century man of the world could not credit magicians with real power.

49. See, e.g., *ANET*, 7bc.

50. Compare, for illustration, the Egyptian spell in which a knife is animated to swallow a snake; *ANET*, 326c.

51. For a full discussion of these matters, see Kaufmann, *Religion of Israel*, 78ff.

52. Ibid., 228.

were performed at the Exodus, so that Israel might know that what is impossible in nature is possible with God. Since Egypt was full of magicians, God chose to work his demonstrations there, so that it would be perfectly plain to all that the miracles were not accomplished through magic. Compare what is said in *Menahot* (85a) about how Yohani and Mamre [legendary Egyptian magicians] taunted Moses, saying "Are you bringing straw to Afraim?"—a city full of straw. To which Moses replied, "To a place of vegetables bring vegetables"—by which is meant that God chose to perform his miracles in Egypt just because it was full of magic: the genuine article might more readily be distinguished there from the counterfeit. For the same reason Moses was deprived of eloquence, so that nobody might think that he got the Israelites to accept the Torah through the power of his eloquence, or that he bested the magicians by his gift of speech.

e. God's address to Moses in 3:7-10 has two main themes: God has taken sympathetic notice of Israel's misery, and he is about to save them through Moses and give them a good land of their own. Verse 10 *ʿammi bᵉne yisraʾel* calls to mind Pharaoh's *ʿam bᵉne yisraʾel* (1:9)—Israel was then alone and unclaimed; now it has a patron. Similarly, verse 8 *lᵉhaʿᵃloto min haʾareṣ hahi* recalls Pharaoh's measures against the contingency *wᵉʿala min haʾareṣ*—the prison in which Pharaoh purposed to keep Israel is now about to be sprung. Pharaoh's declaration of hostility is countered by God's declaration of care.

What has moved God to act on Israel's behalf is stated in verses 7 and 9, whose repetitiveness has been discussed above. Here we note that a certain art is evident in the disposition of their parts, suggesting an attempt to alleviate the monotony of repetition. The main clauses of the two verses are arranged thus:

    Verse 7:   *raʾo raʾiti ʾet ʿᵒni ʿammi*
               wᵉʾet ṣaʿᵃqatam šamaʿti
               ki yadaʿti ʾet makʾobaw
    Verse 9:   *ṣaʿᵃqat bᵉne yisraʾel baʾa ʾelay*
               raʾiti ʾet hallahaṣ

Note the alternation of the position of noun and verb (verb-noun, noun-verb, verb-noun, etc.), then, the chiastic structure (a b c b a), and, finally, the partial synonymy (*ʿᵒni // lahaṣ, šamaʿti // baʾa ʾelay*), all of which is gratifying to the ear.

Comparison of this declaration of motive with 2:23ab–25 shows enough common elements to make understandable the view that the latter passage introduces the revelation at the bush. However, one element of that passage is missing here: remembrance of the covenant. The effect is a one-sided emphasis. To be sure, something of the covenant is evoked by the folk-lists of verses 8 and 17, but it is a minor note (contrast the explicit covenant reference in 6:8), all but submerged in the repeated declaration that it is Israel's anguish in Egypt that has moved God. Not that he was under the obligation of a covenant promise, but that he had taken note of Israel's present distress is the chief moment. Divine compassion is responding to human misery in an act of grace.

In the message to Israel (verses 16–17), the "ground" or motive part of this address (verses 7–8) is reformulated; but the two themes, and thus the stress on the gracious quality of God, remain unaltered. This motive deserves emphasis. The redemption is not a return for anything Israel has done for God heretofore (cf. above, on the implication of 8:22); nor is a promise to do anything for God in the future a condition of Israel's liberation.[53] To be sure, once the redemption has been accomplished, it will become the basis of covenant terms offered to the people (19:4–6); but the relationship that will grow out of the accomplished event does not cast a shadow ahead in the form of terms to which Israel must agree before God undertakes their redemption. According to the message from the bush, no requirement of God is to be answered by the redemption, only a need of man. "This shows how different man's ways are from God's. A man acquires a servant to be fed and sustained by him; but he who created the world by fiat (and thus stands in no need of man) acquires servants so that he might feed and sustain them" (*MHG* to 4:17).[54]

Composition and Redaction

a. The burning bush story contrasts in its continuity and discursiveness with the brief episodes that precede it. Its length and fullness bespeak the importance attached to it, not only as the account of God's self-revelation to and commissioning of Moses, but for its forecast of things to come.

---

53. Israel's worship of God at the holy mountain (3:12) is a prediction of what will be, not a demand that must be acquiesced in (or even told to the people) prior to the liberation.

54. What is implied thereby for the value and meaning of the cult was not lost on later biblical thinkers: cf. Amos 5:22–25; Ps 50:11ff.

The narrative is typical of biblical historiography, which prefaces events with a prophecy of them, thus representing Israel's history as the realization of God's will (e.g., 1 Kgs 11:31–39 and 12:15; 14:7–16 and 15:29; 16:1–4 and verse 12; 21:19–26 and 2 Kgs 9:25–37).

Whether earlier forms of the narrative contained the detailed predictions of 3:18–22, is questionable. Moses' contradiction of God in 4:1 and 3:18 and his accusation in 5:22–23, as though oblivious of 3:19, are disaccords more suitable to a combination of diverse elements than to a free, unencumbered narration.[55] Yet the predictions now flow so naturally from and are so well fused with verse 17 as to make it likely that they were already present before the final redaction. They sprang from the assimilation of our narrative to other narratives of great events that contained anticipatory prophecies. The language of the predictions is that of the subsequent narrative by and large, and was probably inspired by it (cf. 4:29–30; 5:1, 3; 6:1; 11:2–3).

b. Noticeable redundancies occur in 3:9 (paralleling verse 7) and 3:15 (paralleling in part verse 16). The entire block of verses delimited by these redundant passages exhibits features that set it off from its environment. Whereas derivatives of *ra'a* are key terms in 3:16; 4:1, 5 (cf. also 3:2, 3, 4, 7—in all, 10 occurrences), in 3:9–15 the key term is *šalaḥ* (verses 10, 12–15—in all, 5 occurrences). Moreover, whereas the environing narrative refers to God by means of the tetragram, the narrative of 3:9–15 speaks of him exclusively as *'elohim*.[56]

Again, while the topics in the environing dialogue are taken up in the tale of later events (4:27ff.), the issue of Moses' knowledge of God's name never arises in the sequel. It may finally be noted that the removal of 3:9–15 from the narrative causes no break in the continuity; indeed verse 16 connects with verse 8 easily, and 17 repeats 8 with an inversion characteristic of resumptive repetitions. These are indications that the passage in question is heterogeneous with its environment: that it was

---

55. Cf. Rudolph, *Der "Elohist,"* 8. It is true that the present text is the richer psychologically for containing such inner tensions. This is so often the effect of redactorial work that it is hard to suppose that the redactors were unaware of it. How did they regard the complexity they were lending to the simpler traditions they received when they combined them? Perhaps as a restoration of the genuine complexity of the underlying events, which had been dissolved into its elements among the individual tradition-strands.

56. Leaving out of consideration those speeches of God in which he refers to himself as *'ehye* or the tetragram. Note that here too when the narrator speaks of God it is as *'elohim*.

originally part of a variant tradition of Moses' call, from which it was excerpted for its additional data.

The variant offered a different version of God's opening speech (partly preserved in verse 9) which was attached to the main tradition's version (7–8). The shared root ʿ-n-y in verse 7 and 1:11–12, and the shared ʿala/heʿelah min haʾareṣ in verse 8 and 1:10 indicate that the main tradition-strand is A; in both instances the supplemental variant uses synonymous terms: laḥaṣ, hoṣi . . . mimiṣrayim.

The combination of the two produced the literary values of chiasm and emphasis described above. But the chief contribution of this supplemental variant was its account of how Moses learned the name of God. Starting it with verse 9 suggests an interest too in the added emphasis it gave to God's compassion. Above all it heightened the drama by enlarging on Moses' diffidence and God's deep involvement in Israel's plight to the extent of revealing his proper name to them.

Both versions shared common features,[57] a testimony to the similarity of the tradition-variants of the Pentateuch. Such similarity has obvious implications for evaluating the historical foundations of the traditions. It also accounts for the ease with which the traditions were interwoven. The differences among the traditions, on the other hand, account for their preservation. For a primary principle of the redaction, in all of its stages, seems to have been preservation of every significant aspect of any given matter. Insignificant tradition-variants were omitted, with the result that the present text may be regarded as exhibiting the maximal variations and the maximal riches of old Israel's stock of traditions.[58]

c. The striking alternation of YHWH-ʾelohim in 3:4 serves to call attention to a phenomenon that pervades the chapter. We have noted the peculiar tendency of the main narrative (A) to prefer the tetragram while the supplement favors ʾelohim. The preference of the latter may well be due to the subject of 3:9–15—the disclosure and meaning of the tetragram, hitherto unknown to Moses. Using ʾelohim in the narration of verses 9–15 serves to represent vividly Moses' ignorance of the name.

---

57. Note that raʾa, which is so prominent in the main narrative, appears in the supplement too (verse 9), though without repetition; contrarily, šalaḥ appears in the main narrative (4:13) without the emphasis it bears in the supplement. More interesting is the way the sign of worship at the mountain (3:12) now adumbrates the demand to be made of Pharaoh to let Israel sacrifice in the wilderness (3:18, derived from 5:3), though the divergence in terms is enough to indicate separate provenances.

58. So Albright, *From the Stone Age*, 80.

Furthermore, since the interrelated responses of God in verses 12 and 14 make significant use of *'ehye*—a kind of homonym of YHWH, by referring to God as *'elohim*, aural confusion is avoided.[59]

The fact that the introductory verses 3:1–6 show an alternation of YHWH-*'elohim* may be related to the composite character of the rest of the narrative (though the exegetical considerations advanced before are not to be slighted). The alternation may be a reflex of the fusion of the two tradition elements, and be intended to foreshadow the identification of the anonymous *'elohim*, whom Moses knew, with the God known to the reader as YHWH—the narrative thus endeavoring to convey different levels of knowledge of the same object. Perhaps the language of verses 1–6 blends the descriptions of Moses' initial call that once introduced the dialogues of the main narrative and the supplement. Assuming that each told the story of Moses' coming upon the bush in the same climactic form, we may suppose that when the supplement was fused with the main narrative, its language was allowed to color that of the main narrative, so as to provide an adumbration of the issue of the name revelation.

d. This analysis touches on a larger theory concerning the strands of tradition that have been interwoven in the first four books of the Pentateuch. The tradition-strand that we called B is roughly equivalent to what conventional criticism calls P—the priestly tradition-complex. What we call A, on the other hand, is conventionally styled by critics JE—an amalgam of two supposed strands, each characterized by (among other things) distinctive employment of the divine names. The more extensive strand is alleged to use the tetragram throughout, whence its rubric J, for Jahwist (Yahwist); the other, more fragmentary strand is believed to use *'elohim* exclusively in the pre-Mosaic narrative, whence it is called E (for Elohist). E is supposed to hold the view that Moses was the first to whom the tetragram was revealed—in the burning bush theophany, verses 9–15 of which are assigned—with their repeated *'elohims*—to E.[60]

Now, while critics have managed to isolate P's components convincingly on the whole, the disentangling of J from E has always been difficult.

---

59. "It is surely obvious that the author employs [*'elohim*] because he is about to relate the revelation of the name [YHWH] to Moses and the effect would be spoiled by using the name immediately before the account of its revelation" (Winnett, *The Mosaic Tradition*, 22; cf. Rudolph, *Der "Elohist,"* 12).

60. From 6:22ff. it is clear that one tradition-complex, at any rate, held such a view; but, as we shall see, that passage is most likely assigned to B (P). It is nowhere as clear from 3:13ff. that Moses was the first ever to know the tetragram.

To distinguish between them after Exod 3:13ff., when the alleged hallmark of E loses its rationale, is especially problematic. Some weighty opinion tends to doubt that E ever existed as a self-contained tradition complex. The evidence for it is not decisive; indeed several passages claimed for E may be contested on the ground that inner contextual reasons suffice to account for the choice of *ʾelohim* in the passage in question—a position taken above in the discussion of 3:9–15. Nonetheless the presence of heterogeneous elements in A's narrative (conjectured on grounds other than or in addition to the usage of divine names) seems probable. It is best, therefore, to regard these as supplements of unknown provenance, rather than as all stemming from a single second tradition-strand of which only disconnected fragments remain.[61]

e. B's reference to the covenant as a motive of God's attention to Israel, given weight in 2:24b by the naming of each of the three fathers with whom it was enacted, has no echo in the burning bush story, as was indicated above. Not before 6:2ff.—a passage clearly marked by B's features—will that motive be mentioned again. Nowhere in 3:1—4:17 is there any evidence at all of B.

f. To sum up: The burning bush story is a skillful fusion of three elements: the main narrative of the dialogue (3:7–8, 16–17, [18–22], 4:1–17), a supplemental narrative (3:9–15), and an introductory passage

---

61. Volz and Rudolph (*Der Elohist als Erzähler*) deny the existence of an independent tradition-strand E in Genesis with many trenchant observations. They admit, however, that supplementary matter has been added to the main narrative ("J") by a later hand that showed a preference for the epithet *ʾelohim*. The inquiry was carried into Exodus by Rudolph in *Der "Elohist."*

A suggestive, but in the end unpersuasive, attempt to explain the entire phenomenon of name choice on contextual grounds alone is Cassuto's *The Documentary Hypothesis*. There are passages, such as those ascribed to P in Genesis, in which the choice of divine name is clearly an index of a tradition-strand, but there are others, such as our Exod 3:9–15, in which factors other than provenance can account as well or better for the choice.

Having touched on the issue of E, it is fitting to revert for a moment to 1:15–22, the midwives' story, which is assigned to E because of the appearance of *ʾelohim* in verses 17, 20–21. If the evidence of an E strand in the burning bush story is questionable, in the midwives' story it is nonexistent. To be sure, the midwives fear and are rewarded by *ʾelohim*. But since, as has been argued, they were non-Israelites, their piety could have been expressed only in terms of the generic *ʾelohim*, never in terms of the specifically Israelite YHWH.

On the other hand, the use of *ʾelohim* in 2:23b–25 is a characteristic of B (P) which expressly denies to pre-Mosaic times the knowledge of the name of God revealed to Moses (6:2–3). Whatever doubts may be entertained about E do not touch the evidence of the existence of B as a clearly defined, extensive tradition-strand.

(3:1–6) showing signs of formulation after the first two narrative elements had been fused and itself a product of the fusion. While the seams are still detectable, they do not disturb the flow of the narrative more seriously than does, say, the juncture in 2:15b. As was conjectured there, so it may be here, that such relative smoothness bespeaks a process that antedated the final redaction. To the final redactor may be ascribed the conjoining of the ready-made bush narrative (A) to the heterogeneous B section that now forms the transition to it (2:23b–25). Thus he completed the work of his predecessors, supplementing and combining to create the standard synthesis of Israel's traditions concerning the event at the bush, a synthesis richer than any of the elements that entered into it.

The Return to Egypt (4:18-26)

The Movement of the Story

a. 4:18–20. Moses returned to Midian to secure permission of his father-in-law to return to Egypt. There he was told by God of the death of his persecutors, whereupon he took his family and departed.

(1) Moses modestly veils his true motive in returning to Egypt, pretending that he wishes to see how his kinsmen are faring. This is comparable to Saul's silence regarding his secret anointment by Samuel when he was asked by his uncle what happened to him (1 Sam 10:15–16). Both Moses and Saul were paragons of humility (Num 12:3; 1 Sam 10:22b).

(2) After Moses' initiative in verse 18, God's charge in verse 19 comes strangely. To be sure, the passage relates a necessary condition of Moses' commissioning: his safety from persecution by the old Pharaoh; but the verse is formulated as though oblivious of verse 18. IE tries to smooth matters over by taking *wayyomer* as pluperfect (i.e., some time before the event of verse 18 God had said to Moses, etc.); but the pluperfect use of the imperfect consecutive is very rare.[62]

(3) That Moses had "sons" (verse 20) is news, and anticipates what we shall learn in detail only in 18:3–4, namely, that after Gershom (2:22) Moses had a second son, Eliezer.

---

62. Driver, *Tenses* §76. Ramban ties verses 18–20 together ingeniously: Moses had intended to return alone to Egypt (verse 18). After hearing that his persecutors had died, however, he decided to go back with his family and stay in Egypt until the Exodus, thus demonstrating his confidence in the near deliverance of his people.

There is no evidence for the date of Eliezer's birth. But since the events related from 4:27 on leave little room for Moses to return to Midian and father a second child, it is natural to suppose that the two sons referred to in ch. 18 had been born before Moses left Midian. (How Moses' family got back to Midian [the presupposition of 18:3–4] is another problem; however it is solved does not affect the present issue.) No obvious reason suggests itself for the narrative's omitting to tell of the second child's birth until 18:4.[63]

(4) Verse 20 calls the "rod of God" what appeared in verse 2 as Moses' staff and in verse 17 as "this staff." *Onk.* paraphrases "the rod by which wonders had been performed by God." Later legends surround this rod,[64] bolstering the surmise that the phrase is a relic of a more picturesque notion of the rod as endowed with supernatural qualities. Gk's paraphrase belongs to that notion: "the rod that he had from God." The present form of our story plays down that notion, thus heightening the contrast between the magic of Egypt and God's wonderworking, which would have been obscured if Moses' staff were endowed from the start with divine qualities.

b. 4:21–23. God gave Moses parting instructions: he again foretold Pharaoh's resistance and revealed to him that this resistance would in the end threaten Pharaoh's firstborn.

(1) The exhortation to perform before Pharaoh "all the wonders that have been put at your disposal" is not consonant with the foregoing narrative in which wonders to be performed before Israel alone have been given Moses (as noted by *ShR*). (To be sure, 3:20 speaks of all the wonders that God will work on Egypt, but those were not said to be at Moses' disposal.) Like the plural *'otot* of verse 17 (see note thereto), this formulation reflects things to come that have not yet been mentioned.[65]

---

63. That is why some early versions fill the gap by adding to 2:22 the following: "She bore another son, however, whom he called Eliezer, etc. [continue with 18:3]" (Vulgate). This harmonizing addition cannot be regarded as original. Ramban, however, is so disturbed by the silence on Eliezer's birth that he supposes that Moses left Midian with only one son, Gershom; that *banaw* in verse 20 means *b^eno* (he compares Num 26:8); and that Eliezer was born only on the road (before the contretemps of verse 24ff.). The modern inference from 4:25 that the family had only one child (Dillman, *Exodus und Leviticus*) is not necessary; see ahead.

64. See above at 2:18 and *TJ* here: "the rod he took from the garden of his father-in-law; it was made of sapphire taken from the divine throne; it weighed forty *seahs* and had the great and awesome Name engraved on it; through it wonders were performed."

65. Rashi harmonizes by rendering *samti* as future perfect, "I will have placed at

Indeed, comparison of 4:21-23 with 3:19-20 shows that we have here a foreshadowing of the entire plague series with emphasis—a unique emphasis—on the rationale of the climactic plague of the firstborn. Whereas 3:19 speaks merely of Pharaoh's refusal to allow the pilgrimage, and 3:20 refers to a subsequent series of wonder-strokes that would force the king to yield, 4:21 begins with the series of wonder-plagues, ending climactically (verse 23) with the threat against Pharaoh's firstborn. This revelation to Moses of the future recalls too 3:12b's adumbration of the Sinai theophany. All such are intended to display things to come as the working out of a divine plan, known in advance to the prophet. Noteworthy is the increase in specificity and narrowing of scope over 3:19-20—information on the plague series increased; reference to the outcome omitted—with an ominous vagueness present. Does the threat against Pharaoh's firstborn refer metaphorically to his subjects at large, paralleling the firstborn relation of Israel to God, or is it simply a threat to Pharaoh's oldest son? The true nature of the blow remains veiled.

The rationale of the firstborn plague, so strikingly set forth in verses 22-23, is never repeated. It is conspicuously absent in 11:1 where God's warning of the last plague does not describe it at all. As the story now stands, God's message in 4:22-23 was enough for Moses to proceed to warn the king about the last plague after hearing from God that there was but one to go (11:1ff.).[66]

c. 4:24-26. At a night's lodging, a member of the family was assailed by God.[67] Quickwittedly, Zipporah seized a flint and circumcised her son, bringing immediate relief. An epithet had its birth in that event.

(1) Though most aspects of this episode are obscure, its celebration of the apotropaic value of circumcision is clear. The Pal. Targs. specifically ascribe atoning and saving power to the blood of circumcision; IE compares it to the paschal blood that wards off the destroyer;[68] Rashbam accords it the value of a sacrifice. Hizquni suggests more rationalistically that its prophylactic virtue was that of any pious deed.

your disposal [by the end of the plague series]"; Ramban supposes that the signs performed before Israel were to be repeated before Pharaoh, but ch. 5 says nothing to that effect.

66. Ramban supposes that these verses are out of place chronologically, and really were said to Moses just before the last plague. Sam. actually repeats them in 11:4.

67. Gk, Onk.: "an angel of God"—evidently taking Gen 32:25 as a model; by "assault" a deathly illness is meant (IE).

68. Cf. Kosmala, "The 'Bloody Husband.'"

(2) The attack occurred at a night encampment, calling to mind Jacob's desperate night encounter with a divine being at Jabbok (Gen 32:25ff.) (Rashbam).[69] What the motive of the attack was is no clearer here than there. It is not evident that fault lay with any of the protagonists.[70] If a common denominator is to be sought for the two stories it is that the attack came at a moment fraught with susceptibility to harm—at night (the season of danger) on persons journeying toward danger—and that it was warded off, but at a cost to the survivors. Some of the language of Jacob's encounter with Esau in Genesis 33 is so like that of the prior nocturnal encounter of Genesis 32 (cf. 32:31 with 33:10b; and the correspondence of $b^e rakot$ [32:27, 30; 33:11]) that one is led to think that the night event was a premonition of the morrow's confrontation, from which the patriarch emerged tempered. Here too it may be supposed that the nocturnal attack on Moses' family presaged something similar, from which there would be a deliverance, but with bloodshed. That no motive for the attack is given is part of the non-rationality of these stories: the irrational is an accepted part of life, but it serves an indicative purpose—here a premonition of the final plague, God's attack on the firstborn (cf. IE, Hizquni). That Zipporah successfully warded off this attack was a tempering and encouraging omen as the family traveled toward danger.

(3) Who are the cast of this drama? Zipporah is the only unambiguous personage. She takes the active role and this suggests that Moses will not, or for some reason cannot act. Why not?

It is commonly supposed that Moses was the victim of the attack.[71] Seeing her husband failing, Zipporah quickly circumcised a son of hers as yet uncircumcised[72] and touched the prepuce to—whose feet? Some

---

69. Less aptly, Rashbam also compares the angel's blocking Balaam (Num 22:22ff.) and the fish's swallowing Jonah—for Rashbam the common denominator being God's wrath (Moses angered God by his reluctance to accept his charge; taking along his family exhibited half-heartedness; see also his commentary at Gen 32:29).

70. The child's uncircumcision surprised later readers; they regarded Moses' delay in executing the rite as a mortal sin (ShR, see ahead).

71. Rashi; IE; ShR; McNeile, *Exodus*; Driver, *Exodus*; Noth, *Exodus*.

72. The narrative is no more interested in identifying the son than in explaining why he was still uncircumcised. Both matters have therefore been the subjects of later speculation. Some hold that the child was Eliezer, just born and as yet uncircumcised (ShR); others, that he was Moses' firstborn, Gershom, who had not been circumcised hitherto in deference to Midianite custom (Pal. Targs.) and therefore called cryptically Zipporah's ("her") son. Some moderns infer from "her son" that the narrative recognizes only one child of Moses (necessarily the firstborn, Gershom). But that would seem to be pressing the terse language of the story too rigorously. The focus is on the

say, to Moses' feet, daubing him with the saving blood, or conveying to him the virtue of the act of circumcision (IE, Rashbam). Others say, to the feet of the divine apparition, as an act of propitiation (Pal. Targs., Saadya, Hizquni). But it is possible that the legs of the child are meant, the aim being to leave a visible sign there (Kosmala).

The absence of Moses' name from the story has led some to suppose that Moses was not present at all, and that a child must perforce have been the victim of the attack as well as the one circumcised. Saadya assumes that Zipporah and her sons were returning alone to Midian when the attack occurred (cf. 18:2b). R. Hananel supposes that Moses sent his family ahead, and that Eliezer was both victim and circumcised.[73]

The context, particularly the juxtaposition with the preceding, recommends the alternative view that the child involved was Moses' firstborn, Gershom.[74] The echo of "Lo, I will slay your firstborn son" (verse 23) lingers through the beginning of verse 24, and can be heard as a skewed antecedent to the suffixes in verse 24—referring now to Gershom, Moses' firstborn.[75]

---

act and its effect rather than on the participants' identity (hence the absence of names). What is significant is Zipporah's quick wit: sizing up the peril, "she cut off the foreskin of a son of hers"—which one matters not—and thus saved a life.

73. "We learn that to circumcise an infant is to save him from death from the case of Eliezer—'He sought to kill him' (verse 24) refers to the infant, and it was on account of his mother's negligence in having him circumcised. When she realized it, she circumcised him . . . and thus saved him from death . . . It is written, 'If any male should be uncircumcised, that person shall be cut off from his kin' (Gen 17:14). This story shows that a minor is punished for a wrongdoing of his parent" (R. Hananel, Yoma 85b [cited in Kasher, Torah Shelemah, 8, 200, note to § 152; 3/2 (2nd ed.), 915 note to ch. 21 § 33]). IE objects: How could Zipporah have endangered a sick child further by circumcising him? Surely Moses must have been the victim! IE's rationalism inhibits him from appreciating the mysterious saving power of circumcision which it is the purpose of this story to celebrate.

74. Shadal; Morgenstern, Rites.

75. Cf. Blau, "Hᵃtan damim." A bizarre perception of verses 19–26—IE calls it mad—reflecting such a hearing of the end of verse 23 and the beginning of 24, is that of Joseph Kimhi (cited in Kasher, Torah Shelemah, 8, 197 §139): After God's revelation to Moses at the bush and his return to Jethro, Moses procrastinated.. thinking that perhaps the prophecy referred to some distant future. Finally God said to him, 'Go return to Egypt.' Moses took his family along, thinking that, in the event that the redemption would be delayed at least he would have his family with him. Seeing that he was so halfhearted about his mission that he took back his wife—thus inviting the Israelites' suspicion that he was not coming to redeem them at all but to live in Egypt—God again spoke to Moses saying, 'Go say to Pharaoh, Israel is my firstborn!' I said to you, 'Get my people out of Egypt', but you refused to get them out, you refused

(4) The obscurity of the story makes interpretation of Zipporah's statement very difficult. It is commonly held that *ḥᵃtan damim* refers to Moses—supposedly the victim of the attack—as "a bridegroom (i.e. a revived and restored husband) through the blood of circumcision" (NJPS). But *ḥatan* never means husband with reference to a wife, only with reference to his in-laws, (as *kallah* means bride only with reference to her in-laws, never to her husband). Hence an alternative, dating from Mishnaic times and based (it would seem) on a then prevalent usage of *ḥᵃtan* is attractive: "R. Simon ben Gamliel says: the angel of death was not intent on slaying Moses but the infant, as it is said there, 'You are a *ḥatan damim* to me'; observe who is called *ḥatan* and you will find that it is the infant"[76] (*Ned.* 32b; cf. Mishnah *Nidda* 5.3; *Tosefot Yom Tov*; so too Saadya). This suggests the following rendering of verse 25: "You (infant) are a sanguinary 'bridegroom' for me (since at your circumcision death loomed near) . . . Then it was that she called the circumcised[77] 'sanguinary bridegroom.'" Taken this way, the story gives an etiology for the phrase "sanguinary bridegroom," presumably prevalent in biblical times as an epithet of circumcised infants;[78] currently understood as a reference to the blood of circumcision, the epithet was first coined (says the etiology) when once the threat of death in Moses' family was removed by circumcising an infant.[79]

---

to go on my commission to bring them out of Egypt, you go halfheartedly—well, I am going to kill your firstborn son Gershom, ("he met him" refers to the antecedent "your firstborn son.") So Moses explained to Zipporah [when the child was attacked]: 'He is uncircumcised while the rest of his people are circumcised, that is why he wants to kill him.'"

76. In south Egypt, although a boy is three to six years old when he is circumcised, he is still called "bridegroom" [*ʿaris*] (Patai, *Sex and Family*, 203ff.)—evidently a term of endearment.

77. Taking *mulot* as plural of *mul* "a circumcised one," like post-biblical *bᵉkorot* plural of *bᵉkor* "first born son" (cf. Cassuto, *Šᵉmot* [ET = *Exodus*]).

78. Cassuto, *Šᵉmot* (ET = *Exodus*); cf. IE.

79. In Arabic *ḥatana* means "to circumcise" and in several localities in the Near East a connection exists between circumcision and marriage (for which it is preparatory) that accounts for the semantic development of the root in Arabic and Hebrew (Patai, *Sex and Family*). *Ḥatan* has been surmised to have meant originally "the circumcised," namely, the prospective son-in-law whose qualification for marriage it was the duty of the bride's father (the *ḥoten*) to see to (Ehrlich, *Randglossen*). Since among the Israelites, circumcision was moved back to infancy, much before marriage, *ḥatan* in the sense of "circumcised" acquired the qualification *damim* to distinguish it from the unqualified *ḥatan* "son-in-law."

Such an interpretation, which leaves open the identity of the attacked person, allows the focus of the story to remain where the narrator evidently wished it: on the saving power of the blood of circumcision.[80]

Themes and Structure

a. The three brief passages, each three verses long, are permeated with allusions to family—especially sons—and death.

In the first, composite passage (18–20) Moses' return is given in an esoteric and exoteric motive: Moses justified his departure to his father-in-law through a natural yearning to see how his kinsmen were faring. But he departed with his family only after receiving the news that those who sought to kill him were no longer to be feared.

The climax of the second passage (21–23) is the announcement that Israel is God's firstborn, and that if Pharaoh refuses to release it, his own firstborn will be killed.

The third passage deals with a mortal threat to one of Moses' family allayed by the circumcision of his son.

There are clear points of linkage. Verse 20, with its reference to the wonderworking rod "in [Moses'] hand" (cf. 17) links up with the opening exhortation of God to Moses (21) to perform all the portents that have been "placed in [his] hand." Verse 23, with its announcement of God's threat to kill Pharaoh's firstborn, leads to the episode of 24ff. depicting God's assault on the family of Moses. Passages that appear to have little in common are thus connected by linguistic-thematic links.

The undefinedness of the last passage allows at least two perceptions of its relation to what precedes it. If, as is usually assumed, the victim of the attack is Moses, then the bond of father and son, which allows the father to be rescued by an action on the son forms a counterpart to the involvement of "fathers" with "sons" that is the central concern in the immediately preceding verses. Just as God and Pharaoh are involved with their "sons" so is Moses with his.

But if the victim of the attack is Moses' son—and the context points, in that case, to his firstborn, Gershom—then the movement of threat from Pharaoh's firstborn to Moses' is strikingly dramatic. "God met

---

80. The Phoenician scholar Philo of Byblus (64–161 CE) recorded a native myth celebrating the virtue of circumcision: Once, when plagues broke out, the god Chronos offered up his son to his father, Ouranos, and circumcised himself; he also ordered his companions-at-arms to do the same (cited in *EM*, 4:897, s.v. *mila*).

him—i.e. Gershom, Moses' dearest child; of such [juxtapositions] the sages said, 'Everything has its place': this episode was placed here because of the preceding reference to firstborn."[81]

b. To the narrative of verses 18-20 which takes Moses back to Egypt and danger, two appendages are loosely attached: the prediction of verses 21-23 and the night attack. Both turn out to be premonitions of things to come depicted in intensely personal terms. First, the events to be unfolded in the plagues are conveyed in a father-son metaphor with a pithy statement of their rationale. Second, the danger to God's own from his deadly power is experienced and warded off by a blood-rite. We find here an unmistakable foreshadowing of the last plague and the simultaneous saving of Israel's firstborn through the paschal blood-rite.[82] The audience is thus treated to a preview of the denouement of the drama; as a result the narrative exhibits the structure of an *inclusio*: it suggests on the eve of Moses' return to Egypt what will happen at his final departure.[83]

81. Mid. Ḥefeṣ at Kasher, *Torah Shelemah*, 8, 198, §140.

82. Circumcision and paschal offering are associated in 12:43-49 and Josh 5:2-12: the former is a condition of observing the latter. Midrash went further and expressly associated the bloods of circumcision and paschal offering as instrumental in saving Israel: "When the term of the oath made to Abraham about the redemption of his descendants was up and they had no pious deeds to perform so as to merit redemption . . . God gave them two commands, one concerning the blood of the paschal offering and the other, circumcision, so they might merit redemption" (*Mek.*, *Bo*, 5). Or again "The sons of Jacob circumcised their descendants . . . until Pharaoh . . . prevented them from carrying on the practice . . . Yet on the day that the Israelites left Egypt all were circumcised, young and old alike, as it is said 'All the people that came out were circumcised' (Josh 5:5). Indeed, the Israelites took the blood of the circumcision-covenant and put it on the lintels of their houses, and when the Holy One passed over to plague the Egyptians, he saw the blood of the circumcision-covenant on the lintels of their houses mingled with the blood of the paschal lamb and he was filled with compassion for Israel" (*Pir. deRab. El.* 29, [Friedlander 209-10]; cf. Morgenstern, *Rites*, 73ff.). It is not too much to suppose that the association of the two bloods goes back to very early times.

83. Cf. de Groot, "The Story of the Bloody Husband," 16. For Pedersen (*Israel*, III-IV, 736), the message of the night attack story is that circumcision is a prerequisite for participation in the Passover; this is in accord with his theory that Exodus 1-15 comprise the Passover legend (an early Haggada). (This again would make the story the first element of an *inclusio*, corresponding to 12:43-49.) However that may be, the suggestion raises the possibility that an additional or alternative issue in the story is the qualification of Moses' family to join the ranks of Israel. That precisely the foreign mother and her foreign-born child are the protagonists points this way: by circumcising the child the mother caused the entire family to enter into the redemptive event as full-fledged members of the house of Israel.

Some (e.g., IE, Shadal) have supposed that Zipporah and child(ren) returned home

The Redactional Process

This brief passage bristles with difficulties that are most readily accounted for on the assumption that it is a redactorial pastiche. The following pieces of narrative have been strung together:

a. Verse 18: Moses' leave-taking of Jethro after his commission at the bush; apparently he is going alone (cf. Ramban cited above).

b. Verses 19–20a: Moses' departure for Egypt with his family after having been commanded to return there by God; no reflection of the bush commission before 20b; the latter with verses 21–23—whose dislocation was already noticed by Rashi[84] is a heterogeneous element connecting 19–20a with the bush narrative.

c. Verse 21: A reiteration of the substance of 3:18b–20; the reference to portents (*mof^{e}tim*; but '*ot[ot]* in verses 8–9, 17) put at Moses' disposal is new and is generally reminiscent of the signs given Moses in 4:1ff.; however nothing in the bush narrative alludes to signs or portents to be performed before Pharaoh, so that this reference remains ultimately without an antecedent.

d. Verses 22–23: An introductory warning of the firstborn plague, integrally attached to verse 21 but sounding as though it belonged directly before the onset of the plague.

e. Verses 24–26: The enigmatic story of the night attack.

These pieces suggest the existence of traditions setting forth events in differing sequences. Does (a) reflect an account in which Moses' family joined him only later (cf. 18:2ff., now partially harmonized with our passage)? Does (b) reflect a narrative in which Moses received his commission only after he and his family set out for Egypt at God's command?[85]

---

after this contretemps, thus accounting for their later arrival from Midian with Jethro (18:2). The text gives no hint of it (Dillman, *Exodus und Leviticus*, regards the notion as "a sheer figment"); but is there a less objectionable juncture in the story at which to place the antecedent of 18:2?

84. "Scripture does not follow a strictly chronological order of narration." On this, Maharal comments: "Moses of course 'took the rod of God with him' before 'he returned to Egypt.' One must therefore understand the sequence to be as follows: 'Moses took his wife and sons and mounted them on an ass and took the rod of God with him. God said to Moses: When you return to Egypt, etc., Then he returned to the land of Egypt.'"

85. This notion underlies Ramban's expostulation with IE: "What he says is not correct, for God's first address to Moses was at Sinai, not in Midian!" To be sure, IE does not say what Ramban imputes to him, but Ramban's sensibility to the point is telling none the less. Note too Rashbam's exegesis, which ties verse 19 to 2:15 and

Does (c) belong to a story other than the present bush narrative and its sequel in 4:27ff.—these having no hint of portents aimed at Pharaoh?

The roughness of the passage suggests composition at a late stage, at the hand of the final redactor. Evidently, consistency in detail was not a guiding principle in the composition; what was? For one thing, maximal data. Verse 18, while telling how Moses managed to get away from Jethro with a blessing, does not explain how his anxiety over his safety in Egypt (the cause of his flight to Midian) was overcome—all the more necessary for his taking wife and children back with him. Hence verse 19, awkward though it be after verse 18, was retained with its sequel, verse 20.

The conflict of verse 21 with what precedes was overbalanced by its substantive importance: an iterated charge (cf. 3:18b-20) of God encouraging his reluctant messenger as he embarked on his new career. This is not the last such encouraging message; in 7:3-4 God again foretells to Moses Pharaoh's stubbornness and his consequent punishment. Such iterations recall the numerous assurances given Gideon, another reluctant messenger of God. Gideon was twice assured by the angel at his commissioning (Judg 6:14, 16), was given three signs (6:17ff., 36ff., 39ff.), and was afterward assured twice more by God (7:7, 9-15). Each of the three foretellings to Moses has its own style and terms and is likely to have had its own separate provenance. The redactor regarded them as complementary, God having prepared Moses for what was to come at three crucial moments at the start of his career; he therefore included them all, despite some resulting inconsistencies, in his comprehensive version of events.

The rationale of verses 22-23 is a more complex matter. On the analogy of 3:20, 4:21 ought to be followed by an announcement of the consequences of Pharaoh's stubbornness. A warning of the firstborn plague—the last of the portents alluded to in verse 21—now appears. This serves two purposes: it reveals at the outset God's trump card, thus representing all that follows as the working out of a divine plan; and, secondly, it presages the deadly night attack on Moses' family. As a transition to the night attack, nothing could have been as suggestive as the firstborn plague warning, couched as it is in terms of father, son, and death.

The story of the night attack itself is so obscure as to raise doubts that its present form can have been the original one (Cassuto). This contrast with its lucid (if problematic) environment, the enigmatic allusion to Zipporah's ("her") son—why not Moses'?—give ground to suspect that

---

23—quite correctly—and thus bears witness (unintentionally) to the remarkable absence of the commission-motive in 4:19.

the piece is a relic of a fuller tale now lost. Since its scene was a night's lodging (verse 24a), that tale too evidently dealt with a threat to life made during a journey. The redactor, of course, identified the journey with Moses' return to Egypt—with what justice is more than we can say.

In sum: The internal problems of this brief passage suggest that, while the traditions received by the redactor agreed on the major points of Moses' flight to Midian, on his commission as God's agent to liberate Israel and on his return to Egypt, they did not speak with one voice on such details as the question of whether or not he was accompanied on his return by his family, the time-relation of his commission to his departure from Midian, and the nature and intended audience of his signs. The redactor did not venture to iron out inconsistencies; he fused the materials retaining as much as possible of their original form.[86] But in the relocation of verses 22–23 he took a daring liberty for such theological and dramatic purposes as have been suggested above.

Execution and Rebuff (4:27–6:1)

The Movement of the Story

a. **4:27–31.** At God's command Aaron met Moses midway, at the holy mountain; on the way to Egypt Moses revealed his commission to him. Arrived, the two summoned the Israelite elders, announced the good tidings to them, showing them the signs; the people believed them and worshiped in gratitude.

The tale of the fulfillment of God's orders in these verses follows closely the language of the orders. God's command to Aaron ("Go meet Moses in the wilderness," verse 27) is a counterpart to his command to Moses in verse 19 ("Go back to Egypt") and is related closely to verse 14 ("he kissed him" answers to "he will rejoice heartily"). With due allowance for Aaron's mediating role (4:15–16) the events follow God's orders at the bush (3:16–18a). The signs (4:1–9) were performed—apparently by Aaron (so IE at 5:1)—though they were not called for (as God had predicted, 3:18a), and the people believed God's message (cf. 16, 7). So far all went according to plan.

b. **5:1–5.** Moses and Aaron next went to the palace, where they conveyed God's demand to let Israel go celebrate a festival to him in the

---

[86]. Note how he tacked on verse 20b, obviously out of order, so as to avoid breaking up the unit of 19–20a.

wilderness; this elicited from Pharaoh a flat denial of God's authority. A more deferential restatement of the request was then made, which Pharaoh, in turn, answered with a more reasoned refusal.

(1) Events are still following God's forecast at the bush (3:18–19) with the detail now given of how his plan unfolds. The opening statement of Moses and Aaron, patterned after 4:22–23 ("Thus said the Lord," etc.) is, in effect, a provocative challenge. Couched as a peremptory message from the Lord, God of Israel, it commands Pharaoh to release the people unconditionally to celebrate a festival in the wilderness. Such a command, asserting superior authority to Pharaoh and proprietary rights over his slaves (cf. Rashbam) elicits, understandably, the sharpest retort from the king—in the circumstances, a blasphemous retort. He flaunts his ignorance of God, implying he is a nobody and refuses to recognize his authority ("to harken to his voice") with respect to Israel's release.

(2) Moses and Aaron now fall back to the milder language given at the bush: 3:18. "The God of the Hebrews" replaces the tetragram and the proud name of Israel with colorless, less challenging substitutes. More importantly, command has been replaced by humble petition ("Let—go!" by "let us now go"), a time limit has been set for the journey, and a persuasive reason added ("lest he strike us . . ."). "It were better to let us go and return than cause us to die and thus lose all; our God asks no absolute release only that we go three days and return" (BSh).[87]

Pharaoh, on his part, responds more mildly, too, though unchanged in his obstinacy. Focusing on the time-cost element, now that the challenge to his authority has ended, Pharaoh expostulates with the two: "Three days going and three days coming and time for the celebration—that's no small loss. For the people are numerous and the work is much; you'd better go back to your labors" (BSh). That paraphrase aptly interprets verse 4 by 5, apparently its gloss.[88] A similar gloss is 16:8, on 16:7; there as here, a speech is glossed by an explicatory sentence introduced by a new *wayyomer* (cf. also Gen 15:3—explicating the preceding verse 2).

---

87. Several readers have heard in the words "strike us with plague and sword" a foreboding of the plagues—"us" being ambiguous in its scope.

88. Sam. reads *meʿam* for ʿ*am* in verse 5, yielding: "Even now they are more numerous than the people of the land," i.e., the native population (cf. Gen 23:7)—NJPS note. It is an attractive alternative to MT, emphasizing the security orientation of Pharaoh's enslavement policy, explicitly stated in 1:8–12.

But the king has been put on notice of restiveness among his slaves; he loses no time in counteracting it.

c. 5:6–21. That very day Pharaoh took measures to crush the people's restiveness. Diagnosing it as the result of idleness, the king increased their labor by cutting off their supply of straw,[89] obliging them to scavenge for stubble[90] in its stead, and at the same time to produce the same number of bricks as before. When the Israelite foremen, who bore the brunt of the taskmasters' wrath at the people's inability to meet this demand, complained to the king, he angrily[91] accused them of attending to Moses' message because of idleness. Coming upon Moses and Aaron as they left the palace, the foremen charged them with worsening their lot and called down on them God's judgment.

(1) The key word here is *nirpim* "slack" (verse 8; cf. 17), glossed aptly by Rashbam: "and able to do more."[92] Pharaoh supposed that the people's interest in Moses' proposal sprang from idle time; that, therefore, an increased work-load would be an effective antidote.[93]

(2) Caught between the Egyptian taskmasters and the mass of overworked fellow slaves, the Israelite foremen absorb the punishment for the people's inability to perform the impossible task set for them. Their predicament comes out in their ingratiating, thrice repeated reference to themselves as Pharaoh's (loyal) servants, and the king's harsh rejection of their appeal for justice. Their evident expectation that they would be granted a favorable hearing makes his repulse of them the more crushing. Heretofore they considered themselves *personae gratae*, now they found themselves loathsome to the court, and unable to achieve any melioration

---

89. "Chopped straw in mud bricks increases its breaking strength over three times ... due to the binding character of the straw and ... [the] action of, such products of decaying vegetable matter as humic acid upon the clay, which increases its strength and plasticity" (Nims, "Bricks without Straw").

90. *ST* infers that the time was after the harvest ("for when is stubble first found in fields") and correctly dates it in June (Iyyar). "The harvesting of the various crops took place in the spring and was in a normal year completed by May" (James et al., *General Introductory Guide*, 8). Since the Exodus occurred in Nisan, it is assumed by *ST* that the events preceding it, described in the following chapters, filled one year.

91. Pharaoh's exasperation is conveyed through the repetition of *nirpim* "slack" (Gressmann, *Mose*, 65).

92. Cf. Ehrlich, *Randglossen*.

93. The point comes out even more forcefully in Sam. (whose reading is also reflected in Onk.) *wᵉyišʿu bah* "let them pay attention to it (viz. the work)," for MT *wᵉyaʿᵃsu bah* "let them work at it"—thus corresponding perfectly to the verse-end's *wᵉʾal yišʿu* etc. "and let them not pay attention to false promises."

of the people's plight. Their rage at Moses gives rise in turn to his accusation of God in the next passage.

(3) During the developments related in verses 6–19 Moses and Aaron were in the wings. Having set in motion events at God's behest, they wait on him for their next cue. The midrash actually fancies that Moses withdrew to Midian in the interval between verses 10–20 (*ShR*), but that is quite unnecessary. Pharaoh would not deal with them—regarding them as self-appointed upstarts—but only with his regular corvée organization. They on their part could do nothing except as authorized by God, and he was biding his time. For what? Distraught, Moses finally acted on his own.

d. Returning[94] to God with a bitter complaint that he had merely worsened the people's condition, Moses was assured that God would soon act to obtain for Israel a total release from slavery.

(1) Is Moses' complaint inconsistent with the repeated forewarnings given him by God that Pharaoh would not yield to his appeal to release Israel? Not necessarily. For one thing, Moses was not ready for a worsening of their condition after his coming to help them; nothing God had said prepared him for that, and he was embittered by it. For another, God had commandeered Moses to be his agent in a work of deliverance. Yet time had passed and the only thing Moses' message had effected was a worsening of the people's plight. Was that why he was sent? How much longer was the promised deliverance to be delayed? Such complaints, the substance of verses 22–23, are consistent with Moses' foreknowledge of Pharaoh's stubbornness: it had been predicted that Pharaoh would defy God's power; but where was the show of that power?

(2) God answers Moses, "You needn't be worried that this latest suffering is going to last; you will shortly see what I am going to do to Pharaoh" (Abarbanel). The repeated *yad ḥªzaqah* in 6:1 is exquisitely ambiguous. In the light of 3:19 it may be rendered "because of a greater might" both times—referring to God's pressure. On the other hand, 12:33 *watteḥªzaq . . . lªšallªḥam* suggests that "the mighty arm" in question is Egypt's, namely, that they will press urgently on Israel to leave their land, when the final blow strikes them.[95] In any case, the order of the clauses is climactic: not only will he let them go, he will actually drive them out!

---

94. Cf. 9:29, "When I leave the city"; the narrative supposes a place outside the city where Moses communed with God in Egypt.

95. The midrash and Rashi divide the clauses between these senses, taking the first to refer to God's pressure on Egypt, the second to Pharaoh's on Israel.

Themes and Structure

a. In four episodes the first stage of God's plan for liberating Israel unfolds. The framework is the instruction given Moses at the bush, 3:16ff., the events taking us to 3:19, where the mighty arm of God is called into play. The development is calamitous: initial trust and hope give way to disbelief and frustration.

b. The narrative dwells upon Pharaoh's reactions to God's message and the consequent worsening of Israel's lot. The motif of the whole course of the contact between God (Moses) and Pharaoh is sounded in the stark opening confrontation between them: God commands Pharaoh, thus asserting his right over him and his slaves. Pharaoh does not recognize God (i.e. his authority) or his right over Israel. The king epitomizes human pride, refusing to acknowledge a power superior to itself, a recurrent topic of biblical thought. Sennacherib echoes Pharaoh: "Which of all the gods of these lands saved his land from my power, that the Lord should save Jerusalem from my power (Isa 36:20). The Mesopotamian tyrant of Isa 14:14–15 thinks: "I will ascend heaven, set my throne above God's stars . . . mount the back of clouds, be like the Most High"; Nebuchadnezzar boasts as he threatens the three Hebrew youths, "Which god will be able to rescue you from my power?" (Dan 3:15). And the wicked, as Job tells us, say "Who is Shadday that we should serve him?" (Job 21:14–15; *ST*).

By provoking Pharaoh to this blasphemy the narrative presents the main theme of all that is to follow. A gauntlet has been thrown down, and in the nature of things Pharaoh will eventually have to yield on every point. "You said, 'Who is the Lord'—you are destined to say 'The Lord is in the right' (9:27); you said, 'I know not the Lord'—you are destined to say, 'I have sinned to the Lord your God'" (10:16) (*ShR*); he who scoffed at releasing Israel would in the end, as predicted, press them to leave his country. In all that follows, Pharaoh's insolent Godlessness, here expressed quintessentially, must be kept in view; his challenge to God provoked the ensuing calamities that befell him and Egypt.

c. How Moses' mission came to grief is told in echoes of speeches previously made by God and Moses—the language of redemption turned sour. Moses and Aaron had said to Pharaoh, "Thus said the Lord"; the taskmasters said to the people, "Thus said Pharaoh." Moses and Aaron had asked, "Let us go now . . . and sacrifice to the Lord our God"; Pharaoh twice repeats their request as the reason for the heightened oppression.

Moreover, the introductory "Let us go" (*nelᵉka*) is repeatedly echoed in the orders given the people: "Go to your tasks!" "Let them go gather straw"; "Go take straw!" God's demand was "Release my people that they may serve me (*wᵉyaʿabdeni*)" (4:23); Pharaoh's scheme was "Let the labor (*haʿᵃboda*) bear down on the men, and let them keep at it, and not pay attention to false promises." Pharaoh counters God's claim on Israel's service with his own. This is underscored by the sevenfold occurrence of derivatives of *ʿabad* in verses 9–21, all expressive of subjection to Pharaoh. In the king's speech to the foremen the two thematic verbs are combined: "Go work" (*lᵉku ʿibdu*) he tells them, epitomizing the conversion of the words of hope to words of despair.[96]

For the full appreciation of these themes their prevalence in the sequel must be noted. Far from burying God's demand by his orders, Pharaoh was destined to hear it over again in every one of Moses forewarnings in the course of the plagues (7:16, 26; 8:16; 9:1, 13; 10:3). Pharaoh would eventually be brought to terms and then routed; and as he gives way he would again utter *lᵉku ʿibdu*, this time in another context: "Go serve the Lord your God" (10:8), "Go serve the Lord" (10:24), "Go serve the Lord as you have stipulated!" (12:31).

d. The failure of his mission sends Moses back to God with a bitter complaint. He opens with the charge, "Why have you made it worse for this people?" and continues with recriminations in the idiom of the bush commission, which he now depicts as cruelly misleading. In a newly assumed role, Moses no longer waits for God, but, exploiting his intimacy with him, returns on his own initiative to give vent to his anguish over his people's worsened state. His own frustration is bound up with his people's agony; he thus becomes their spokesman. The other side of the classical mediating role of the prophet here finds its first expression: he not only speaks for God to man, but, on his own, advocates man's cause to God.

Inasmuch as Moses came to Pharaoh speaking "in the name of God," the crisis transcends his own and even the people's stake. The name of God wherewith Moses and Aaron sought to move Pharaoh had not only been ineffective, it had roused the king's self-assertiveness to new heights. He had left no room to doubt that servitude to him ruled out

---

96. A related irony is conveyed by having the foremen "come upon" (*wayyipgᵉʿu*) Moses and Aaron and accuse them of putting a sword (*ḥereb*) into the court's hand—an evocation of Moses' argument that unless Pharaoh would release the people God would "come upon us with a sword" (*yipgaʿenu . . . beḥareb*).

service to God. Surely now God must show his power and redeem his dishonored name.

Composition and Redaction

The bush narrative finds its sequel in 4:27—5:5; the terms of the two passages are almost identical. But the story of the intensification of Israel's bondage, while on the whole smooth-running, raises a question. That the predicted development in 3:18–19 fails to anticipate this event is perhaps less remarkable than the fact that Moses and Aaron take no part in it.[97] To be sure, their absence is explicable (see above); but the awkwardness of their reappearance in verse 20 leaves room for doubt that their absence, reasonable as it may be, was part of a literary design.

One suspects that underlying 5:6–23 is an elaboration of the bondage theme—not only were Israel forced to work in bricks, they were denied the regular supply of straw—that had as little to do originally with Moses as the basic statement of the theme in 1:11ff.[98] This elaboration was incorporated into the sequel of the burning bush story to provide a thematic foil to the plague narrative. The plague narrative will tell how God forced Pharaoh by gradually intensified blows to surrender his exclusive claim to Israel's service (*ʿaboda*); this sequel to the bush story tells how Pharaoh tightened the screws on Israel in arrogant and unjust assertion of that claim.

The generally smooth integration of the intensification theme indicates that it was accomplished before the final redaction. All of 4:27—6:1 appears to have been in its present form (part of the A tradition-complex) when the final redactor took it into his work.

---

97. Cf. the conclusion drawn from this in the midrash: "After Pharaoh issued this decree Moses returned to Midian and spent six months there, while Aaron remained in Egypt" (*ShR* at 5:10).

98. The thematic connection of 5:6–23 with the bondage statement of chapter 1 is so strong that the midrash overlooks the present distance between them and boldly fills out the generalities of chapter 1 with the particulars of chapter 5; see *ShR* at 1:13–14. Noth remarks the peculiarity of Moses' absence in verses 6ff.; his inference therefrom that a variant tradition of the Exodus existed in which Moses played no part goes far beyond the evidence.

The Commission Renewed (6:2—7:13)[99]

The Movement of the Story

a. **6:2-9.** God[100] affirms that, having, as El Shadday, made a covenant with the patriarchs to give them the land of Canaan he has now heard Israel's cry and recalls his covenant. Moses must announce to the Israelites that, as he is YHWH: he will liberate them, take them for his people, and bring them to the promised land. Moses delivers the message, but the people are too distracted to listen.

(1) The iterated "I am YHWH"—verses 2, 6, 7, 8—indicates the entire passage's intense concern with the cargo of the name—the character of God. The need for self-identification may be enough to account for its occurrence in verse 2 (cf. 3:6); it does not explain the occurrence in verse 8, or the sense of "You shall know that I am YHWH, your God ..." in 7 (cf. 7:5). Indeed, more than mere self-identification is conveyed by the formula even at the opening of a theophany. When "I am X" in that position is qualified in some way, the qualification is intended to comfort or encourage: "I am the God of Abraham, your father" (Gen 26:24; cf. 28:13; 46:3; Exod 3:6); "I am YHWH who brought you out of Ur of the Chaldees ..." (Gen 15:7). Egyptian examples: "See me, look at me, my son Thutmose! I am thy father, Harmakhis-Kepri-Re-Atum. I shall give thee my kingdom upon earth";[101] "I am Khnum, your creator. My arms are round about you ..."[102]

When a mixture of qualified and unqualified self-identifications occurs, the effect is the same; e.g., "I am the great divine lady, I am the goddess Ishtar of Arbela, who will destroy your enemies from before your feet. What are the words of mine, which I spoke to you, that you did not rely upon? I am Ishtar of Arbela. I shall lie in wait for your enemies..."[103] This is no different from the unqualified form, standing alone thus: "I am

---

99. The problems of this difficult passage are discussed in an illuminating way by Jacob, "Mose," 187ff.

100. *ᵉlohim* is a general term for the Deity whose self-revelation in two stages is about to be alluded to through distinctive names. Cf. the identical usage in 3:11, 13, 14, 15 in a somewhat analogous context.

101. *ANET*, 449b.

102. Oppenheim, *The Interpretation of Dreams*, 251.

103. *ANET*, 449d.

Ishtar of Arbela, O Esarhaddon, king of Assyria. In the cities of Ashur, Nineveh, Calah, protracted days ... unto [you] shall I grant."[104]

That the self-identification does more than answer the question "who are you/what is your name?" comes out strikingly in the royal declaration of Gen 41:44: "I am Pharaoh; and without your consent no man shall lift up hand or foot in all the land of Egypt." Rashi glosses aptly: "*I am Pharaoh* who have the capacity to issue decrees over my realm, *and* I decree that *without*, etc." Just such a connotation is carried by the closest analogues to our passage, the opening "I am El Shaddai" of the theophanies to Abraham (Gen 17:1) and Jacob (35:11). Kimhi glosses: "*I am El Shaddai*, and nature is under my control, and I have the power to alter it as I will" (at 17:1). Whether Kimhi's speculation about the meaning of the epithet is correct is less important than his appreciation of the fact that the phrases "I am X" is designed to convey a cargo beyond mere identity. It must never be lost sight of that the name of a god is so inextricably bound up with his nature and capacity, that every self-identification is at the same time a message of power and authority." I am YHWH" in our passage means nothing less. We shall soon see that it connotes, more particularly, sanction and guarantee.

(2) Verses 3–5 are the historical basis of the asseveration (*laken*) of 6ff. (cf., e.g., Judg 10:11–13a; 1 Sam 2:27–29; 1 Kgs 14:7–9; Ezek 5:5–6; 20:1–29). God appeared to the patriarchs, and indeed (*wᵉgam*)[105] he promised them Canaan, and now (*wᵉgam*) he has heard Israel's moans and remembers his promise (the climactic *wᵉgam* as in 1 Sam 4:17).

That God did not make himself known to the patriarchs by his name YHWH is on the face of it contradicted by Gen 15:7; 28:13 and many other passages showing the patriarchs' familiarity with the tetragram (12:8; 14:22; 15:2, 8; 24:3; 27:20, 27). An interesting adumbration of modern critical views is a medieval theory that all occurrences of the tetragram in the patriarchal narratives are anachronisms from the hand of Moses (R. Yehoshua, cited by IE). A representative harmonization posits a difference in the extent of the patriarchs' grasp of the connotation of the tetragram: they knew it, but its cargo was only that of *El Shaddai* (whose meaning, whatever it was,[106] conveyed less than YHWH). "The

---

104. *ANET*, 450b.

105. That the primary meaning of *gam* is to emphasize rather than to add is argued by Labuschagne, "The Emphasizing Particle *gam*."

106. The conventional translation of Shaddai as "Almighty" derives from a fanciful analysis of the term as if from *ša-day* ("self-sufficient"). Modern scholars prefer a

text does not say, 'I did not let them know (*hoda'ti*) my name YHWH,' but rather 'I did not make myself known (*noda'ti*) to them,' i.e., I was not recognized by them, in my attribute of verification, for which I am called YHWH—he who may be trusted to carry out his promises. For I only made them promises, but did not fulfill them" (Rashi; cf. Rashbam: "My name [YHWH] signifies that I am capable of fulfilling my promises").

The insistence on *noda'ti* is supported by Ezek 20:5, 9; but the difference from *hoda'ti* is questionable[107] and the nuance "trustworthy" for the tetragram is at least arguable.

There is warrant, however, for understanding the tetragram as "the name of greatness and capability" (Mey.), This is explicit in such passages as Jer 16:21, "I will make them know my arm and power, and they shall know that my name is YHWH"; or Isa 52:6 "[After the final redemption] 'truly my people will know my name [viz. YHWH]"; and pervasively in the prophecies of Ezekiel, where mighty acts of God are repeatedly made the ground of the assertion "they/you shall know that I am YHWH" (6:7; 7:4; 12:15; etc.). In that light, Meyuhas' interpretation of the historical implication of our passage is noteworthy: "When I revealed myself to the patriarchs it was as El Shaddai—as God merely; but my proper name, connoting my greatness, is YHWH the mighty; and in the character of that name I did not make myself known to them—that is, I did not show them prodigies . . . We find throughout Scripture that when God works wonders he boasts that his name is YHWH. For example, below, 'Then Egypt shall know that I am YHWH when I stretch forth my hand over Egypt . . .' (Exod 7:5). Our text is thus elliptical [the equivalent of 'I appeared to Abraham, Isaac and Jacob as El Shaddai, but my proper name is YHWH, and by that name of mine, YHWH, I did not make myself known to them']."

However the passage is interpreted, and whether or not it (as it seems) denies the patriarchs' knowledge of the tetragram (as opposed to denying them merely an awareness of its full sense), it must mean that with the advent of Moses a new and fuller perception of God was achieved. Virtually no explication of this momentous advance in the history of Israelite religion is given anywhere in the Bible. Its trace, the antique epithet Shaddai, appears henceforth only in poetic or archaizing

---

derivation from Akkadian *šadu*, "mountain," employed as a divine epithet. A satisfactory etymology of Shaddai is yet to be proposed, just as is that of YHWH (Speiser, *Genesis*, at 17:1).

107. N.B. *Onk.* and Gk who render as though *hoda'ti*.

contexts. What is more, the vehicle of this crucial information, verse 3b, is actually no more than a parenthetical statement, incidental to the main sentence: "I appeared to the patriarchs as El Shadday (not making myself known to them by my name YHWH) and indeed established, etc."[108] Its function in context is to identify the speaker with the deity that opened theophanies to the patriarchs with "I am El Shadday"—this theophany being intended as a continuation of those. All of verse 3 is designed as an assertion of continuity (the equivalent of 3:6); thus the change in divine names is not only unexplicated, it is not even stated for its own sake.[109]

(3) The message to the people (verse 6–8) is a solemn undertaking, as is indicated not only by *laken*[110] but also by the repeated sanctioning "I am YHWH." "He made them a promise, beginning and ending it with an oath by his glorious name" (*ST*). This view of the force of "I am YHWH" in our passage is borne out by an allusion to it in Ezek 20:5–6:

> [5] On the day I chose Israel
>> (a) and raised my hand (in an oath) to the seed of the house of Jacob
>>> (b) and made myself known to them in the land of Egypt
>> (a') When I raised my hand to them
>>> (b') saying, "I am YHWH your God"—
>
> [6] On that day I raised my hand to them to bring them out of the land of Egypt, to a land that I scouted for them, (a land flowing with milk and honey).

In this paraphrase the self-revelation of God (b, b' = "I am YHWH" of Exod 6:6, 8) is said to have constituted an oath (a, a') whose substance was the Exodus and landgiving. Zimmerli's comment to the Ezekiel passage is germane to ours: "The elective encounter of YHWH with Israel

---

108. So Ramban.

109. Cf. Lohfink, "Die priesterschriftliche Abwertung der Tradition." It is thus doubtful that the chief aim of 6:2–3 is, like that of 3:14–15, a revelation of a new name. It is that only incidentally; 6:2, like Gen 17:1, 35:11 assumes that the hearer knows immediately the character conveyed by the deity's self-identification. The stress is not on the revelation of a new name (any more than in the address, "I am Ishtar of Arbela"), but on conveying to the hearer a signal of comfort and encouragement—he being supposed to know what the name means as soon as he hears it.

The midrash seems puzzled by the inorganic quality of the clause in question. The *ShR* homily (cited by Rashi) beginning "Too bad about those dead and gone" tries to justify what looks like a gratuitously denigrating reference to the patriarchs by turning it into praise of them (cf. Ramban).

110. *ShR*; Goldbaum, "Two Hebrew Quasi-Adverbs."

signifies at once self-revelation and a pledging of faith . . . The noetic and voluntative aspects of divine revelation are singularly intertwined . . . YHWH's turning to Israel is an oath, . . . a freely undertaken obligation."[111]

Ezekiel calls this self-revelation the moment of God's electing Israel. (This illuminates the significance of the two stages of God's self-revelation as set forth in Exod 6:2–8: If the self-revelation to Israel signifies their election, the appearance to the patriarchs must signify theirs.) It is, of course, a problem that Ezekiel should have spoken of the moment of election in terms drawn from Exod 6:2–8 (though, cf. Ezek 20:6b with Exod 3:8, 17), while the decisive turning of God to Israel is related much earlier, in Exodus 3–4. Exodus 6:2–8 cannot in its present position be regarded as the account of God's turning-election, but only of its reconfirmation; see the discussion below of the relation of chapter 6 to chapters 3–4.

(4) The promise has three parts:

a. redemption (three verb-clauses with God as subject)—the reference is to the Exodus;
b. adoption, Israel having experienced God (two verb-clauses with God as subject)—the reference is to the events at Sinai (cf. 19:4–6);
c. settlement of the land (2 verb-clauses with God as subject).

Is it accidental that the oath ($š^eḇuʿa$) contains seven ($šebaʿ$) clauses in which God obligates himself?

The central verse 7 regards the liberation from Egypt as constitutive of Israel's "knowing"—the word means "having experience of"—YHWH (by the same event Egypt too will come to know who YHWH is; 7:5). "Through the . . . Exodus and the adoption as God's people the sentence 'I am YHWH' which Moses now proclaims to them will become an object of their experiential knowledge and conviction."[112] Compare Hos 13:4: "I have been YHWH your God ever since the land of Egypt; you have never known (= experienced) a God other than me; there is no savior but I." For Israel the tetragram means deliverer.

(5) "The Israelites did not listen to Moses this time, though they had the first time (4:31); for they had expected relief from their hard labor, but instead had been worked even harder" (Rashbam). So when God commanded Moses to approach Pharaoh he demurred, arguing *a*

---

111. Zimmerli, *Ezechiel*, vol. 1, 443 (ET = *Ezekiel*, vol. 1, 407–8).
112. Dillman, *Exodus und Leviticus*.

fortiori: If Israel, who had only to gain from my message, and who had once believed me will not listen, how much less will Pharaoh, who has only to lose and who never believed me; and still less considering my ineloquence.

b. 6:13-30. The story is interrupted by a genealogical list supplying details about Moses and Aaron that have been wanting till now.

(1) The relation of verse 13 to the context is vague. Aaron's inclusion in God's charge is taken by many (Rashi, Mey.) as a foreshadowing of 7:1-5—God's concession to Moses' diffidence by the appointment of Aaron as his spokesman to Pharaoh; heretofore Aaron had been appointed only Moses' spokesman to the people (4:16; cf. verse 30). On the other hand, the allusion to a charge concerning the Israelites as well as Pharaoh suggested to BSh that a new start was being made here of the entire commission narrative (BSh takes verse 29 as having occurred at the burning bush!): "The account is summarized briefly in order to set forth the whole negotiation with Pharaoh uninterruptedly."

Verse 13 and verses 26-28, which derive from it, constitute the frame of the genealogy, stating that it is here to tell us about Moses and Aaron.

(2) The antecedent of the pronoun in the phrase "their clan heads" (verse 14) could be either the Israelites or Moses and Aaron of verse 13. Verse 25b inclines the balance in favor of Moses and Aaron.

(3) The omission of known persons from the genealogy (e.g., Moses' wife and sons who have already been mentioned) indicates selectivity. The inclusion of persons whose line is not carried down to the latest stages of the list suggests that they are mentioned only so that other contemporaries, in whom the genealogist is interested, can be ranked in relation to them.

Thus brief mention is made of the clans of Reuben and Simeon (on information drawn from Gen 46:9-10) only in order to rank Levi among the sons of Jacob; for it is Levi alone whose descendants are followed beyond the second generation. The latest stages of the list have this in common: the lifetime of Moses spans them all. Indeed, all the sibling groups from the generation of Moses and Aaron on contain figures out of the history of Moses' later activity. "Yizhar's sons are mentioned because of Korah (Numbers 16); Uzziel's because of Mishael and Elzaphan (Lev 10:4); Korah's sons, because of '"but Korah's sons did not die' (Num 26:11) . . ." (Rashbam); "The sons of Moses, Hebron, Ithamar [etc.] are not mentioned because they do not figure in the narrative" (Hizquni).

An hereditary-aristocratic (in this case Aaronic priestly) interest in pedigree is reflected in the naming of the mothers of Aaron (a Levitess), Elazar (the sister of a Judahite chief [Num 1:7]), and Phinehas (unknown). One is reminded of the notices of royal mothers in the book of Kings (1 Kgs 14:21; 15:2; 22:42; etc.).

For Levi, Kohath, and Amram, life spans are given, after the manner of notices given throughout Genesis of patriarchal lifespans. Thus that line is singled out as continuing the succession of ancient worthies reaching back behind Abraham to Noah and Adam.

The list as we now have it is thus multipurpose; neither the summation of verse 25b nor the iterated references to Moses and Aaron in verse 26-27 reflect adequately its plurality of focuses. The list evidently was tailored for its present use out of diverse sources; its mixture of data is untypical of genealogies.

(4) The strange *parasha* separation of verse 28 from its continuation in verse 29 (Rashi et al.) may be due to an interpretation reflected in the M^{e}kilta (*Bo* 1) that, while God charged both Moses and Aaron, he actually spoke to Moses alone (a denial to Aaron of prophetic status equal to Moses'). Render according to this artificial division: 27 "It was they who spoke to Pharaoh . . . , namely Moses and Aaron; 28 and that was, when the Lord spoke to Moses in Egypt." This is an uncommon case of doctrine overcoming literary sense.[113]

c. 7:1-7. God responds to Moses' demurrer by appointing Aaron as his spokesman to Pharaoh. Pharaoh will prove obdurate, suiting God's purpose to multiply his prodigies in Egypt and thus let the Egyptians experience his power.

(1) The hardening of Pharaoh's heart (verse 3) is to make him an example for all time of the consequences of prideful defiance of God (cf. 10:1). The narrative has established the heinousness of his crimes[114] and

---

113. Another such case may be Deut 2:16, whose connection with the following verse is patent (IE, Bahya). Why a *parasha* separates them is suggested by Rashi's comment: "From the story of the spies (Deut 1:22ff.) to this verse the verb *wayy^{e}dabber* never occurs in this *parasha*, only *wayyomer*, to indicate that during the 38 years that Israel were out of favor Moses never received an oracle intimately, face to face, in calmness of spirit . . ." The *parasha* break will thus be intended to mark off the period of disfavor and signal the renewal of intimacy between God and Moses, allegedly expressed by the change from the prior series of *wayyomers* (1:42; 2:2, 9) to *way^{e}dabber* in 2:17 (*Mek.*, *Bo* 1; cf. Chavel's note to Bahya at Deut 2:16-17).

114. "Pharaoh and his company voluntarily defied God, without compulsion, and did violence to the aliens resident among them, imposing on them a total subjugation"

their root in a heathen obliviousness of God's authority. The aim of the exemplary punishment to be visited on Egypt is to impress that authority on them: "Up to now they have said, 'I know not YHWH' (5:1), let them know that I am he who is called YHWH, and the name befits me in accord with my power, my might and my prodigies" (Rashbam and Mey. on 7:5).

For the punishment to suit a crime of such proportions and achieve its desired end, it must itself be grand and prolonged till the country be devastated and its pride brought low. It was necessary to avert premature repentance on Pharaoh's part, which, had he been only normally obdurate (as were his courtiers), would have occurred before the plagues had run their course (cf. 8:15; 9:20; 10:7). Extended, small doses were also necessary so as to measure the plagues to what the people could tolerate (cf. 9:16).[115] That God deliberately managed the affair only heightens its fearsomeness. Such is the fate of the proud who flaunt God; they are frozen in their blind defiance to their doom.

How thoroughgoing God's control of Pharaoh's reactions is supposed to be is far from clear. Notwithstanding the language of 7:3, Pharaoh's obduracy during the first five plagues is consistently represented as self-motivated (7:22; 8:11, 15, 28; 9:7). God is said to have hardened his heart in plagues six, eight, and nine (9:12; 10:20, 27; cf. also the summation in 11:10 and the further case of 14:8). In plague seven, obduracy is self-motivated (9:35), though later (10:1) God takes credit for it. This fluctuation in verse 9:35 and 10:1 would have sufficed by itself to cast doubt on the significance of the shift in the expressions—it being arguable that "self-motivation" was illusory, the facts being governed by 7:3 and 10:1. But the distribution of expressions is otherwise so markedly unequal as strongly to indicate the narrator's preference for self-motivation during the first half of the plague series and for divine compulsion during the second half. The implications of this preference are nowhere spelled out;

(Maimonides; see below, n. 116).

115. Saadya (*'ᵉmunot wᵉDeʿot* lv, vi) took the phrase "harden the heart" to mean "give courage, bolster the spirit" so that it would not give way under adversity (cf. also R. Yehoshua, cited in IE. A nuance of the same notion is Albo's view (*'Ikkarim*, IV, 25; ed. Husik, 227) that the hardening consists of "removing from his heart the softening effect which comes from misfortune, so that he may return to his normal state and act freely without compulsion" cf. Abarbanel). Both views are ingenious answers to the objection that God's intervention made the punishment of Pharaoh for obduracy unjust.

nor may the narrator have in fact worked them out. But the following midrashic comment cannot be altogether amiss in its interpretation of the facts: "God gives warning a first, a second, a third time; and if a man does not repent he closes his heart to repentance in order to punish him for his sin. Wicked Pharaoh received God's emissaries five times and ignored their warnings; so God said, 'You have chosen to stiffen your neck and harden your heart—now I on my part will add to your guilt: that is the sense of 'For I have hardened his heart'" (10:1) (*ShR* 13.3).[116]

On any reading, then, Pharaoh loses his freedom of choice in the course of the plagues. That freedom is regarded as a privilege whose abuse may be punished by revocation. Only God knows when such a drastic step must be taken, hence no man may despair of repentance; but that on the road of a transgressor a point of no return may be reached is the plain teaching of this and other passages in Scripture (1 Sam 2:25 [cf. Kimhi]; 1 Kgs 18:37; Ezek 20:25).[117]

Notwithstanding these deterministic pronouncements, and in accord with biblical historiography, Pharaoh's behavior in the course of the ten plagues is psychologically quite intelligible. This two-story depiction of the motives of history will be discussed below.

d. 7:8-13. The brothers are provided with a sign of their divine commission, which Aaron is to perform upon demand. When they appear before Pharaoh, Aaron performs the sign, but its effect is cancelled by the ability of Pharaoh's magicians to do the same, in spite of the ultimate superiority of Aaron's sign.

(1) The purpose of the sign (*mofet*) is to meet the same skeptical reaction on Pharaoh's part as Moses anticipated in 4:1 on the part of the people. Not God's power, but Moses' and Aaron's agency is in doubt; that is conveyed by *lakem*: "provide a sign for yourselves," i.e., to confirm your claims. This episode, therefore, must not be counted with the plague series that follows; that as we shall see, has to do with demonstrating God's

---

116. Following out this implication, God's announcement to Moses in 7:3 that he would harden Pharaoh's heart will thus allude to a measure to be taken later on, in the last plagues only; it is evidence of God's omniscience, no different from the prediction of 3:19, not a denial of Pharaoh's freedom from the start (Ramban). Interpretation of the hardening of Pharaoh's heart as a denial of repentance is worked out by Maimonides in his Mishnah commentary, Introduction to *Abot*, ch. 8 (briefly in Code, *Teshuva*, ch. 6).

117. Greenberg, "Y^ehezqel 20 v^ehagalut Haruḥanit," 435-37.

power, not that of the brothers (Abarbanel). Moreover, while this sign is innocuous, all that follow do harm.

(2) The instrument of the wonder is Aaron's staff, mentioned here for the first time. IE attempts, with little conviction, to identify Aaron's staff with Moses', which alone has heretofore been mentioned as a wonderworking instrument. The difficulty crops up again in the inconsistent account of the blood plague.

However, the prominence given Aaron and his staff here is part of a design. It signifies the low level of the action at this early stage of the proceedings. Each party is represented through "seconds": Moses commands Aaron, and Pharaoh commands his magicians. This level is maintained through the first three plagues as well. Moreover, the sign itself is of such ordinariness that the magicians can duplicate it—a circumstance that all but cancels the effect it might have had on the king. This is another theme that will last through the first three plagues, making psychologically plausible Pharaoh's hardness of heart: so long as his men were able to duplicate the Hebrews' wonders there was no reason for Pharaoh to take them too seriously. That the Hebrews' serpent was able to swallow the magicians' was of course portentous—but only for one who was not predisposed against the significance of the sign.

(3) In crediting the Egyptian magicians with the ability to animate inanimate objects, the biblical authors and native Egyptians were at one.[118]

What significantly distinguishes Aaron's mode of operation from that of the magicians is that the latter worked through "their spells," while Aaron worked silently. For him who had eyes to see, the magicians were activating the familiar forces of magic, while Aaron called on some unknown power—which he himself identified as that of Israel's God. Moreover, that mysterious power ultimately bested the others. But Pharaoh was not impressed with a show that his own men could largely duplicate. "Pharaoh began to laugh and crow over them like a hen, saying: 'Are those the signs of your God! People usually bring wares where there's a market for them; do you bring brine to Spain or fish to Acco? Don't

---

118. Cf. *ANET*, 326c: an Egyptian spell in which a mottled knife (evidently representing a snake) "goes forth against its like" and swallows it; Erman and Black, *Literature of the Ancient Egyptians*, 36: Ubaoner animates a wax crocodile (which eats a man), then turns it to wax again by seizing its tail. See at length Montet, *L'Égypte*, 90ff.

you know I control all kinds of magic?' He summoned children from school, and they in turn, did the same; he even called his wife, and she did it too . . . Said Yohani and Mamre to Moses: 'Are you bringing straw to Afraim?' Answered he, 'One brings vegetables to a place of vegetables'" (ShR 9:6-7).

Themes and Structure

a. The section prepares the way for the grand encounter between God and Pharaoh: the plague narrative. In a programmatic speech God reiterates his design for Israel with a new emphasis on his purpose to reveal to them the meaning of his name. Then the agents of his dealing with Pharaoh on behalf of Israel are fully introduced. The charge laid on them is solemnly announced; its essence is to let Egypt too know what the name YHWH means. Moses and Aaron come before Pharaoh and fail to obtain credit with him, so God must set in motion the plague series.

b. The main theme ("I am YHWH") appears at the very outset in 6:2, is repeated in verses 6, 7, 8, in the recapitulating verse 29 (where it sums up all of vss. 2-8), and in the concluding 7:5. Its assertiveness answers the challenge of Pharaoh's "Who is YHWH . . ." (5:2) and to Moses flaunting his failure to achieve anything ever since he came to Pharaoh "to speak in your name" (5:23).

As it is the identity and capacity of God that has been questioned, so it will be these precisely that the plagues will vindicate.

c. A motive of God's action beside his compassion (already mentioned in 3:7-9) is newly proclaimed in 6:4-5: faithfulness to his covenant with the patriarchs. Although 2:24 alluded to the covenant, nowhere in the bush theophany does God mention it as a ground for his action. But now, in this moment of despair, Moses is authorized to speak to Israel of God's covenanted obligation. Moses is to reveal the full extent of God's stake in their redemption in order to strengthen their belief that he will act. Not merely his compassion is involved (as had been stressed in the bush theophany), but his reputation for keeping his promises—an essential part of his "name." God's determination to vindicate his name by fulfilling his word to give Israel the land of Canaan is to be announced as the warranty of Israel's redemption. But the people are beyond the power of words to comfort, so Moses must go on to press Pharaoh for their release.

d. Just when Aaron is mentioned as Moses' partner in the mission to Pharaoh a genealogy is intruded into the story, sundering 6:12 from its continuation in 7:1. Its intrusiveness is underscored by the seam-like recapitulation (28–30) leading back to the narrative. An attempt has been made to incorporate the foreign body artfully in a chiastic framework:

Vss. 6:	(1–) 10–12	A
	13	B
	14–25	C
	26–27	B'
	28–30	A'

Within this framework other chiasms appear: the reversal of the order of Moses-Aaron in verses 13, 26, and 27, and of the major clauses of verse 12 in verse 30. Such chiastic variations mitigate the monotony of the repetitious editorial framework.

"Why wasn't this genealogy given before, at the time when the brothers were first commissioned? Our answer is that Aaron's partnership with Moses at the first commissioning was *ad hoc* [an assumption promoted by Aaron's absence in 6:9 and no mention of Pharaoh in 4:16] and applied only to the first stage of the mission. The genealogy was reserved for the time when the partnership of the two became enduring. That is the point of the participle in verse 27: 'They are the ones *speaking*—viz. constantly—to Pharaoh . . .' The narrator reserved the genealogy for this point in the story, when Aaron became Moses' permanent partner in all his dealings with Pharaoh connected with liberating Israel from Egypt" (Ralbag). To this it may be added that just before the account of these dealings was a suitable place for setting out the honorable pedigree of the Hebrew representatives. It is as if to say, that, stemming as they did from Israel's aristocracy, the men were not assuming too much in addressing the Egyptian king.

The break made after 6:12, unnatural from the viewpoint of the action, thus marks the beginning of the uninterrupted account of Moses and Aaron's joint negotiations with Pharaoh that ends only with the announcement of the last plague in chapter 11.

e. The notice of 7:5, anticipating "all the wonders that will occur as the story unfolds" (Abarbanel), looks like a counterpart to 11:10—all the more so when interrelation of 7:1–6 with 11:9–10 generally is recognized.

These two passages form an *inclusio*, defining the beginning and end of the account of Moses and Aaron's negotiations with Pharaoh. The existence of such an *inclusio* indicates that this account was felt by the ancient narrator to comprise a thematic entity. The assumption of such an entity made in the preceding section is thus strengthened.

The age notice of 7:7 marks a station or a milestone in life's journey (cf. Gen 16:16; 17:24-25; 25:20, 26; 41:46). It signals the end of the commissioning narrative.

f. The oracle of 7:8-9—the first to Moses and Aaron jointly—opens a preliminary to the plague story. Whether 7:8-13 is to be associated with the foregoing or the following is problematic because of its transitional character. The Samaritan Pentateuch and many moderns[119] attach it to the following plague narrative, with whose first three episodes it has obvious formal connections (cf. 7:22; 8:3, 11, 14-15). Such a judgment is favored also by 7:6-7, which has the character of a pause. I attach it to the foregoing[120] because of its substantive difference from the plague episodes. As argued above, it relates a proffer of credentials rather than a plague; a response to a challenge, not a threat.

Furthermore, the episode functions as an analogue to chapter 5: both describe Pharaoh's defiance of God that led to the plagues. This analogy, it will shortly be argued, rests on an original relation of 7:8-13 to what precedes it paralleling the relation of chapter 5 to its precedent. As much to facilitate this argument as to keep together the pre-plague episodes, 7:8-13 has been attached to the foregoing. It must be acknowledged, however, that in the formal structure of the present narrative 7:6-7 marks a pause, and that 7:8-13 functions as a preparatory to the plague account.

The Literary Problem of 6:2–7:13: Its Relation to 3:1–6:1

While the gist of God's response to Moses in 6:2-8 reads as an encouraging message to disheartened Israel, a fitting sequel to chapter 5, details in it and the subsequent narrative are perplexing and the whole seems suspiciously repetitive of what has gone before.

---

119. E.g., Cassuto, *Šᵉmot* (ET = *Exodus*); Noth, *Exodus*.
120. With Driver, *Exodus*; McNeile, *Exodus*, tends so.

a. The evoking of the patriarchs and the incidental allusion to the shift in divine nomenclature (6:2–3) recall 3:6, 15–16, and 3:13–14, without being identical, or brought into connection with those passages. Why these topics had to be touched on again is not explained. Similarly, 6:6ff. repeat the substance of parts of the bush theophany, though in different terms and without reference to the earlier theophany.

b. Moses' *a fortiori* argument (6:12) against appearing before Pharaoh is surprising. Why did he not simply refer to his rebuff, recorded in chapter 5, since God had done nothing to make his appeal to Pharaoh more persuasive than before? In other words, 6:12 ignores Moses' experience at the court described in chapter 5.

c. Moses' allusion to his speech difficulty in 6:12b and God's appointment of Aaron as his spokesman in 7:1–2 repeat topics dealt with in chapter 4—again without being identical in their terms, but close enough to make the absence of cross-reference puzzling. Harmonists have pointed out that since 4:15 appoints Aaron to speak for Moses only before the people, his appointment in 7:2 to speak to Pharaoh is really new. The force of that argument is diminished by the dual consideration that in 5:1 Aaron already accompanied Moses into the palace while 6:9, on the other hand, represents Moses as speaking to Israel directly. It is hard to adjust the terms of Aaron's appointment in 7:1–2 to his role in the foregoing narrative.

d. Moses is equipped with a sign to convince Pharaoh—a strange omission in the narrative of chapter 5[121]—in terms that betray no recognition of his previous, thwarted mission. Moreover, one is struck again by the similarity without identity of the staff-serpent sign in chapter 7 to that of 4:2–3.

e. The movement of the story falters palpably after God's speech to Moses in 6:2–8. What is wanted is not further talk and preliminary sparring but the onset of God's action against Pharaoh. That we must wait for this until 7:14 is perhaps the most awkward feature of the entire section. It must also be remembered that—notwithstanding our title, "the commission renewed," based on the larger context—not a hint of renewal is given within the text itself. Were this section standing alone it would not appear to presuppose the failure of an earlier commission.

---

121. Josephus (*Ant.* 2.13.3–4) remedies the difficulty by merging the accounts of 7:10–13 and ch. 5: Moses performs signs (plural) before Pharaoh, including the staff-serpent sign, in his very first meeting with him.

THE LITERARY PROBLEM OF 6:2—7:13: ITS RELATION TO 3:1—6:1   117

f. The similarity of the two commissioning narratives and their sequels may be best appreciated by outlining them side by side:

3:1—6:1	6:2—7:13
a) Revelation to Moses at the holy mountain of God's plan to save Israel;	a') Revelation to Moses in Egypt of God's intention to save Israel;
b) Moses made God's agent to Israel and Pharaoh;	b') Moses to tell it to people;
c) his objections—including clumsy speech;	e') Moses does, and is rejected;
d) Aaron made his spokesman;	b') Moses told to go to Pharaoh;
e) Moses returns to Egypt, conveys message to people, who believe him;	c') objects with an *a fortiori* argument and on account of his clumsy speech;
f) goes with Aaron to Pharaoh, who rejects them.	d') Aaron appointed spokesman to Pharaoh;
g) told by God he is about to act against Pharaoh.	f') Moses and Aaron have an audience with Pharaoh, who rejects them;

BSh was so struck by the recurrence of the complaint regarding clumsy speech (especially surprising after God's assurance in 4:15) that he identified it (at least its occurrence in 6:29) with 4:10, and regarded 6:13ff. as a supplementing recapitulation of 3:1—6:1. But the consensus of moderns regards each of the two accounts in its entirety as variant narratives of one and the same sequence—Moses' commission and his initial failure. While 3:1—6:1 represent JE (our A) traditions, 6:2—7:13 attaches itself linguistically and thematically to 2:23b-25 and is therefore to be ascribed to P (our B).[122]

---

122. Note, e.g., the covenant theme (2:24b; 6:4, 5), the phrase *šamaʿ naʾaqa* (2:24a; 6:5a), *ʿaboda* (2:23; 6:6).

The present state of the B section, with its intrusive genealogy and seam, does not look original. Whether or not the genealogy itself belonged to the B tradition, its introduction here and its seam may be ascribed to the redactor. By placing it before 7:1 he showed awareness of a thematic entity "Moses and Aaron's dealings with Pharaoh," delimited by the *inclusio* 7:1-7; 11:9-10 (both B), directly before which he saw fit to

This view explains the surprising repetition of elements without reference (and at times in contradiction) to earlier occasions which they echo. But it raises in turn a new question: Why did the redactor include the doublet?

For it is not the case that the redactor included everything that was transmitted to him. It may be assumed that B's narrative of the bondage said something about how Israel came to be enslaved, yet when the redactor excerpted 1:13–14 from it, he omitted the account of the enslavement as unnecessary after verses 8–12. And if the next piece of B after 2:23b–25 sets in with 6:2, the redactor must have omitted B's accounts of Moses' antecedents as well, favoring A's circumstantial narrative of 2:1–22.[123] Why, then, did he see fit to include this intrusive doublet of the commission narrative?[124]

There are two possibilities: (1) The redactor was aware that 6:2–7:13 was a doublet and included it for its variants (the new form of the liberation announcement, the genealogy, the assignment of Aaron as a spokesman to Pharaoh, etc.). Such a redactorial procedure is implied in BSh's view that a new start of the bush commissioning story is made in 6:13. The difficulty with that supposition is that heretofore the redactor has woven maximal narrative variations into a single running story (in

---

preface the brothers' pedigree.

123. The idea that the genealogy of 6:13ff. was B (P)'s equivalent of Moses' birth story (Noth, *Exodus*) is implausible. Genesis 11:26ff. shows that even when genealogies are located so as to introduce new characters (as Moses' is not), they are not by themselves adequate for the job: the narrative interspersed through the genealogical details concerning Abraham is indispensable for introducing him; nothing like it is found in Moses' genealogy.

Winnett (*The Mosaic Tradition*, 28), on the other hand, doubts B (P) ever had an account of Moses' beginnings; he cites "the abrupt manner in which Abraham is introduced in Gen. 12" as a parallel to the sudden introduction of Moses he supposes in Exod 6:2. But Genesis 12 can begin abruptly because the genealogy and narrative of Gen 11:26ff. now precede it. Whether or not they were originally part of the story (Winnett doubts it), their presence now relieves the abruptness and furnishes an introduction to Abraham. That a presumed new story now starts in 12:1 without introducing Abraham does not prove it was ever thus since, even had that new story once possessed an introduction, it would have been dropped by the redactor after 11:26ff.

Winnett is right in asserting that new characters may be introduced abruptly: witness how Elijah is introduced in 1 Kgs 18:1. But even that remarkably abrupt start contains more of an identification of the new character (in the words *mittošabe gilʿad*) than does Exod 6:2 of Moses.

124. Note by the way that 6:2, like 4:18, suggests that Moses was called by God only after he returned to Egypt.

ch. 1 and 2) and we shall see him doing so consistently in the plague story. So a second possibility must be considered: (2) that he viewed this account as, in fact, sequential to what preceded.

Several factors could have contributed to this view: first, the location of this commission in Egypt necessitated placing it after the story of Moses' return from Midian, The people's refusal to listen to Moses, because of hard bondage fits well after the account in chapter 5 of the increased work load. Finally, providing the brothers with a sign was a reasonable outcome of their first failure.

To this may be added the *a priori* likelihood that the A narrative's sequel to 6:1 "must have told of a comforting speech of Moses to his own people, its ineffectiveness, and Moses' doubt about prospects of getting anything more out of Pharaoh"[125]—roughly the substance of 6:2-12, On the basis of the similarity between B's commissioning account and this hypothesized sequel of the A narrative, a replacement of the latter by the former might have been assayed. In so doing, the redactor would have done no more than dispose available materials as best he could in a sequential narrative. Resulting inconsistencies and difficulties were neither obliterated nor allowed to frustrate the synthesis.[126]

The variant strands of tradition concerning Moses' commissioning shared enough elements in common to make their interweaving feasible and on the whole convincing. The significant thematic constant is the self-revelation of God's name and nature. The challenge of Pharaoh's defiance and Moses' complaint (ch. 5) provokes God solemnly to promise that he will vindicate his name (6:2—7:7). How he did so is the main burden of the story to come. Thus our problematic section serves as a pointed introduction to the plague narrative.

---

125. Dillman, *Exodus und Leviticus*.

126. The phrase *mittaḥat siblot miṣrayim* in 6:6, 7 raises intriguing questions. In B, the usual complement to *hoṣi* is not this unique phrase but *me'ereṣ miṣrayim* (7:4; cf. 5; 12:17, 42); *siblot-* otherwise appears only in A (1:11, 2:11; 5:4, 5). Dillman, *Exodus und Leviticus*, regards its appearance here as a trace of A's hypothesized sequel to 6:1, worked into B by the redactor. But it is a question whether the redactor is to be credited with such seamless intrusions into otherwise integral passages. Either *siblot-* is original here (does this imply B was under the influence of A?), or entered some time in the course of transmission—but before the redaction—under A's influence.

III. The Plagues of Egypt (7:14–11:10)

The Movement of the Story (7:14–11:10)

a. **7:14-25.** Moses was commanded to come to Pharaoh at the Nile's edge in the morning and to demand, in the name of the Hebrews' God, that he let Israel go to worship him. Otherwise, Pharaoh would come to know the Lord's power through a plague that would turn the Nile to blood, kill its fish, and make its water undrinkable, Aaron was charged to extend his staff over all Egypt's waters, the Nile was struck and it, together with all the rest of the country's water, turned to blood. The magicians duplicated the feat, confirming Pharaoh in his stubbornness. The Egyptians had to dig around the Nile for water, but Pharaoh went into his palace, heedless. And so a week passed.

(1) Pharaoh's morning business at the Nile is not stated, nor do we have native Egyptian information that would support any of the various guesses as to what it was.[1] What is clear is that since this plague was to start right before the king's eyes (7:20), Moses had to meet him at the river. Why Moses was ordered to meet Pharaoh there again for the fourth plague (swarms of insects) is not clear. It may be connected with the pattern of the narrative, which will be discussed below.

(2) Although Moses warns that he will strike the Nile with the staff he holds, verse 19 has God commanding that Aaron stretch his staff over Egypt's water to bring on the plague. As in the accreditation sign (7:10)

---

1. Was he bathing (Gressmann doubts it), or taking a morning stroll—as was the aristocratic custom (Rashbam, BSh)? Was he making his daily check of the level of the Nile ("to this day the king of Egypt is accustomed to go out during the summer months to check how many degrees the Nile has risen, for that is when it rises" [IE]), or perhaps coming to worship it (*MHG*)?

so also in the following two plagues (lice, insects) it is Aaron who, at Moses' command, initiates signs with his staff. Verse 20 can just be read with Aaron as the subject of *wayyarem* "he raised," though verse 17 and verse 5 below lead us to expect that it was Moses who struck the Nile with his staff. Harmony can be had here only by the strained assumption that there was one staff, that of Moses, and that Aaron used it at Moses' command for the performance of the first three signs (to increase Moses' prestige [Rashbam]); wherefore it is called Aaron's staff (*ST*, IE). The confusion over the staffs (like that over the names of Moses' father-in-law) indicates that there were conflicting traditions concerning the roles played by Moses and Aaron in this plague.[2]

Motions of the hand and the use of the staff by Moses and Aaron, though similar to magical practices (cf. Naaman's expectations in 2 Kgs 5:11) and derived ultimately from them, do not serve as magical in our story; i.e., they are not intrinsically powerful, nor do they set in motion occult forces. The only power invoked by the Hebrews is God's, and they can invoke it only as agents doing his announced will.

The aim of such gestures in this story is "to show that through [Aaron's] agency the plague comes, for as soon as he extends his hand it will commence" (Hizquni, IE). The gesture links the plague to the just-announced threat of God on the lips of Moses: by its commencement at the moment that Aaron fulfills Moses' command it is identified as the work of the power in whose name Moses speaks.

(3)Another inconsistency appears with respect to the extent of the plague. According to verse 24 the Egyptians succeeded in finding subsurface water that was drinkable, since only the Nile was plagued—agreeably with verses 17–18, 21a. But verses 19, 21b say that all the waters in Egypt turned to blood. *ShR* reflects the difficulty in conflicting opinions of R. Yehuda and R. Nehemiah, the former maintaining that only Nile water was affected, and citing verse 24; the latter, evidently relying on the other passages, maintaining that the plague affected all water, including subsurface. For R. Nehemiah, verse 24 describes what the Egyptians tried, unsuccessfully, to do to get drinkable water (*MHG*). As before, it appears that divergent traditions have been combined in the narrative, but in this

---

2. Early rabbinic exegesis understood the first plague, like the next two, to have been brought on by Aaron: "Why weren't the waters struck by Moses? Said God to Moses: 'The waters preserved you when you were cast into the Nile; it is not fitting that they should be struck by you'" (*ShR*).

case harmonization is easier: surface water only was affected; subsurface was not (BSh, IE).

(4) The narrator, intent on having the magicians successfully duplicate the Hebrews, and thus serve to harden Pharaoh's heart, encouraging him to believe it was just a question of magic (*ShR*), has not spelled out where they obtained unspoiled water. Surmises range from the assumption that the plague was momentary, and that the magicians reproduced it when it was over (BSh),[3] to reference to the aforementioned subsurface water (IE), to the notion, unlikely for Egypt, that they used rain water (*ST*). At any rate, unspoiled water must soon have been available to the Egyptians, not only because the magicians had some at their disposal, but because there is no appeal to Moses to remove the plague, as there is in subsequent plagues whose duration was intolerable. The Egyptians had to labor to find water by digging; but Pharaoh turned and went into his palace; "Said Pharaoh to Moses: 'You don't trouble me, for if I can't have water I'll have wine'—but his people suffered and had to dig" (*ST*).

(5) Since no other episode either ends or begins with a time-duration notice (verse 25), the traditional joining of verse 25 to the preceding (making a *parasha* after 25) seems no more compelling than the modern (RSV, NJPS) joining of it to verse 26. Either way, the first plague is said to have lasted one week. The only other measured duration is for the darkness, which is said to have lasted three days (10:23). Three, like seven, is a typical number of completeness.[4]

There is no way of calculating the duration of the other plagues or the time between each. Traditionally each plague—including warning time in between—lasted a month (*ShR*), the total period of the "judgment of Egypt" being reckoned at a year (Mishnah *Eduyyot* 2.10; "Stubble for straw is available in Iyar [April–May] and they were redeemed [the following] Nisan [March–April]"; Rabad, cited there by *Tosefot Yom Tov*). While the guess of a month per plague is unpersuasive, the estimate of a year's duration for the whole of Moses' work in Egypt is not only indicated by the internal evidence cited but accords with the explicit biblical chronology that makes Moses eighty years old when he came to Pharaoh and, figuring forty years for his desert period, makes him one hundred and twenty at his death.

---

3. Dillman, *Exodus und Leviticus*.
4. Pope, "Number"; Pope, "Seven."

b. 7:26—8:11. God sent Moses in to Pharaoh's palace to warn him that if he refused to let Israel go worship him, his whole land would be plagued with frogs. At Moses' command, Aaron extended his staff over all the waters calling up swarms of frogs that penetrated everywhere, from Pharaoh's palace down. The magicians again duplicated this feat, but Pharaoh, greatly annoyed, asked Moses to pray to the Lord and remove the plague, promising to let the people go. Moses invited Pharaoh to set a date for their removal, and his prayers were answered. The heaped carcasses of dead frogs made the land stink, but when Pharaoh got relief he reverted to his obduracy.

(1) During the blood plague, Pharaoh had a place to escape from Moses and the plague: he had merely to turn from the Nile and enter his palace to put the plague out of mind (for while his subjects had to dig around the Nile, he of course did not). Now Moses is to "come into Pharaoh('s palace)" and threaten him with a nuisance that would begin by "coming into his house, his bedroom, and his bed" (cf. also the order in verses 29; 8:4, 5, 7; n.b. Ps 105:30). Personally affected this time, the king is forced into making his first concession. Ignoring his magicians,[5] he recognizes prayer to the Lord as the only efficacious means of removing the plague; he even promises to let the people sacrifice to the Lord (how sincerely is seen in verse 11; referring to this Moses later warns Pharaoh "not to trifle" with him again [8:25]).

(2) Moses exploits the king's rout to demonstrate God's incomparable power—8:6, a variation of the basic theme set forth in 7:17a. The term of a day, doubtless viewed as an incredibly short period in which to remove the myriads of frogs, suffices for God to put an end to the swarming pests. There is a touch of grim humor in the after-effect of the plague. Yes, he killed off the pestilential creatures, only to create a new nuisance—the stink of their carcasses.

(3) Moses' invitation to Pharaoh to "have this triumph over me" by setting whatever term he wishes for the plague is an unauthorized venture, and has been compared to Elijah's bold venture of a test between the Lord and Baal (Abarbanel). Just as Elijah prays that God acquiesce in his initiative and show thereby that "I am your servant and have done all these things in accord with your command" (1 Kgs 18:36), so here Moses assures Pharaoh that it will be "as he ordered" (*kid⁽ᵉ⁾bar⁽ᵉ⁾ka*) and

---

5. Whose ability to reproduce the plague is so essential to the contest that its baleful consequence—the intensification of the nuisance—is overlooked. Why the magicians were not asked to remove the first set of plagues is discussed below.

proceeds to cry to God over the promise (*dabar*) he had made to Pharaoh in the matter of the frogs.[6] And "God did in accord with Moses' stipulation (*dabar*)." Such boldness is exhibited again in 8:25, and there too it is said that "God did as Moses had stipulated" (verse 27). Job 22:28 says of the righteous, "You will decree a thing and it will happen for you," which was glossed later, "The righteous decrees and the Holy One, blessed be He, carries it out."

Moses' diffidence has all but vanished in the crucible of events.

c. **8:12–15.** God charged Moses to have Aaron strike the dust of the earth with his staff, at which it would turn to lice, plaguing man and beast. Aaron did so, and the lice came. When the magicians tried to duplicate the feat and failed they confessed to Pharaoh that "it is the finger of God," yet Pharaoh remained unmoved.

(1) The choice of "dust of the earth" is determined by its similarity to lice. This is the same as the principle underlying sympathetic magic: "Like produces like,"[7] though here the transformation is not magical but the work of God. A formal similarity to magical practice is found again in the episode of the boils (see below).

(2) The magicians' inability to produce lice completes their rout. Whereas formerly they were at least able to produce, if not to remove, the plague, this time they cannot even produce it. They admit that this plague is divinely sent, and is no work of magic of which they are masters. Never again do the magicians emulate Moses and Aaron.

At this point, the issue raised in 7:11 has been settled. The power manifested through the marvels of Moses and Aaron is not wizardry, but something beyond the reach of wizards; it is the "finger of God." The magicians do not allow that the Lord, God of Israel, is the cause; but they confess, at least, that it is not mere magic.

Pharaoh however is unmoved; perhaps he, like several exegetes, chose to take his magicians' confession to mean that the plague was "an act of God," a natural calamity not at all the work of Moses and Aaron—for had it been that, the magicians could have reproduced it (Rashbam).[8]

d. **8:16–28.** Moses was to meet Pharaoh in the morning at the river and warn him that if he did not let the people go serve God, his land, starting again from Pharaoh's palace, would be filled on the morrow

---

6. So render verse 8b; Abarbanel; Ehrlich, *Mikra*; and Ehrlich, *Randglossen*.
7. Gressmann, *Mose*, 91.
8. Dillman, *Exodus und Leviticus*.

with swarms of noxious creatures. Goshen alone, where the Israelites lived, would be exempt from the plague—which would show Pharaoh the Lord's presence in the land. As the plague ravaged Egypt, Pharaoh declared himself ready to let the people celebrate their festival in the land. Moses argued for and obtained the right to worship in the desert nearby, expressing the hope that this time Pharaoh was in earnest, Moses then prayed for the removal of the pests, which, when it happened, encouraged Pharaoh to remain stubborn.

(1) The ʿarob are said, in Ps 78:45, to have "consumed" the Egyptians as the frogs are there said to have "ruined" them, whereas in Ps 105:31 the ʿarob are conjoined to the lice. Hence the two definitions of the pest that have come down from the past: from Josephus (*Ant.* 2.14.3) through rabbinic literature, "a mixture of wild beasts"; from the Septuagint through the moderns, "dogflies" or "swarms of mixed insects."[9]

In favor of the first view is a passage in the Egyptian "Prophecy of Nefer-Rohu" describing a time of anarchy, when "the wild beasts of the desert will drink at the rivers of Egypt and be at their ease on their banks for lack of *someone to scare them away.*"[10] In favor of the second is the fact that the most common mixture of pests in the Near East is "mosquitoes, fleas, flies and the like" (*Bᵉreshit Rabba* 20.8).

(2) Once again the text goes out of its way to name Pharaoh and his court as the first victims of the plague (verses 17, 20, 25, 27); accordingly, we find him again ready to concede a point for relief. He opens on a bargaining note: "Since the Lord evidently is in the midst of the land (cf. verse 18) why must you go out to the desert? Worship him in Egypt; you'll find him here, as you yourselves say!" (Abarbanel). Moses parries with the allegation that popular fanaticism will react on the Israelites, whose alien mode of worship must give offense to the Egyptians (cf. the taboos mentioned in Gen 43:32; 46:34). He insists on the desert site of worship and wins his point, though Pharaoh has the last word—a warning against going too far off, meaningless in itself, but making it quite clear what he fears. Moses acquiesces in Pharaoh's brusque request to pray on his behalf, and God removes the plague to his order on the following day. As predicted, Pharaoh's obduracy again prevails.

(3) With this plague the element of separation between Israel and Egypt in the extent of the plagues sets in; it recurs in the pestilence (9:4,

---

9. The two definitions are recorded in *ShR*: R. Yehuda maintained that they were a mixture of wild beasts, R. Nehemiah, that they were kinds of hornets and mosquitoes.

10. *ANET*, 445b.

6), hail (9:26), darkness (10:23), and first-born death (11:7). It is designed, says verse 18, to teach that "I, the Lord, am in midst of the land." As may be gathered from such passages as Deut 31:17, "Surely it is because our God is not in our midst that these evils have befallen us," or Exod 17:7, "Is the Lord present in our midst or not?," the phrase signifies a controlling providence, dramatically illustrated by singling out the innocent from the guilty during the infliction of a general plague.

A second new feature (repeated in pestilence, hail, locust [10:4] and first-born) is the announcement in advance of the time the plague will strike. The innovation of Moses in 8:5 is adapted to underscore the origin of the plagues in the will of the Lord; they are not merely "divine," as the magicians had admitted; they are specifically the work of the Lord, whose agent, Moses, foretells their coming to the day. Thus step by step the narrative builds up the overwhelming evidence of God's power and control over events. Only men blinded by their arrogance fail to recognize it.

e. 9:1–7. Moses was charged to go into Pharaoh's palace and warn him that if he refused to let the people go to worship God, all the livestock in his fields would be struck with a severe pestilence. Israel's livestock was exempted, and a time fixed for the plague's onset. After the blow fell, Pharaoh checked and found that Israel's livestock was indeed unscathed; this only confirmed him in his refusal to let the people go.

(1) Since in both following plagues livestock are victims (verses 9–10, 19, 22, 25) harmony requires that the pestilence not kill "all of the livestock of Egypt." *Kol* in verse 6 must be taken as hyperbolic for "most": even though "all" is explicitly there, one cannot rely on generalizations (*ST*). So it must be also in 8:13 if the magicians are to have had any dust to operate with; so again in 9:25—contrast verse 32. Another tack is to limit the victims, in accord with a strict reading of verse 3, to those in the open field (Rashi).[11]

(2) Pharaoh does not entreat Moses to call off the pestilence because "what was to die had died, what was to live remained alive" (BSh), and so there was nothing for which to pray.

f. 9:8–12. God charged Moses and Aaron to take handfuls of kiln-soot, which Moses was to throw skyward in front of Pharaoh (without warning him of the consequences). The soot would turn to fine dust, spread over the country and cause an inflammation breaking out in boils

---

11. Dillman, *Exodus und Leviticus*. Abarbanel takes yet another tack: the later victims were newly purchased from foreigners in Egypt or from Canaan, or from the Israelites.

on man and beast. This was done, the boils broke out—the magicians weren't even able to appear in court so badly were they afflicted. But God stiffened Pharaoh's heart so that he still refused to yield.

(1) Moses and Aaron are both commanded to take the handfuls of soot—though only Moses was to toss it in the air—in order to provide four handfuls, perhaps one for each of the cardinal points (Abarbanel). The action is in the presence of Pharaoh—though the king is not given forewarning—in order to make it clear to him that the plague is due to God and not to accident. The choice of kiln-soot to "induce" fever-boils[12] is best accounted for on the assumption that it was to be taken when still hot (BSh, Abarbanel). Conformable with this quasi-magical gesture (cf. above, on lice), is the mention of the magicians, who have gone unnoticed since their lice discomfiture. This time they not only failed to duplicate the sign but, being among its victims, were unable to confront Moses and Aaron at all.

In line with the mention of the magicians is the momentary reappearance of Aaron for the first time since the lice plague. The two parties, Aaron and the magicians, are counterparts: the activity of the first in the inducement of the plague is a foil for the passivity of the second, who here receive their *coup de grace*.

(2) God's hardening of Pharaoh's heart is mentioned here for the first time in the plague narrative. "Perhaps in the first plagues it was the magicians who caused his heart to harden. After this one they never showed up again, so he had no aid and comfort and might have yielded had not God intervened" (Ramban).

g. 9:13-35. Moses was to appear before Pharaoh in the morning and warn him that if he did not release the people he would be struck this time with all of God's remaining plagues, to teach him that God is incomparable. God might have destroyed Pharaoh along with the livestock in the pestilence, but he had kept him alive to display his power and broadcast is fame throughout the world. Should Pharaoh persist in his obstinacy, God would strike Egypt with hail of unprecedented severity—but animals taken indoors would be spared. Pharaoh's God-fearing courtiers heeded this warning. At a signal from Moses the hail came with thunder and fire. Exposed humans, beasts and vegetation were struck, except in the land of Goshen. Pharaoh summoned the brothers, confessed

---

12. Though the nature of the disease is obscure, the etymology of $š^eḥin$—derived from a root whose Aramaic and Arabic cognates mean "be hot, inflamed"—amply justifies the NJPS rendering, "inflammation."

his sin and his people, and begged them to pray for the cessation of the plague promising to release them. Moses agreed, not that he believed in Pharaoh's repentance, but to prove God's control over the earth. Early ripening plants had already been crushed by the time Moses left to pray, though not late ripening. When the hail ended Pharaoh reverted to his hardheartedness.

(1) As the story of the seventh plague starts, the astonishing survival of Pharaoh up to now—susceptible to a misconception unflattering to God—is taken note of in an expansion on the message of 7:3–5: "You villain! Do you suppose I could not wipe you off the earth? Take a lesson from the pestilence: when I unleashed it, had I let it affect you and your people, you would have perished from the earth. That I did not let it affect you was only to show you my power" (*ShR*). The restraint in the use of annihilative force was deliberately intended to display God's repertoire of visitations. Now, however, with plague seven, God announces his intention to let out the stops and loose the incomparable force of his blows. "All my remaining plagues will be directed at you this time"; the force of *kol* in verse 14 is the same as in 29:12, "all the rest of the blood." Strictly speaking "all the remaining plagues" were not loosed "this time," in the hail plague. But the language is hyperbolic and means only to convey the idea that henceforth restraint will be dropped. The Lord's incomparability will now be shown in blows of unprecedented severity (verses 18, 24; 10:6, 14; 11:6).

(2) Since a primary purpose of the plagues is to get respect for God's authority, and the proper target of the hail is plant not animal life, God advises Pharaoh how to avoid harm to men and livestock during the hailstorm. It is another chance to accept or reject God's authority, and for the first time we hear of God-fearing subjects of Pharaoh who took the warning seriously and saved their men and animals. The solidity of Egyptian defiance of God has been shattered.

(3) This narrative has a notable amount of significant cross-allusions. Pharaoh's confession echoes God's threat: "This time," God had said, it was going to hurt; "This time" Pharaoh confessed, "I stand guilty"—the sense probably is, I admit I have been in the wrong all along (Ramban). Pharaoh has here adjudged the entire process in God's favor and against himself and his people; he yields unconditionally to Moses' demand. Moses, however, avows that the submission is insincere, coerced, not truly God-fearing. Yet, seizing the opportunity once again to show God's control of the earth he agrees to pray for the plague's cessation. Note how

Pharaoh's distinction between the Lord and God in verse 28 is deliberately cancelled in Moses' "the Lord God" (verse 30)—never again found in Moses' speech in the whole of the Pentateuch. Finally, the unique use of *haṭa* in the formula of obduracy in verse 34 echoes Pharaoh's confession: he acknowledged guilt but went right on being guilty.

(4) Flax is in the bud at the end of January, as barley is then in the ear (it is harvested in Egypt in February–March). Wheat, on the other hand, ripens later, and is harvested only in March–April. This provides a date in the year for this plague as well as for the next—which presumably occurred when the wheat and the emmer had grown sufficiently to be attacked by the locusts; say, a month later.

h. **10:1–20**. God commanded Moses again to go in to Pharaoh notwithstanding his God-sent obduracy, which was intended to give scope to God's wonderworking—a topic on which Israel should dwell in generations to come and through which they would come to recognize God's power. The brothers warned Pharaoh that persistent refusal to submit to God would bring a Locust plague of unheard-of severity: what vegetation had been spared by the hail would be consumed wholly. And the homes of Egypt, from Pharaoh's down, would be afflicted with the pest. The two Hebrews having gone, Pharaoh's courtiers urged him to let the men go worship their God, lest Egypt be utterly ruined. So Pharaoh recalled the brothers and began to negotiate the release. Moses' unwillingness to bargain enraged Pharaoh and he expelled the brothers. The plague came, darkening the face of the land with swarms of locusts; all vegetation was consumed. Pharaoh quickly summoned the brothers, begged them to forgive him this once and to pray for removal of this death. Moses prayed, the plague was ended, but God hardened Pharaoh's heart.

(1) God's lesson to Moses is a counterpart of the lesson to Pharaoh in 9:13–16; here, however, the value of events to Israel's religious training is stressed. "Since Pharaoh has wickedly defied me and I have no expectation of sincere repentance on the part of the heathen, it suits me that he remain stubborn that I might increase my signs against him and thus enable you to recognize my power." It is God's practice to visit punishment on the heathen in order that Israel learn to fear him as it is said, "I have cut off nations, their chiefs are desolate . . . I thought, surely you will fear me, you will accept correction" (Zeph 3:6–7) (Rashi at 7:3).

Thus the object of the plagues is not only to teach Egypt (7:5), but Israel too "that I am the Lord." For that it is desirable that the series be drawn out in a crescendo that will leave an indelible impression on Israel for all time.

A lesson to Moses replaces the usual announcement by God of the plague that will follow should Pharaoh refuse to let the people go. It complements the admonition to Pharaoh in 9:14–16, and serves a similar purpose: there Pharaoh was given to understand that the prolongation of the plagues does not bespeak God's impotence, but his purpose to make of Pharaoh an object lesson to all men. Here Moses is to understand that Pharaoh's invincible stubbornness does not make nugatory Moses' continued demands on him; it is a providence of God for the edification of Israel. Both lessons arise from the untoward length of the series (known in advance only to God; cf. 11:1) and are intended to remind and instruct the protagonist what the meaning of that length is. A manifest sign of the protagonists' concern over the unlooked-for duration of the process is the repeated "till when/how long" in both Moses' (God's) message to Pharaoh and the courtier's speech to the king. Everybody's patience is wearing thin.

(2) Although the announcement of the plague appears now only in Moses' speech to Pharaoh (verses 3–6), God must have told Moses of the locust plague and charged him to warn Pharaoh of it (otherwise why should he "come in to Pharaoh"?) except that this first appears in Moses' speech to Pharaoh; the text of verse 1, then, is elliptical. Similarly above, in the plague of hail, the text gives God's dictated speech to Moses but omits Moses' presentation of it to Pharaoh, obviously to avoid setting it out twice; "thus once this, once that element is omitted" (Ramban). Over against Masoretic Text's elliptical style, which is, indeed, constant throughout the plague narrative, is the Samaritan Pentateuch's consistently full one. Wherever God puts a speech into Moses' mouth, Samaritan repeats the speech in the direct discourse between Moses and Pharaoh. Here, conversely, Samaritan previews Moses' direct discourse (verses 3–4) in God's address to Moses after verse 2. However, one has only to compare the variable repetition of the story of Abraham's servant (Gen 24:35–48 and 1–27) or of Pharaoh's dreams (41:17–24 and 1–7) with Samaritan's literal repetitions of the plague speeches to see how different the authentic style of biblical repetition is from its later, mechanical imitation.

(3) Earnest negotiation with Moses (what preceded was not that, cf. 8:25 and 9:30)[13] is set in motion by the courtiers' urgent plea to Pharaoh to come to his senses before Egypt's food supply is lost. Their own ambiguous formulation is, "Let the men (*ᵃnašim*) go and worship the Lord their God." Do they mean (as did Pharaoh) to oppose men to women and children? When Moses and Pharaoh touch the point neither uses the courtiers' term so it is not likely. More likely they refer to Moses and Aaron who, with representatives of Israel, might be supposed to be enough to fulfill the cult requirement; cf. 12:31 in which Moses and Aaron are a separate party in Pharaoh's final listing of all those he has agreed to release.

However it was meant, Pharaoh's opening ploy to the recalled envoys sounds quite restrictive. "Unquestionably Pharaoh intended from the first—as he finally allowed explicitly—to release all adult males. But so as not to encourage Moses to demand more he asked, 'Just who will be going,' as if he never intended to let any but certain specified persons go" (Abarbanel). Moses' response is to demand the unqualified release of the entire people together with their livestock—this last he never mentioned before. In context this sounds not like a cool insistence on what must inevitably come to pass but rather like a deliberate provocation. Pharaoh takes it poorly and vows he'll never release them and their little ones—not to speak of their livestock—but only adult males (which is what he was prepared, as a reasonable man, to bargain for), for surely they only were required for a festival. (The reasonableness of Pharaoh's claim is evident from 23:17 [34:23]: Israel's cult law required only males to appear at the three great festivals of the Lord. Nonetheless it was presumptuous of Pharaoh to prescribe to God's prophet who might go to celebrate his festival.) What Moses was demanding sounded mischievous: Pharaoh hints darkly that what he really meant to do was spirit Israel away. Indignantly he orders the two men expelled from his presence.

The episode reveals for the first time an Egyptian readiness to negotiate seriously. The courtiers appear to be on the point of surrender, and Pharaoh is moved to adopt—from his viewpoint—a reasonable position (his asking for terms signalizes a greater seriousness in his offer than ever before). Moses now discloses the true dimensions of his demand—the inclusion of the livestock was a surprise, and is ignored in

---

13. Abarbanel conjectures plausibly that one reason for the new weekly *parasha*'s beginning here is that this plague begins the negotiations concerning the Exodus that ended with the actual event.

Pharaoh's response—and thus strains Pharaoh's accommodating mood to the breaking point. Far from joining in real bargaining, which is what Pharaoh invited, Moses shows himself the inflexible advocate of a position that challenges the established power-political relationships. But capitulation is not in Pharaoh's mind, and so he expels Moses and Aaron ignominiously. Though ready to compromise, Pharaoh is far from relinquishing his hold on Israel and acknowledging God's claim on them, so the plagues must continue.

(4) Pharaoh plainly hints in verse 10 that he knows whither the Hebrews' demand is tending, namely, toward escape (IE). This is a clearer expression of his apprehension than his warning not to go too far in 8:24, though that betrayed a definite suspicion of Moses' purpose. It is wholly in character that, in spite of this awareness of the intention of the Hebrews' leaders, Pharaoh never explicitly agrees to the final departure of Israel from his land, even after his claim on the people has been bargained away. In the very extremity of the first-born plague he cries, "Go worship the Lord as you said, and say a blessing for me too" (12:31–32), thus still maintaining the pretense of a temporary exit permit for worship only. Such pretense is altogether credible and illustrates the psychological truth of the narrative.

(5) While the plague raged, Pharaoh quickly summoned the brothers and confessed himself guilty toward their God and toward them—an allusion to his angry words and to his peremptory dismissal of them. He begs that they forgive him and make one last appeal on his behalf to God, implicitly suggesting that he will now finally act. In 9:30 Moses expressed his disbelief that Pharaoh had come to a true fear of God; this time he does not even mention it, for he knows there is no prospect.

i. 10:21–29; 11:4–8, 1–3. Moses was commanded to bring on a dense darkness over the land of Egypt without warning Pharaoh. The darkness was so dense it could be felt,[14] and no one could leave his place for the three days it lasted; for the Israelites, however, there was light. Pharaoh summoned Moses to resume negotiations. He was now ready to concede everything Moses demanded only excepting the livestock, which must be left as hostages. Moses replied that not only must every last beast of theirs go—for God's requirements in the festival were

---

14. From the fact that the darkness could be felt it has been supposed that it consisted of something of cloudlike density—moderns have thought of dense *hamsin* sandstorms; cf. Josephus, *Ant.* 2.14.5: "darkness so thick that their eyes were blinded by it and their breath choked..."

unknown—but that Pharaoh himself would supply sacrificial beasts for the Lord. Pharaoh's restraint ended and he angrily banished Moses from his presence, warning him against seeking further audiences under pain of death. Moses seconded this severance of relations, leaving the king with the announcement that at midnight every first-born in Egypt would be struck dead, while Israel would go unscathed. Then, he predicted, the court entourage would come and prostrate themselves before Moses, crying to him to take Israel and get out; and Israel would leave. Having spoken, Moses stalked out in a rage.

(God told Moses that there would be one last plague, after which Pharaoh would unconditionally drive Israel out of Egypt. Anticipating that, Moses was to have the people ask the Egyptians for silver and gold vessels. The Egyptian mood toward Israel had been disposed favorably by God. And Moses himself was held in esteem by the Egyptian people.)

(1) Pharaoh has moved halfway toward Moses' position (verse 10) in allowing all the people, minus their livestock, to leave. He emphasizes this by ending with the concessive "Your little ones may go with you too": Moses on his part not only refuses to yield an inch, but audaciously demands an additional royal contribution to the cult of the Lord. This is in line with the consistent aim to humiliate Pharaoh before God. However, even though Moses "never intended to press this point . . . but said it only to re-enforce his argument" (Ramban), Pharaoh was understandably outraged. It was now clear that Moses would settle for nothing short of a complete surrender by Pharaoh of any hold on Israel. Pharaoh may well have had doubts over Moses' good faith when he ascribed so total a demand to his God. "It was incredible that the Lord should command celebrants on a three days' journey to take along with them every last head of cattle. Heretofore it had always been a question of releasing the people, not their cattle. So Pharaoh grew furious and said, 'Since I have complied entirely with the command of your God, while you add on demands he never made, you deserve to die:' Pharaoh had never said such a thing to Moses before, because Moses had always spoken in God's name; but now that Pharaoh suspected him of making up things on his own he issued this decree" (Abarbanel). Pharaoh was willing to be "God-fearing" within the bounds of his sovereignty; to grant the freedom that Moses was demanding for Israel was tantamount, in Pharaoh's view, to abdicating the throne.

(2) Moses thereupon announces God's last blow. As Pharaoh has threatened him with death, so he now foretells the death of every

first-born in Egypt, human and animal—whatever belongs to the national possession. The interpretation of this plague given in 4:22–23 ("Israel is My first-born, etc.") must be supposed to have been told Pharaoh at this time; Samaritan, in fact, repeats it after "Thus said the Lord" in 11:4.

In this climactic plague, reminiscences of the foregoing are to be found. It will be without parallel—as were the hail and locusts; it will make a separation between Egypt and Israel—as in the case of insects, pestilence, and hail; and, most humiliating of all, it will compel the court's obeisance not merely to almighty God, but to his human agent and Pharaoh's antagonist, Moses (11:8).[15] Thus Moses ringingly seconds Pharaoh's definitive breaking-off of further relations: Moses would certainly not seek another audience with Pharaoh; the next time it would be Pharaoh who would desperately seek to communicate with Moses and Aaron (12:31).

(3) How Moses knew that Pharaoh "spoke rightly" in barring any further audiences, and how he knew what to foretell in response is set forth in 11:1–3. "On some prior occasion this message had been conveyed to him together with the instructions concerning the Passover [cf. 12:12—those instructions too must have preceded the announcement of the last plague; see below]. It appears out of chronological order and was placed here to give the background of Moses, 'Thus said the Lord' in verse 4, informing the reader that Moses spoke from revelation. Thus God had already told Moses [earlier] that he would bring only one more plague, and that he must tell the people to be ready. So when Pharaoh said, 'Get out of here and never seek another audience with me,' Moses replied, 'You've spoken rightly; thus said the Lord, etc.' and walked out" (Mey.). 11:1, like 10:1, omits the description of the plague given in verses 4ff. Samaritan dutifully and needlessly inserts verses 4–7 after verse 3 in the form of a direct address of God to Moses.

Why this section was displaced will be discussed below.

(4) The favor in which the Egyptians held the Israelites accounts for their agreeing to give them what they asked for (12:36; cf. 3:21). Notice of the high esteem in which Moses was held is unique to this passage.

That the man who induced the great calamities that befell Egypt should have been held in awe is understandable. Is the favor shown toward Israel wholly miraculous, or has it too some grounding in a psychological

---

15. That *yarad* in 11:8 is not physical but prestigious, was sensed by *ST*: "It will be a descent in status for them." cf. Köhler and Baumgartner, *Lexicon*, and for the contrary use of ʿ*ala*: Gen 46:31; Num 16:12; Deut 25:7.

possibility? "When the Egyptians saw the great plagues that struck them on account of Israel at Moses' command they began to recognize Israel's merit in having a God who saved and fought for them. They also began to perceive the wrong that they had been doing them, and that they were human, too.[16] Prosperous people generally regard the miserable poor as belonging to another species. Adding to their misery is no particular crime. But when these unfortunates begin to rise a bit, the prosperous begin to have regard and sympathy for them" (Shadal).

Esteeming Moses was a normal reaction to what he had accomplished; compassionating Israel was a paradoxical reaction of the oppressors to their own misfortune. Though unusual, and thus regarded by the narrative as a work of God, it does not go beyond what experience has shown to be a possible human response in such a situation.

j. 11:9-10. Thus it was that events were just as God had predicted (7:3-4):[17] Pharaoh had refused to yield, enabling God to display his great wonders. Moses and Aaron had done their duty and God had made Pharaoh obstinate so that he refused to let the Israelites go.

Moses' and Aaron's appearances before Pharaoh are over as is their active part in the plagues; hence the summary conclusion of their activity in the court. What follows is a new topic, the preparation in Israel for the great day of deliverance.

Themes and Structure

a. The theme of the plague narrative is sounded in the preparatory exhortation to Moses and Aaron (7:5): "The Egyptians shall know that I am the Lord when I stretch My hand over Egypt." It is repeated variously throughout the individual episodes: "By this you shall know that I am the Lord" (7:17, blood); "that you might know that there is none like the Lord our God" (8:6, frogs); "that you may know that I, the Lord, am in the midst of the land" (8:18, swarms); "so that you know that there is none like me in all the earth . . . for this I have let you live, in order to show

---

16. "After the plagues the Egyptians were conscience-stricken over their wrongdoing, and they became friendly and compassionate toward Israel, unable to withhold anything from them" (*ST*; cf. Ramban).

17. *Wayyomer* (11:9), "(Now the Lord) had said"—pluperfect, in accord with the summarizing or recapitulating use of *waw*-consecutive (e.g., Josh 10:40; 1 Sam 17:50; Ruth 1:22; see Joüon, *Grammaire*, §118h, p. 323 [ET = Joüon, *Grammar*, §118h, p. 363]).

you my strength" (9:14, 16, hail); "that you may know that the earth is the Lord's" (9:29, hail).[18]

The plagues are thus an answer to Pharaoh's retort in 5:2, "Who is the Lord that I should obey him and release Israel; I do not know the Lord, nor will I release Israel." Accordingly the plagues are all described as divine wonders; pains are taken to distinguish them from the products of magic on the one hand, and, on the other, from natural calamities. The magicians' failure to duplicate the plagues establishes their origin in a higher realm. Their onset precisely after an announcement by Moses, and often at a signal by Aaron or by Moses, links them to the God whose agents these men are. Their removal to order by Moses, usually effective by a predetermined date, demonstrates the control of events by the God to whom Moses appeals. Natural calamities do not set in and are not removed so predictably, nor is the accumulation of such a series of disasters normal—not to speak of the unheard-of severity of the hail, the locusts, and the terrifying selectivity of the first-born death. Add to this the separation made between Israel and Egypt in almost all of the injurious plagues and little will have been left undone to convince even the stoniest heart that "the earth is the Lord's."

The effect of the report of the plagues on others than the Egyptians is twice touched on. In 9:16 it is anticipated that the story of what happened in Egypt will broadcast the fame of God throughout the earth. And in 10:2 the plague history is expected to play a role in the education of future generations of Israelites in the knowledge of God. Both these remarks are found in passages designed to justify the extraordinary length of the process, and go well beyond the immediate context in their reflections on its ultimate import.

b. The plague narrative is not monotonous for all its repetitiveness, owing to an unusually rich weave of its basic elements—formulas, motifs, and changing reactions. Although the line of the story does not always advance explicably or systematically from stage to stage the final effect is nothing less than architectural: an unfolding drama of gradually increasing tensions, climaxed by flaring passion on both sides. How has this effect been achieved?

---

18. Ancillary to this theme are the confession of the magicians that the lice represented the finger of God (8:15); Moses' dour "You and your servants—I know that you do not yet fear the Lord" (9:30), or "How long will you refuse to humble yourself before me" (10:3); and the need of Pharaoh repeatedly to beg Moses pray to YHWH to remove the plagues.

(1) Early readers noted the gradual escalation of severity in the plagues beginning with nuisances and pests, passing through destruction of livestock and crops, and ending (in the first-born plague) with the death of human beings. The tendency is clear even though every item will not neatly fall into place. A picturesque comparison is found in several midrashim: God used the tactics of kings against the Egyptians. First he cut their water supply; then he created a din around them [frogs]; then he shot arrows at them [lice]; then he brought legions against them [swarms of insects]; then he brought on a pestilence; then he threw naphtha at them [fever boils]; then he rained missiles on them [hail]; then he sent hordes against them [locusts]; then he imprisoned them in dark dungeons; finally, he had their chiefs executed (*Tanḥuma, Bo,* 4). The increasing severity is perceived here as the progressive reduction of a rebellious population. Others have detected a deliberate, gradual heightening of the harm inflicted by the plagues:

> At first God commanded that a harmless wonder be performed before Pharaoh: the change of the staff to a serpent. Then he commanded a slightly harmful wonder: the change of water to blood. Then a slightly more harmful one: the frogs, which entered their houses and bedrooms causing people discomfort. But that was far less than the discomfort of the lice that lived on their bodies, beneath their clothes, and stung them as lice do . . . It befits a benign sovereign to punish a rebellious people with such a gradation. And that is indeed just how kings deal with rebels: first they cut off their food supply, then they afflict their persons, chastising them with whips and scorpions. Note that God began his disciplining with the mildest punishments; of their victuals he withheld only water—which was not wholly cut off from them only made more difficult to obtain. Next, their persons were mildly harmed.
>
> Afterwards he began again in the same order to inflict increasingly heavy blows on them. First the mixture of noxious creatures that ravaged their livestock and food in and out of doors; next another blow to their food supply—the severe pestilence that afflicted their livestock worse than the noxious creatures . . . then he afflicted their persons severely with a fever breaking out in boils.
>
> Afterwards he began yet another round of worse plagues in the same order: the hail, destroying whatever it could of exposed vegetation, thus depriving them of food; next that wondrous plague of locusts, to destroy what had been left over by the hail,

and so completely wipe out their food stocks (the locusts also created discomfort in that they entered their homes). Then he inflicted on them a plague that grievously afflicted their persons just short of death—the darkness that kept them three days immobile and unseeing—not even a candle could give light due to the dense black envelope—so they couldn't get their food those three days. The last plague, the death of the first-born, was worse than all its predecessors. (Ralbag, end of *Wa'era*)

(2) This attempt to find order in the escalation of the plagues operates with a pattern of three series of three, capped by the last, most injurious plague. That pattern[19] was first sketched by Rashbam (at 7:26): "Twice Moses warned Pharaoh, the third time he did not, and so through the whole series; in every group of three, the third carries no warning." A refinement was made by Bahya (at 10:1): "You will notice that of the two that carry warnings, the first reads always, 'Take your stand before Pharaoh'; the second, 'Come into Pharaoh's palace).' ... I explain it thus: Moses gave warning at the Nile the first time and at the palace the second because these were the two chief sources of Pharaoh's pride (cf. Ezek 29:3 and Dan 4:1 [concerning Nebuchadnezzar]); precisely in the seats of his pride came the warnings of the plagues." Irony aside, it is an accurate stylistic observation and discloses what the design of the narrative is.[20] This is the second factor that contributes to the architecture of the story.

(3) The agent through whom the plagues are induced varies, not altogether randomly. In the first three plagues Moses commands but Aaron executes the signal for the plague. On the Egyptian side the magicians are the responders. This is the same array of characters as in the accreditation sign (7:10–12); clearly whatever else the first three plagues aim at, they are a continuation on a heightened level of the contest left undecided by

---

19. Reflected earliest in the mnemonic of the tanna R. Yehuda: DṢaK, ʿADaŠ, Bᵉʾ AHaB.

20. The pattern 3.3.3.1 augments by a unit the creation story pattern of 3.3.1 (Cassuto, *Genesis*, 1.8), as ten is the next number of completeness after seven. Whereas the last of seven items marks a consummation conventionally in Near Eastern literature (e.g., Babylonian flood story, *ANET*, 94cd; Keret epic, *ANET*, 144a, d), the peculiarity and greater intricacy of the biblical pattern reside in its breaking up the prior six items into groups of three. In the plague narrative there is a double climax: in place of the seventh item comes a third group of three, markedly more intense than the preceding, and only then comes the capper, the tenth plague, worse than all. Cassuto (*Šᵉmot*; ET = *Exodus*) and Winnett (*The Mosaic Tradition*, 3ff.) are among the few moderns who have noted this pattern in the plagues; cf. Loewenstamm, *Masoret*, 34ff. (ET = *Evolution*, 87ff.).

the accreditation sign. Whether the Hebrew envoys were merely magicians or not is finally decided in the third plague, when the Egyptian magicians confess their inability to reproduce lice and ascribe the plague to the finger of God. Neither the magicians nor Aaron play any active role thereafter though both reappear in a subsidiary role two plagues later. Aaron and the magicians are thus correlatives, both serving as seconds to the principal antagonists. This accounts for the active role of Aaron in the first triplet of plagues.

In the last triplet Moses alone announces and induces the plagues. Aaron may be occasionally glimpsed accompanying his brother, but this is *pro forma* (i.e., in accord with the mediating role assigned to him and which the narrator does not permit to obtrude in the story). Now the last triplet is the climax of the nine; its effects are the most disconcerting and force the court to negotiate with Moses. It is appropriate therefore that they be delegated to God's chief negotiator, Moses. Their effect also was to make Moses esteemed by the Egyptians—a matter of importance for the final spoliation of Egypt.

The division of labor in the middle triplet of plagues is harder to understand. God himself brings on the first two—Moses only warns of them—while Moses, with the assistance of Aaron, brings on the third. One might have expected an ascending line of inducers—Aaron, Moses, then God. The actuality does not accord with that. Yet the thematic aptness of the choice of inducers in the first and third triplets leads one to inquire whether some reason may not underlie the choice in the second triplet as well.

(4) Just as the first set of plagues has as its distinctive aim to show that the Hebrew envoys act in the name of a power mightier than magic, so two of the second set are explicitly distinguished, and the third at least partially so by the separation said to have been made in them between Israelites and Egyptians (8:18; 9:4).[21] Two again of the third set offer an-

---

21. In the third plague of the second set, boils, there is no explicit mention of the separation. However, from the notice that the magicians "could not stand in the presence of Moses and Aaron" it is plain that a separation was made at least among these characters. The notice taken of the magicians in this plague recalls the first triplet, but with this difference: only here, agreeably with the motif of this set, is a point made of the magicians suffering a plague in contrast to Moses and Aaron. In the first set it is a question of who can produce the plague, not who is its victim.

Whether there was a separation between Israelites and Egyptians in the first triplet is not noted by the text, because it would not contribute to deciding the issue in this set—whether or not Moses and Aaron were magicians. For that, a single-minded focus is maintained on the success the magicians enjoyed in their efforts to keep up with

other new feature: an emphasis that they were unparalleled in all Egypt's history (9:18, 24, hail; 10:6, 14, locusts). The third triplet is thus expressly depicted as the most prodigious.

It is notable that in the initial plague of each triplet a purpose clause appears in God's message to Moses that embodies the motif to be featured in the triplet. The first set is prefaced by an echo of God's second commission to Moses, "You [Pharaoh] shall know that I am the Lord"—meaning, as we have seen, "You shall know me as a power," a fit description of what was demonstrated by the failure of the magicians in the first triplet. The second set is keynoted by the clause, "that you may know that I, the Lord, am in the midst of the land"; the idea of an overseeing providence embodied in this clause conforms with the separation theme of the second triplet. The third set opens with the purpose clause, "that you may know that there is none like me (*'en kamoni*) in all the earth"[22]—an expression repeatedly echoed in the next two plague narratives (but not in the darkness narrative).

Thus the first triplet establishes God as a power beyond and other than the magic of Egypt, the second shows his presence in the land

---

Moses and Aaron. Any other difference between the parties than in their capability to work a given wonder would have been distracting. The magicians are not put out of the competition by their inability to remove the plagues, for the issue is not whether they can undo the Hebrews' work, but whether the Hebrews' work is or is not of an entirely different order. Even though their inability to undo it must have been an embarrassment, so long as they could reproduce it, the Hebrews' claim to speak in the name of an entirely nonmagical power was unconvincing.

Later readers disagreed over the scope of the first set of plagues. Rabbinic exegesis assumed—in line with its tendency to augment the wonder of every plague—that in the first set, too, the Israelites were unaffected. Ibn Ezra, however, took the absence of an explicit notice of separation before plague four to mean that heretofore the effects were general—but did little harm. Only in the injurious fourth plague did God make a separation. While this seems reasonable, Ibn Ezra has gone too far in regarding the omission of an explicit separation notice in the plague of boils and locusts as meaning that no separation was made in these. Moses and Aaron represent all Israel's exemption from boils, as the magicians represent all Egypt's suffering from them. As for the locusts, the text may be elliptical; on the other hand, since the Israelites were not farmers, they would not have been adversely affected by a plague whose major effects would be felt only months later after the harvest (after they had gone).

22. Moses' similar admonition in 8:6, "that you may know that there is none like the Lord our God," is not out of place in the first triplet, and yet it is not as thematically significant as the analogous clause in 9:14. For the latter occurs in God's message at the head of a triplet, and is reiterated four times in the following narrative. This is not the case of the clause of 8:6, nor, again, of that of 9:29. These utterances of Moses relate to the general purpose of the whole plague series without being connected closely to the distinctive themes of the triplets.

through a discriminating application of punishment, and the third gives scope to his power, more than anything that history has to tell.[23]

This analysis suggests why God himself brings on the first two plagues of the second triplet. Since the second theme is God's presence and providence in the land—proven by discriminating plagues—it is appropriate that its triplet should contain two instances in which God directly induces a plague without the mediation of Moses or Aaron. What proves the link between the presence-discrimination theme and the direct action of God is the tenth plague. Verse 11:7b makes the main lesson of the first-born's death God's discriminating punishment, and verse 4 (even more emphatically, 12:12—n.b., the final "I, the Lord!") stresses that it is God alone who will inflict on the plague.

This analysis has not shown the presence of the themes equally in each triplet. The first theme is the most thoroughly pervasive in its triplet and offers no difficulty. The second theme shows up in the first two members of the second triplet but only partially in the third (the sixth plague, boils) where the separation phrase is lacking. In the third triplet it is again the third member (the ninth plague, darkness) that lacks the distinctive thematic expression of unprecedentedness—though it is perhaps implicit in the unique phrase "a darkness that can be touched" (10:21).

Here as elsewhere the narrative displays tendency without systematization, a symmetry but not a perfect one.

(5) As the narrative proceeds its complexity increases. There is an accretion of motifs in the second and third triplets, climaxing in the tenth plague. Thus, the second triplet ends with a backward look to the first's routed magicians; and in the third, the separation theme of the second triplet reappears (though not in the same language) twice alongside its own distinctive theme. The warning of the tenth plague includes both the second and the third themes, and recalls the first in the predicted discomfiture of Pharaoh's courtiers who will come to bow to Moses.

Similarly, the fixing of a time for the onset of the plague sets in with the first plague of the second triplet (swarms), and appears thereafter in every forewarning speech.

While there is no significant difference between the lengths of the first and the second triplets, the third is markedly longer and more

---

23. Abarbanel recognizes the motif-setting significance of the three purpose clauses. Influenced by later theology he describes the three themes as, first, the demonstration of God's existence; second, of his providential guidance of the world; third, of his ability to alter nature at will.

complex as befits a climax. Each of its members is about as long as both corresponding members of the first and second triplets combined:

I	II	III
A 12 verses	A 13	A 23
B 15	B 7	B 20
C 4	C 5	C 9[24]

This length is due in part to the rationalizations given Moses and Pharaoh of the astonishing duration of the series. Furthermore, the third triplet is the only one in which every member contains a dialogue between Moses and Pharaoh. This is so because in these three plagues there is a serious movement of accommodation by Pharaoh to Moses' demands making for genuine dramatic tension (see below). Finally, the complexity consists in an unusual amount of cross referencing: the recurrence of the second triplet's theme; the reference in the hail plague back to the pestilence and ahead to the locust plague in the mention of the surviving plants; the many internal cross-allusions in the hail narrative as set forth above; in the locust plague, reference back to the hail, and a hint of the darkness to come; the negotiations after the darkness picking up where they broke off before the locust plague; and finally, the threat of death to Moses dramatically turned upon Pharaoh in the immediate sequel. In sum, while there has been occasional cross referencing heretofore, in the third triplet it is much denser and makes for a more tightly knit consecutive narrative than before.

Thus by the end of the ninth plague the narrative has worked up such an intensity that the reader is caught up in the passions that have flared forth at its climax, and awaits their imminent resolution.

c. A remarkable feature of the narrative is its depiction of the protagonists. Pharaoh is far from a one-dimensional caricature of wickedness. Enough is related to give us a credible portrait of his mentality and motives. As a prototypal anti-God his portrayal has importance for the biblical understanding of human sinfulness.

(1) Pharaonic policy toward Israel from the very start has been posited on the king's absolute right over them. It takes for granted their total subjection to his will, identified in 1:5ff. with the good of Egypt, and includes even the license to murder (the condemnation of male infants to

---

24. I.e. 10:21–29.

drowning) This policy is manifestly concurred in by the great bulk of the Egyptians, who give no sign of protesting it at any point. From this position Pharaoh rejects both the unknown God's title to command him and his authority over Israel. His initial reaction to Moses' importunings is that they threaten the productivity of his work force. From a shrewd imperial viewpoint the appearance of Moses signified idle time on the part of his slaves in which they could dream up ways of escaping their tasks. Pharaoh's response is tailored to this diagnosis: his subjects are held in a tighter vise and their would-be spokesman derided as a purveyor of lies.

(2) Pharaoh's position rests on his command of all the power in Egypt. His word is law and is executed by a well organized bureaucracy (we hear of corvée officers, taskmasters, foremen). His arm reaches everywhere in Egypt; there is refuge from him only in flight. Even supermundane forces are at his disposal in the expertise of his magicians. The heathen monarch is thus portrayed as entirely self-contained and self-confident, as the fountainhead of power, the director of his people's destiny who commands the obedience of his subjects even to criminal policies, if they are represented as in the national interest. He has no consciousness of mundane or supermundane checks on the free exercise of his authority.

(3) The challenge to this self-sufficiency posed by the demand of Moses was a new thing to which Pharaoh could not adapt himself readily or consistently.[25] His initial response (5:2) was disdainful rejection in

---

25. Pharaoh's reactions and concessions are the least ordered elements of the plague narrative:

Plague	Pharaoh's Response
Blood:	unmoved
Frogs:	begs relief, concedes release unconditionally
Lice:	unmoved
Swarms:	concedes conditional release (two stages), begs relief
Pestilence:	unmoved
Boils:	unmoved
Hail:	confesses guilt, begs relief, concedes release unconditionally
Locusts:	willing to negotiate before plague for conditional release, later confesses guilt, begs relief
Darkness:	concedes conditional release; when rejected, refuses further negotiation.

While the general trend of responses is intelligible, as will be argued, their particular order—particularly between lice and boils—is not. Gressmann's attempt (*Mose*, 70 n. 3) to rearrange them reasonably in an ascending line entails radical rewriting of the text, and even then leaves him unsatisfied.

harsh and decisive words. He is unmoved by the accreditation sign and the blood plague; his magicians' partial successes must have given him some comfort, but now (as noted by Ramban) he has turned silent, a token of his anxiety. When he is unwontedly annoyed by the frogs, he breaks down and seems to yield all—deceptively, it turns out later. But this deception is the sign of weakness; Pharaoh must resort to duplicity because he can no longer have his will openly. Moses does not shrink from rebuking Pharaoh to his face later over this unseemly behavior (8:25).

The second triplet begins. Affected by the swarms of pests Pharaoh makes a second insincere concession to Moses. Later the pestilence and boils find him defiantly clinging to his obduracy (see especially 9:7).

The first scenes of the last, climactic triplet are marked by an erosion of support for Pharaoh's policy. In the hail, some of his own ministers show a genuine fear of God. Pharaoh's manner now changes; adapting his words to the evidence of God's might Pharaoh confesses his guilt toward him, but he has not yet given up the attempt to buy relief by large and empty promises. With the threat of locusts, Pharaoh's situation worsens; his isolation from his courtiers becomes critical as they impatiently urge him to yield. Now at last Pharaoh must make a substantive, not merely a verbal, change: he declares himself ready to negotiate.

(5) The principle of Pharaoh's negotiation is to preserve his hold over Israel while conceding enough to get respite from the destructive blows. Pharaoh is ready to entertain "legitimate" demands of his slaves. He therefore reacts in hurt and outrage to Moses' flat insistence on total surrender. (We hear no more from the courtiers, who may be supposed to have regarded the king's course as both prudent and honorable, and have shared his outrage at Moses' flagrant disregard of the king's claim over his subjects.) Pharaoh so far assumes that Moses is acting in deliberate bad faith that he artlessly calls his ultimate aim (escape) "evil"—thus mistakenly assuming a shared estimate of that aim. Nothing is more expressive of Pharaoh's enclosure in his own view of things as his exclamation to Moses, "Look, you are bent on evil" (10:10).

He explains the disorder by assuming "that the concessions stem from another recension" of the story. But since not even analysis of the story into its components results in a straight-line development of responses, such an assumption is unfounded.

Unevenness of response must be a primary feature of the story (see below in the discussion of the redactorial work).

(6) As he is pressed to the wall by the darkness, Pharaoh resumes negotiations and shows himself ready to meet Moses halfway. By now he has reversed himself fully in his own terms (compare 10:24 with 10:10). The rub is that these terms still presuppose his rightful authority over Israel. Hence they cannot go far enough for Moses. When Pharaoh finally faces squarely the full extent of Moses' demand—nothing short of total surrender of any hold on Israel—his indignation knows no bounds. All his accommodation has been spurned, all his retreats for nothing. This fellow Moses would be satisfied with nothing short of the king's abject humiliation—his surrender of every parcel of his sovereignty with respect to Israel. The man was a rebel and deserved death.

(7) In this dramatic evolution of Pharaoh's reactions, there is a consistency of principle—the core of his intransigence—namely, the maintenance of his sovereignty. That is the crux of the matter; that is the offense to the Godhead's kingship; that is what cannot coexist with God's authority. Thus the opposition of Pharaoh is the archetypal opposition of human power, of human authority to the claims of God. Under pressure it will show flexibility and accommodation, even reversing itself—first by crying for help, then by confessing guilt and making concessions. But after all its retreats, it clings to its last redoubt, a core of self-assertiveness and independence, to surrender which would mean the end of its claim to ultimate, self-sufficient power. Here it resists, careless of the cost, unto death.

(8) Moses' position vis-à-vis such a principle is equally consistent. He refuses to recognize Pharaoh's authority. In each of his six warnings he repeats unchanged God's demand, "Let my people go serve me." He is uncowed, inflexible, finally disdainful as he pursues his goal of complete liberty for Israel. As Pharaoh's manner mellows, Moses' grows sharper. Early there is a sporting note in his invitation to Pharaoh to set a time for the removal of the frogs (8:5); clever parrying of Pharaoh's quasi-concession to worship in the land of Egypt (8:22–23), followed by an earnest rebuke (8:25); the next remark on Pharaoh's intransigence is gloomier and dour (9:30). In the final bargaining scenes, Pharaoh's concessions not only fail to move Moses toward meeting him halfway, but actually provoke Moses to his most trenchant and extreme rejections of Pharaoh's game. At each concession, Moses provocatively raises the ante, throwing the king into a paroxysm of rage. With a power resting on a Godless foundation there can be no compromise and no dealing. The only acceptable outcome is victory for God and humiliating overthrow for the Godless.

d. In all of the foregoing behavior, particularly in that of Pharaoh, there is nothing marvelous and unnatural. This moves one to look again into the declared framework of the events, God's announced and reiterated hardening of Pharaoh's heart. The narrative certainly regards the obduracy of Pharaoh, his clinging to his pride and his defiance of God, as a work of providence. At the same time, the narrative is at the last remove from a wooden, mechanical representation of its villain. On the contrary, it provides all that is needed to make Pharaoh's motives and behavior intelligible. In spite of the deterministic framework, events are depicted as flowing from the ambitions and conflicts of normal human beings—that is, of human beings seized with the everyday delusion of self-sufficiency.

We are at the heart of the biblical conception of the drama of history. Events unfold under the providence of God, yet their unfolding is always according to the motives of the human actors through whom God's will is done without their realizing it. That is the view of Joseph when he said, consoling his brothers, "It was not you who sent me here [though it was through your envy that it happened] but God" (Gen 45:8). That is the view of the historian who says of Rehoboam's stupid and stubborn policy that it was of God, "in order to fulfill the prophecy that he had spoken through the agency of Ahijah the Shilonite" (1 Kgs 12:15). That is the view of our narrative as well. God had determined that Pharaoh should act as he did, indeed he saw to it; but Pharaoh conducted himself throughout conformably with his own motives and his own Godless view of his status. God made it so, but Pharaoh had only to be himself to do God's will.[26]

---

26. Jacob ("Gott und Pharaoh") rationalizes the biblical view as follows: *ḥazaq/kabed leb* are peculiar to the plague narrative (cf. 1 Sam 6:6), and hence may be considered coinages of this narrator. Their meaning is determined by Pharaoh's *lo yadaʿti ʾet YHWH* "I do not know (i.e., recognize) the Lord": since *leb* is the organ of *yadaʿ*, *ḥazaq/kabed leb Parʿo* means in effect "Pharaoh remained unaffected, unacknowledging; *wayeḥazzeq YHWH ʾet leb Parʿo* means "the Lord let Pharaoh remain unaffected." Jacob explains these expressions as short-cuts: that which is mediated through human psychology is ascribed to the direct action of God. Pharaoh's behavior is a function of his temperament [which is, indeed, of God], but the biblical author, with "prophetic passion" ascribes that behavior directly to God. So too Deut 29:3, "To this day the Lord has not given you a mind to understand (*leb ladaʿat*), etc."; the sense is, God has made you too weak to understand. And when Deut 2:30 says that God "hardened Sihon's heart," what is meant is that he let him form a mistaken estimate of Israel's strength which led him rashly to oppose its passage through his land (so too Josh 11:20); no special change of human nature is intended.

The Redactional Process

a. Notwithstanding the design of the plague narrative, there is considerable evidence that the present text is not of one piece.

(1) In the first two plagues, inconsistencies regarding the identity of the brother who is to signal the blood plague (7:17 and 19), the nature of the signal, and the scope of the waters affected in both plagues (7:17, 21 and 19; 7:28; and 8:1) suggest that elements of two versions of the story of these plagues have been combined.

(2) The last plague of each triplet (lice [3], boils [6], darkness [9]) differs from the rest in having no forewarning to Pharaoh. This formal divergence, in itself quite tolerable and innocuous, becomes suspicious when it is combined with further evidence of heterogeneity.

In the story of the boils:

(a) the sudden unmotivated reappearance of Aaron and the magicians after their absence since lice;

(b) the backward glance in the introduction of the hail plague to the pestilence (9:15) skipping over the intervening plague of boils;

(c) the absence of the direct action of God, thematic for the second triplet.

In the story of the darkness:

(d) the incongruity of darkness intervening between the destruction of food and livestock (hail, locust) and the death of the firstborn—aggravated by the implication of 10:17 that the series of plagues had reached its climax;

(e) the absence of the thematic clause of the third triplet ("never the like before or after").

To this must be added the appearance of doublets now given by the pairs, lice-swarms of insects, pestilence-fever boils, and—because of the darkness motif in locusts (10:5, but especially verse 15)—locust-darkness. Were these three plagues always part of the same series as the other six? The suspicion that they were not is strengthened by the omission of just these three in the poetic evocation of the plague story in Ps 78:44–51.[27]

b. When the elements making for inconsistency in the first two plagues are isolated, they turn out to be homogeneous with the narrative of the lice plague (cf. 7:19, 8:1 with 8:12; then 7:20, 22, 8:2 with 8:13). The

---

27. In the other poetic echo, Ps 105:28–36, boils goes unmentioned. Of all the plagues, boils is thus the most poorly attested: Loewenstamm, *Masoret*, 39–40 (ET = *Evolution*, 95–96).

agency of Aaron, a leading motif in these passages harks back, in turn, to the accreditation sign (7:9ff.), which is obviously cast in the same mold. That clue leads to the further realization that the notice of the magicians' success (or lack of it) (7:11–12, 22; 8:3, 14) and the obduracy formula of 7:13 also belong to this narrative strand (7:22; 8:15; cf. the fragment in 8:11). Inasmuch as the accreditation sign is part of B's narrative, we may assign these elements of the plague story to B as well.

The selfsame elements—Aaron, the magicians, and the obduracy formula—are present in the tale of the boils (9:8–12) and indicate that it too belongs to B.

The association of the darkness plague (10:21–23, 27)[28] with this narrative strand is more problematic. It lacks forewarning like lice and boils; like boils, it lacks the thematic motif of its triplet; it is substantially unlike the environing plagues. These features argue for heterogeneity with the preceding narrative. Against a connection with B, however, is the absence of Aaron and the magicians. Critics have noted that the onset of darkness by a signal from Moses is like that of hail and locusts (9:22–23; 10:12–13) and unlike that of the other plagues (blood, frogs, lice—by a signal from Aaron; boils a variant thereof; swarms, pestilence—by direct action of God). Moreover, the obduracy formula in the episodes of hail, locusts and darkness differs from all the rest in the clause, "so he did not let the Israelites go/so he would not let them go" (9:35; 10:20, 27). Hence some critics postulate three distinct narrative traditions in the plague story, P (contained in our B), J (contained in our A), and E—the longest stretch of which comprises the darkness plague.

However, the elements assigned to E are so fragmentary[29] that its reality is dubious. As concerns darkness, E's supposed hallmark—Moses' staff—is wanting: Moses outstretches his hand, not his staff, toward the sky (10:22; contrast 9:23 and 10:13).

As for the obduracy formula, the phrase, "let the Israelites go" is, in fact, part of B's formula in 6:11 and 7:2 šillaḥ 'et B. Y. me-'arṣo. As early as

---

28. The rest of the text (verses 24–26, 28ff.) contains no allusion to the darkness plague but links up with the locust plague's negotiations; see below.

29. References to Moses' staff are supposed to be a sign of E: 7:15, 17; 9:22–23; sporadic "redundancies" such as 9:24a, 25a are assigned to E. Such redundancies may, in fact, reflect an epic-poetic substratum of the language of the narrative, in which parallelism was the norm (Cassuto, "Rešit," cites natan qol(ot) and tihᵃlak in 9:23 as evidences thereof).

8:11 the predominance of B's formulas is felt, so that in the present form of the story its elements occur in all but two episode endings:

Accreditation sign: *ḥazaq leb, lo šamaʿ, kaʾašer dibber Y.* (B)

Blood: ditto (B)

Frogs: *hakbed leb* (A, cf. 7:14; 10:1), *lo šamaʿ, kaʾašer dibber Y.* (B)

Lice: *ḥazaq leb, lo šamaʿ, kaʾašer dibber Y.* (B)

Swarms: *hakbed leb, lo šillaḥ ʾet haʿam* (A)

Pestilence: *kabed leb, lo šillaḥ ʾet haʿam* (A)

Boils: *ḥizzeq leb, lo šamaʿ, kaʾašer dibber Y. ʾel Moše* (B)

Hail: *hakbed leb* (A), *ḥazaq leb, lo šillaḥ ʾet B. Y. kaʾašer dibber Y. bᵉyad Moše* (B)

Locust: *ḥizzeq leb, lo šillaḥ ʾet B.Y.* (B)

Darkness: *ḥizzeq leb* (B), *lo ʾaba lᵉšallᵉḥam* (free variant)

Summation (11:10): *ḥizzeq leb, lo šillaḥ ʾet B. Y. meʾarṣo*[30]

As a detachable stereotype, the obduracy formula is by itself a poor index of ascription for the entire episode to which it is attached.[31]

All in all, then, the supposed components of E may be left in one or the other major tradition-complex whose postulation has until now been adequate to account for the present text. To which shall we assign the darkness episode? The divergences between it and its environment (A) have already been listed: these stand in the way of an ascription to A. But does not the absence of Aaron and the magicians rule out ascribing it to B?[32] Not necessarily. For if it be so ascribed, the following pattern in B's narrative may be discerned:

(1) The accreditation sign having been imitated by the magicians,

(2) Moses has Aaron produce blood, which is imitated by the magicians;

---

30. The minor variations are typical of the style of repetitious passages in biblical narrative. On the alternation *ḥazaq–ḥizzeq*, see the discussion above at 7:30.

31. How free-floating the elements of the formula were is suggested by 4:21's combination of *ḥizzeq leb* (B) and *lo shillaḥ ʾet haʾam* (A) in a passage whose contents precludes ascription either to B or the main narrative of A.

32. Rudolph, *Der "Elohist,"* 21, at a loss to connect darkness with any major tradition-strand, declares it "a supplement of unknown origin."

(3) Moses has Aaron produce frogs, which is imitated by the magicians;

(4) Moses has Aaron produce lice, which the magicians could not do;

(5) Moses, helped by Aaron, produces boils; "the magicians could not stand before Moses because of the boils";

(6) Moses produces darkness, and "for three days no one could get up from where he was";

(7) God puts Egypt's firstborn to death, finally moving Pharaoh.[33]

The climax in the order of agents of the plagues—Aaron, Moses and God—is matched by the plagues' increasing severity: the first three are imitable by the magicians, the second three overwhelm them and then all Egypt. This climax accounts for the disappearance of the correlatives, Aaron and the magicians, in the darkness plague. All told, B's plagues number seven, six (3 plus 3) capped by one, a classic pattern found as well in the creation story (Gen 1:1—2:3). Not one of these plagues is destructive or lethal before the very last. Demonstration of God's might through prodigies that humble men is their primary object, rather than punishment.

In identifying the narrative tradition of this series with B, a certain difficulty arises. The episodes narrated purely and entirely in B's style—lice and boils—contain no address of Moses and Aaron to Pharaoh, and the lack of such an address in the darkness episode argued for identifying it too with B's narrative. Yet 7:2—B's commission narrative—expressly prepares the ground for Moses and Aaron to address Pharaoh with the demand to let Israel go. Where does B relate those demands? In the present residue of B, nowhere; but in the tale of blood and frogs where the B element is supplementary to A's narrative, demands occur in the A narrative. It must be surmised that B's narrative of blood and frogs told of a demand made of Pharaoh in the style of 7:2, but that it was replaced in the final redaction by the richer equivalent found in the other narrative strand.

c. What remains after B has been isolated is the A strand. It contains the following episodes:

---

33. That pharaoh was unmoved until the last plague of B's series is inferable from lice and boils, whose formulation is pure B. The pleas and concessions that now appear in frogs and darkness are to be assigned to A, in which they regularly appear (see below). That B told of the firstborn plague and made God its direct agent may be inferred from the anticipatory notice in 12:12, a B passage.

(1) After warning Pharaoh by the river, Moses strikes the Nile and turns it to blood; Pharaoh is unmoved.

(2) After warning Pharaoh in his palace, frogs from the Nile cover Egypt;[34] Pharaoh begs Moses to pray for relief and promises to release Israel.

(3) After Moses warns Pharaoh by the river, God brings on swarms of creatures, separating Goshen from the rest of Egypt; Pharaoh promises a conditioned release and begs Moses to pray for relief.

(4) After Moses warns Pharaoh in his palace, God strikes down Egypt's livestock with a pestilence, sparing Israel's herds; Pharaoh is unmoved.

(5) After Moses warns Pharaoh (by the river?), he signals the onset of unprecedentedly severe hail, destroying vegetation and exposed men and animals; Pharaoh begs Moses to pray for relief and promises to release Israel.

(6) After warning Pharaoh in his palace and rejecting a conditioned release of Israel, Moses signals the onset of an unprecedented plague of locusts, wiping out the rest of Egypt's vegetation; Pharaoh begs just one more pardon which, when granted, does not result in his allowing Israel's departure.

(7) The final firstborn plague (7) is announced.

The river-palace pattern of introductory formulas orders A's series into three pairs (blood-frogs, swarms-pestilence, hail-locusts). The last two pairs are, in addition, internally bound by express themes (separation, unprecedentedness). (In the present text the theme of the first pair is governed by B's interest in demonstrating God's superiority to the magicians.) But the substance of the plagues suggests rather two sets of three plagues each: the first set consisting of nuisances, the second, of destroyers of non-human life. Accordingly, the entire series has the character of graduated punitive blows, capped by the death of the firstborn. Once again the pattern of seven (3 + 3 + 1) appears.[35]

---

34. By whose agency is unknown since B has been given exclusive right to speak on the matter.

35. Smend (*Erzählung des Hexateuch*, 126–27; cited by Fohrer, *Überlieferung*, 71 n. 29) has further noted that plagues 1 and 4, 2 and 5, 3 and 6 have similar effects on Pharaoh (cf. the correspondence between days 1–4, 2–5, and 3–6 in the creation story of Genesis 1), and that the effects intensify (a) within each series from 1 to 3

A's plague series, unlike B's, gives the impression of being itself the product of a development. One wonders whether the incongruity between substance (3 + 3) and form (2 + 2 + 2) was there from the first. The wider implications of the plagues referred to in 9:15–16 and 10:1–2 give the appearance of later reflections. The inconsequence that has arisen from the extension of certain plagues beyond their expected limits also points to evolution in the tradition. Thus the problematic reappearance of cattle as victims of the hail (9:19) after their "total" destruction by the pestilence (9:6) can be resolved on the verbal level (see above); but what underlies the problem is more than a verbal nuance: it is the extension of what is properly a vegetation plague (n.b. 10:5b) to human and animal victims. Similarly with the swarms: they are described as ubiquitous nuisances, just like the frogs (cf. 8:17 with 7:28), yet the "whole land of Egypt was ruined" by them. The phrase, while vague, is yet enough to constitute an unwanted anticipation of the later vegetation destroyers, the hail and locusts. The tendency to expand the scope of the plagues endured; it is responsible for the final sum of ten, synthesized by the redactor, as well as for the continued elaboration of the plagues found in the midrash.

The elaborations that in the course of time gave A's narrative its complex character do not amount to or hang together as a third narrative strand. They were natural extensions of the material in A. Their integration into A's text is so smooth as to justify the assumption that it was already accomplished by the time A reached the final redactor.[36]

---

and from 4 to 6; (b) in the second series in relation to the first. Pharaoh's responses, then, vacillated in an ascending spiral according to A. This regularity of vacillation was destroyed by the combination of A and B, but neither depicted Pharaoh's responses in an ascending line, as Gressmann tried to do (see above).

36. Evidence that this is the case is the reference in the reflective expansion 9:15–16 to the pestilence, ignoring the intervening boils; evidently the expansion antedates the final fusion of the narratives of A and B, at which time boils came in between.

That the plague tradition was fluid during biblical times may be inferred from the variants in Ps 78:45ff. Both frogs and swarms are there called consumers and destroyers of the land; they are directly conjoined to the locusts. Plants and animals, but not men, are victims of the hail. Men and not animals are struck by the pestilence. The divergences have been perceptively treated by Loewenstamm, *Masoret*, 26ff. (ET = *Evolution*, 71ff.).

On the assumption that the original series of A's plagues was symmetrical, Gressmann (*Mose*, 77) reconstructed it thus: the first two were Nile plagues (blood, frogs); the second two struck livestock (swarms, pestilence); the third two, vegetation (hail, locusts).

d. The redactor thus had at his disposal two seven-membered versions of the plagues, overlapping at the beginning and end, each with its own inner rationale and climax. He proceeded to mesh them as follows:

Since B's first item, the accreditation sign, differed from all the rest in not inflicting discomfort or harm, it was excluded from the patterned block of plagues. These began, accordingly, with blood and frogs which stood at the head of the plagues proper in both versions. The theme of these plagues was determined by the narrative of B, which made them continuations of the Aaron-magicians contest started in the immediately preceding accreditation episode. Hence just so much of B's narrative as was needed to bring this to the fore was introduced into A's version (viz. 7:19–20a, 21b–22; 8:1–3). The third plague had to be B's lice, in which the contest was decided.

A sequence of three formally distinct episodes was now constituted that decided the disposition of the rest of the episodes: two plagues preceded by warnings (the first in the morning by the river, the second in the palace) followed by a third without warning.

A traditional number sequence of six (3 + 3) items augmented by one more was elaborated upon by the redactor to make room for the total of ten different plagues related by the two versions. Three sets of three, with the capper at the end, would accommodate the material nicely. With formal criteria governing the arrangement, the intermeshing of the remaining items was reasonably smooth. The second series was made up of A's swarms and pestilence (warnings), followed by B's boils (no warning), which associated well with pestilence. Next came A's hail and locusts (warnings), then B's darkness (no warning) which was linked through the darkness motif to the locusts. Since both series were in a climactic order, their interweaving did not produce an inept result. The presence of the key motif "coming to know YHWH" in both A (7:16, etc.) and B (cf. 7:5) helped too. But strict ascending order, pattern in Pharaoh's responses, and consistency of theme throughout all parts had to be sacrificed (perhaps happily, from an artistic viewpoint).

With the interweaving of traditions, adjustments had to be made. B's theme now prevails in the first two plagues, perhaps displacing a different one of A. The formulation of the penultimate plague, prior to the death of the firstborn, posed a special problem. In B's version the death of the firstborn followed the plague of darkness—a symbolic premonition of it; in the other version, it followed the locust plague (note the premonition of it in 10:17, "this death"). Arranging darkness and locust in series resulted in some awkwardness. The locust plague, which Pharaoh states is the last he'll undergo (10:17), is now followed, when he reneges, not by the last plague but by the last-but-one. The negotiations of 10:24ff., now following the darkness, in fact make no reference to the darkness but link up well with the preceding locust plague (10:19). It may therefore be assumed that in A's account the locust plague was followed by another round of sterile negotiations ending in the announcement by Moses of the final plague.[37] With the interposition of B's darkness episode the last round of negotiations had necessarily to be attached to this last-but-one plague.

B's narrative of the plagues was contained within the *inclusio* by 7:2–6 and 11:9–10. This framework having been retained, its formulas of obduracy came to dominate the episode endings, in which a formula of obduracy regularly occurred. A's formula still appears at the endings of swarms and pestilence (8:28; 9:7; cf. 9:34; 10:1); but in 8:12b (frogs) and everywhere else the richer variety of clauses found in B's formulation has prevailed. It is reasonable to attribute this prevalence to the effect of B's *inclusio*.

The strange placement of 11:1–3 is unlikely to be original, though it is hard to find a smoother context without radically rewriting the present text of the ninth plague. The displacement of these verses together with the removal of the warning of the last plague to 4:22–23 seem to be results of the redactorial reshaping of the beginning and end of the entire plague series.

To sum up: The plague narrative is the product of an elaborate growth of traditions, which reached the redactor in two crystallizations partly overlapping, partly divergent. The present shape of the material was arrived at by intermeshing the two in as unforced a manner as possible. While the prefinal components influenced the final form, the latter, with its original structure, is one of the most striking evidences of the redactor's art. Moreover, through him A's conception of the plagues as punishment has been fused with B's conception of them as demonstrations of God's power. The result is an added dimension: a sense of the multivalence of events. Such enrichment of the values of the narrative is characteristic of the redactorial work throughout the Pentateuch.

---

37. Fohrer, *Überlieferung*, 65 n. 17.

Excursus
Exodus and History: Preliminary Reflections

The relation of the narrative of Exodus to history has two aspects: the authors' conception of fidelity to events, and modern critical assessments of that fidelity.

To what extent can we suppose that biblical authors intended their words to be taken as exact representations of events? If our assumption is valid, that the present text is the product of development (however it may be described), considerable artifice and elaboration of received tradition materials must have gone into its shaping. When the resumptive 6:29 inverts the order of Moses' statement in 6:12, conscious art is at work rather than a precise reporting of what Moses said. Our view of every one of the major narrative units takes them to be deliberately constructed, with dramatic and formal considerations playing a significant role. Even the prefinal stage of the material shows complexity. In the hypothesized A narrative of the plagues, for example, we have interpreted certain "bulges" as later reflections on the meaning of the plagues. The role of the sister in the birth story of Moses appears to be likewise the result of early elaboration of the tradition-kernel to answer a specific need.

When we ask whether the author of such elaborations, or the redactor, regarded his work as historical—as an accurate account of what happened—we employ a conception that, so far as we can tell, was foreign to these men. Their primary purpose was to communicate *torah*—guidance for right living—and narration of past happenings no less than law was considered *torah* (cf. Ps 78:1 and the content of the psalm). Edification was the chief value of such narratives, and whatever served to edify might fittingly be incorporated into them. The intent was not so much to describe as to celebrate events as saving acts of God. In this, the latest transmitters of the tradition were at one with the earliest.

We picture the primary stage of the tradition (mostly now beyond recovery) as a saga, an enthusiastic relation of great events by participants in them. Already in this primary stage the message conveyed was more of the event's impact than of the detail of its occurrence. The sense of transcendent meaning was expressed in the literary form of poetry (the event was non-prosaic), couched in metaphors, in hyperbole, in set forms habitually used to convey highly charged contents. The tale was told dramatically, with simplification of motives and personages (two or three characters in an episode) and a climax. Later historical and biographic anecdotes in talmudic aggada give partial prosaic analogues to the early stage of biblical traditions. Retellings of the saga gave rise to embellishments, and in time original simplicity gave way to complexity.[1]

Complication is an essential feature of transmission of the saga. The impression the story made on successive generations was embodied in the accretion of motifs, deeds, and circumstances, in which new layers of meaning were added to the story. Sobriety led to prosification, and here and there reflection brought the progress of the story to a halt in a "bulge" of commentary or interpretation. Thus the burning bush story, at first comprising probably no more than instructions to Moses of what to say and do, now includes predictions of coming events after the pattern of later prophetic revelations. The conception of prophecy as a sign of God's lordship of history has added a dimension to the primary story.

In the work of the redactor, this enrichment of the tradition reached its culmination. Now God's assurance of diffident Moses is expressed not in one, but three separate charges. The plagues are depicted not as punishments or signs of God's power, but as both at once. The redactor did not prefer the one to the other, since indeed both were legitimate comprehensions of the events. Did the redactor believe God assured Moses three times, or that there were fully ten plagues? His mode of combining the material suggests he may never have asked the question in the sense that we ask it. From later analogies in aggada, where divergent versions of a story are laid side by side (in the form of "some say, others say"), it appears that concern about the congruence of a story to events as they happened was wholly subordinate to presenting and preserving what could enrich and edify. The more angles one could approach an event from, the more handles one had by which to grasp its meaning,

---

1. Cassuto, "Rešit," argues for a poetic origin of the Exodus saga. A fine characterization of saga is in Buber, *Moses*, 13–19 (Heb. ed., 2–6). Halevy ("Lelimmud") applies Buber's insights to talmudic aggada.

the more adequately the transmitters appear to have deemed their work accomplished.[2]

The chief formal difference between the operation of the redactor and that of the compiler of aggada is that the former alone seems to have been intent on forging a continuous narrative. He therefore incorporated significant, complementary variants side by side, attempting to elaborate a single, reasonably effective narrative out of them. At times we suspect he may have regarded the result as a restoration of the true complexity of the event—a complexity dissolved into its elements among the various traditions he received (perhaps that is how he understood the two narratives of Moses' commissioning). Where outright inconsistency and conflict resulted from his combinations—difficulties we cannot suppose he ignored—it may well be he let them stand in the conviction that, since taken by themselves the items made sense, there was value in them despite their conflict when combined. Perhaps a wiser head than he would some day harmonize the conflict. His chief aim was after all not to depict how things happened, but how the traditions of Israel, in all their richness, pictured how things happened.

Considering this, we will not expect a close relation between every detail of the narrative and actual events. As far as the portrayal of beliefs and institutions that underwent an inner Israelite evolution is concerned, there is an everpresent likelihood that the realities reflected belong to later periods than that about which the narrative tells. The cargo of the epithet "Levite" used of Aaron, for example, is explicable only on the basis of the later use of "Levite" for priest.

---

2. Two examples from the aggada will illustrate our meaning: "When [R. Huna] had some medicinal preparation, he always filled a water pitcher with it and hung it over his doorsill, inviting anyone who wished to take some of it. Another version (lit. But others say): He would learn the lore of demons, and he used to hang up a pitcher of water, inviting anyone who needed it to come in [and wash from it] so that he would not risk [demonic] danger" (*Taanit* 20b).

Hospitality toward multiple relations is also found in aggadic exegesis of biblical passages: "*The Egyptians worked the Israelites ruthlessly (beparek)*. R. Elazar said: Soft-mouthedly (*bepe rak*); [through seductive talk they got them to work energetically the first day] then the amount of bricks they produced on that first day was imposed on them every day thereafter. R. Samuel b. Nahman said in the name of R. Yohanan: Crushingly (*biprika*); imposing men's work on women and women's work on men" (ShR).

The thought process underlying aggada (and to a considerable extent applicable to the redaction of the Torah, if we have rightly grasped it) is described with penetration and originality by Max Kadushin in *Organic Thinking* and *The Rabbinic Mind*.

What is the situation with regard to the Egyptian background of the narrative? Can that be authenticated from extrabiblical sources?[3]

The one and only clue to the place in Egyptian history of the Exodus narrative is the mention of Pithom and Raamses in 1:11. No Egyptian king is named though two reigns are mentioned in the story; no event of history recorded in Egyptian sources appears. But the city Raamses is almost certainly the delta residence of the Ramessides of the 19th dynasty, founded by Ramses II (1304–1237) and named after him. His long reign suits the representation of Moses as being born and growing to manhood under a single reign. Egyptian records are silent about Israelite slaves,[4] but the story's assumption of their nearness to the capital (which makes Moses' movement between them and the court easy) agrees with New Kingdom evidence that parties of Asiatic shepherds were occasionally permitted entry to the eastern delta for pasture.[5] That such immigrants dwelling in the vicinity of the capital should have been subjected to corvée by Ramses II in the course of his extensive building operations is natural.

The picture of Pharaoh as absolute master of the population (cf. Gen 47:13–26) agrees with modern assessments of his status.[6] The Egyptian king was an absolute monarch in the strictest sense of the term. Law was his formally expressed will; the few laws and edicts that have come down to us begin with the clause, "His majesty has commanded," or "The king himself has said" (cf. Exod 5:10). The basis of his power was his complete control of the machinery of government—the civil service, the police and the army.

Even the priests of Egypt were his agents and representatives, and it was he who normally appointed and removed them. As to the common man, while it is wrong to suppose him utterly without rights,[7] the lot of the forced labor recruited from foreign and captured populations was harsh.[8] The juridical status of the land and people of Egypt as Pharaoh's

---

3. A good survey of the present state of the question is Herrmann's "Israel in Ägypten"; see also Montet, *L'Égypte,* 24ff., 54ff.

4. ʿApiru captured in Syria-Palestine and put to work in Egypt throughout the New Kingdom cannot with any confidence be identified with the Israelites.

5. *ANET,* 259.

6. The following is taken from Edgerton, "The Government."

7. The parade example is the strike of laborers recorded in Ramses III's twenty-ninth year; cf. Edgerton's study "The Strikes."

8. See Bakir, *Slavery.*

property, described in Gen 47:13-26, cannot be verified from Egyptian sources. But the subservience of the people to their rulers—not a single uprising against a native king is attested in two and a half millennia of history—is enough to account for the biblical derogation of Egypt as "the house of slaves" (*bet ʿᵃbadim*).

The name of Moses, now generally taken to be Egyptian (in spite of an irregularity in the sibilant), speaks for the authenticity of the background of Moses' birth-story. On the other hand, the similarity of the story to the commonplace motif of the cast-away infant hero has raised doubts about its historicity. The legend of Sargon is usually compared:

> My mother was a changeling (?), my father I knew not . . .
> My changeling (?) mother conceived me, in secret she bore me.
> She set me in a basket of rushes, with bitumen she sealed my lid.
> She cast me into the river which rose not over me.
> The river bore me up and carried me to Akki, the drawer of water.
> Akki, the drawer of water lifted me out . . . took me as his son and reared me . . .[9]

If the Mesopotamian legend served as the model for Moses' birth-story, there is no point in examining the latter for Egyptian local color. However, the matter is not so simple. Benno Jacob observed that whereas in the legend of Sargon (and similar tales) the child is abandoned to protect others (apparently to hide the shame of his mother, in Sargon's case), the disposition made of Moses was for his own protection.[10] Now the closest analogue to that motif occurs precisely in Egyptian myth, in the allusions to Isis' concealment of her infant child Horus in a Delta papyrus-thicket, to save him from death at the hands of Seth.[11] In view of this, the derivation of Moses' birth-story from Mesopotamia seems uncalled for. It must also be noted that in its present form the biblical story is not a typical exposure narrative. It emphasizes the care bestowed on the infant after, as well as before, he was placed (not cast[12]) into the river. The sisterly surveillance that succeeded in restoring the baby to its mother gives the story a turn almost directly opposed to exposure tales. How the infant

---

9. *ANET*, 119.
10. Jacob, "The Childhood," 247.
11. Helck, "Ṯkw und die Ramses Stadt," 48; Redford, "The Literary Motif," 222-23. The goddess Nephthys, Isis' sister, is said to have thrown a mat over the child, an interesting parallel, as Helck points out, to the role of Moses' sister.
12. The point is well taken by Cogan, "A Technical Term."

was saved for his family and his people, not how he was lost to them, is the main burden of 2:1–10.[13]

In the story of Moses' adoption by a high-born Egyptian lady and his eventual assumption of leadership over his enslaved fellow tribesmen there is nothing impossible—though none of it has been verified from Egyptian sources, and the lady's being a princess seems more a dramatic (ironic) than a historical feature.[14]

The local color of the stories is sometimes of doubtful authenticity. The notion that the princess took her bath in the Nile is dubious. The ancient Egyptians regarded the Nile as dangerous for laundering as well as for fishing because of the crocodiles that infested it.[15] The custom of the wealthy was to have pools in their gardens;[16] that and considerations of privacy, in addition to the danger, would have militated against an aristocratic lady's bathing in the Nile. The notion appears to be a reflex of Palestinian habits of bathing in rivers (cf. 2 Kgs 5:10, and the later recourse to the Jordan for baptism).

Repeated efforts have been made to verify the local color of the plague narratives. But aside from the magical features, whose density and suitability to Egypt have already been remarked, there is less of a

---

13. D. B. Redford has treated the motif of the exposed child at great length ("The Literary Motif"), dividing the material into three groups, the third of which, containing the Moses story, is the smallest (five examples—biblical and postbiblical Moses, and three others, none of which—Redford admits—is firmly comparable [e.g., Jesus' flight to Egypt]). Redford persists in associating the Moses Story with such legends; he regards the Sargon story as archetypal and discounts Helck's proposal to consider the Horus myth relevant. Redford sums up the similarities as follows: Like Sargon's mother, Moses' places him in an ark; as do the servants of Amulius, she places him in shallows; like wild animals in other versions, Miriam stands guard; like Oedipus, Moses is found and cared for by a female member of the royal household. Could one say in plainer language that the Moses story has no real parallel among these?

14. From the time of Ramses XI (11th century) comes a record of an Egyptian woman who adopted the children of a female slave and emancipated them to make them her heirs (Gardiner, "Adoption Extraordinary"). Against this background Herrmann can say of Moses' career: "Nothing is against the possibility that Moses, as the son of a dependent beduin, was born in Egypt, and received, for unknown reasons, an Egyptian name, if not from Pharaoh's daughter then from an Egyptian woman in whose service he was. She also may have adopted the child and raised him to independence. All this need not exclude Moses' contact with his tribal brothers. This exceptional sojourn between the desert and settled land made it possible for a Semite with an Egyptian name to launch on his own an effort to escape" ("Israel in Ägypten," 77).

15. Erman, *Literature of the Ancient Egyptians*, 70.

16. Montet, *L'Égypte*, 78; Montet, *Everyday Life*, 23.

dividend here than one might at first think. From antiquity it has been suggested that the plagues strike at Egypt's gods: the bloody Nile, says the midrash, humiliated the Nile god; the darkness, moderns assert, terrorized the Egyptians for they believed the sun to have been swallowed by its enemy, the serpent Apophis; and so forth. These attempts to see reflexes of Egyptian god-beliefs in the plagues are unpersuasive because the plague stories in fact know of only one God, the God of Israel, and his antagonists are not the gods of Egypt (mentioned only once and incidentally in 12:12) but Pharaoh and (at first) Pharaoh's magicians. These magicians operate "atheistically," through spells, never once invoking the gods (as did the real-life magicians of Egypt known to us from native sources). When once they do mention God, it is only to acknowledge his superiority to them. The notion that the plagues involve a battle of gods is utterly alien to the biblical account of them.

Another line of argument seeks to authenticate the plagues in the physical conditions of Egypt. A reddened Nile is normal for the period of its annual rise; frogs, insect swarms, and locusts have been known to create serious trouble in Egypt.[17]

A notably thorough effort to fit the biblical sequence to the realities of Egypt was made by Greta Hort.[18] Hort expressly sets aside the Moses-Pharaoh interviews (with their heavy stress on God's intervention) as beyond the scope of an empirical investigation, limiting her study to the phenomena that can be externally tested. She starts out with the assumption that the bloody Nile was in reality an unusually high Nile, carrying an abnormal amount of the red earth that abounds in the Nile's basin, together with a large number of blood-red flagellates from the high mountain lakes at the sources of the blue Nile (summer). The flagellates caused the death of the fish; swarms of frogs were driven out of their haunts by the decomposing fish and sought refuge in the shade of homes and fields. But all had contracted a deadly disease from the foul water (internal anthrax) and died (late summer). The flooded countryside was a fertile breeding ground for abnormally large numbers of mosquitoes (October); and when in October–November the Nile receded the organic debris that covered the land bred flies. The pestilence that struck the cattle was the anthrax, ingested from the infected ground (January); the boils were skin anthrax spread by the flies. Hail is rare in northern Egypt

17. Montet, *L'Égypte*, 94ff., adduces real or literary examples of all the plagues.
18. Hort, "The Plagues."

but may come there at any time; the state of the various crops indicates the beginning of February. Locusts migrate from the Sudan in February-March; blown across Sinai and North Egypt they were finally driven off by a sea-wind (i.e., a north wind from the Mediterranean) frequent in December-February but also occurring as late as April. By early spring the bare earth, parched and powdery, with a thick layer of red earth, was raised in great masses by the first *hamsin* winds of the year coming from the south; three days is typical for such a *hamsin* (early March). The last plague resists being incorporated into a natural order.

Hort has thus shown that the biblical plague sequence comprises elements native to the Egyptian scene. She cannot show that such a remarkable chain of calamities did in fact result from a high Nile—no such chain is on record. "The assertion that an especially high rise of the Nile, something that can be shown to have happened often, set in motion such a chain of plagues only once in the course of centuries and millennia, is not convincing."[19] To that extent her theory leaves room for the main burden of the biblical account; namely, the divinely managed character of the plagues. But with all the good will in the world her further attempt to account for the various circumstances and effects of the plague —e.g., the exemptions of the Israelites—does not persuade, not to speak of her total breakdown in the face of the last plague. Nor, if the truth be told, is there a hint in the narrative of a high Nile (n.b.: the Egyptians digging for water around the Nile—which cannot, therefore, have flooded its environs).

Apart from these intrinsic difficulties, Hort's effort is unconvincing because it ignores the evidence that the "ten plagues" are the product of the redactor's combinatory art, rather than a primary tradition of a historical event. When that is taken into account, the more modest judgment will have to be made that the plague narrative reflects the elaboration of certain now unrecoverable troubles that befell Egypt at the time of the Exodus. Some of the episodes seem to be intensifications of familiar Egyptian maladies; others (pestilence, hail) are not specifically Egyptian. All have been brought together here for the greater glory of God.

Assessment of the fanaticism of the Egyptians, alleged in 8:22 is difficult. The expression of popular hostility through stoning seems a particularly inept projection of hilly Palestinian conditions onto the alluvium of the Delta. Xenophobic attacks on alien cults are attested in Egypt from Persian times (Elephantine) onward.[20] Information in Herodotus (II, 38,

---

19. Fohrer, *Überlieferung*, 76.
20. *ANET*, 492.

41, 42, 45) about sacrificial usages in the various cities of fifth century Egypt shows that the Israelites did sacrifice animals that were regarded as taboo by reason of their sacredness (e.g., the cow, sacred to Isis). And late Egyptian sources cited by Josephus (*Against Apion* 1.26) tell of outrages of the "impure" of ancient times (among whom were supposedly the Israelites) including the violation and eating of sacred animals.[21] But this does not amount to evidence that during the Ramesside age the Egyptians were fanatically opposed to Asiatic cults. Indeed that age was hospitable to Semitic deities. Ramses II established in his new capital temples to Anat, Horon, and Astarte. To be sure, there is no evidence that when Egyptians worshiped Semitic deities they followed foreign usages; and how Semitic worshipers in Egypt practiced their cult is unknown. "That Asiatics in Egypt retained their cult and gods unchanged is not probable, because they assimilated very quickly to Egyptian conditions ... and merged into the Egyptian people."[22] Still, the possibility that religious resentment against the Hyksos lingered on in Ramesside times and found expression in hostility toward Asiatics in Egypt practicing their native cults, cannot be ruled out;[23] and it cannot be said of the Israelites that they assimilated, since the whole point of 8:22 is their distinctiveness in religious customs. On the other hand, in view of the projection onto Egyptians of stoning, an alternative explanation of 8:22's allegation must be considered: that from correct knowledge of Egyptian dietary taboos (Gen 43:32) and loathing of Asiatic beduin (Gen 46:34),[24] the author extrapolated their hostility to foreign cults, ascribing Israelite attitudes and reactions to the Egyptians where they may not have applied.

To sum up: The gross features of the Exodus story—the sojourn in Egypt of Israelite tribes, their bondage and escape under an inspired leader—are too unflattering to have been late inventions, and have enough (though meager) contacts with extrabiblical evidence to be creditable. But in the rich detail of the narrative, what emerges is not history but Israel's celebration of its history as the saving acts of God. The vivid

---

21. These and related texts are discussed by Yoyotte in "L'Égypte ancienne." He regards their currency as due to xenophobic feelings aroused by the Persian domination and continuing to Greco-Roman times.

22. Stadelman, *Syrisch-palästinensische Gottheiten*, 150.

23. In the 13th century (Ramesside times) Papyrus Sallier I, containing a legend about the Hyksos king Apophis was written. It opens with a pathetic evocation of the misery of Egypt during Hyksos rule, and underscores the religious offense the Hyksos king Apophis gave Egyptians through his religious innovations (*ANET*, 231).

24. Montet, *L'Égypte*, 99ff.

impact of events has been transmitted through artful narration, in which hyperbole, dramatic structure, and modernization served to convey to generation after generation the wonder of those who participated in the events. The reality that the tale intends to convey is not past historical but present affective: the experience of events as they were taken in first by eyewitnesses, then through the consciousness of the generations who perennially relived and reflected on them as the basis of their own living faith.[25]

---

25. Of great relevance to the assessment of the Exodus narratives are the issues discussed in the controversy between G. Ernest Wright ("Modern Issues") and Gerhard von Rad ("History and the Patriarchs") over the relation of history, faith, and literature in the patriarchal narratives, in *Expository Times*.

Appendix
Questions for Uncovering the Message of a Biblical Text[1]

Editor's Note: In the years following the publication of *Understanding Exodus*, Moshe Greenberg developed his holistic method further and adapted it for use with non-narrative texts as well, including the book of Ezekiel. In addition to his published descriptions of this methodology,[2] he prepared for his students a hands-on list of "Questions for Uncovering the Message of a Biblical Text" that, among other things, puts the holistic method into practice by directing attention to factors in a text that maintain or disturb its unity. It is published here because of the methodological value of the entire list as well as its illustration of Greenberg's method.

1. What are the boundaries of the unit? Are there opening and closing formulas? Any structure that maintains its unity? Contents or linguistic usages that unify it?

2. To what extent are the components of the unit connected to each other? How are they connected?

3. Regularity or irregularity—in grammar (unusual forms?), vocabulary (rare? unique?), length of sentences (equal or not?).

4. If the ideational continuity is incomplete, is there some other basis for the juxtaposition of the parts (verbal connection, some other external connection)?

5. In addition to the plain sense of the passage, what other things that make an impression, or other message-bearers, exist (assonance?

---

1. Translated from the Hebrew by the editor.

2. Greenberg, "The Vision of Jerusalem in Ezekiel 8–11: A Holistic Interpretation," in *The Divine Helmsman: Studies in God's Control of Human Events Presented to Lou H. Silberman*, edited by James L. Crenshaw and Samuel Sandmel (New York: Ktav, 1980) 143–64 (see pp. 146–47 for a similar list of questions); Greenberg, *Ezekiel 1–20*, Anchor Bible 22 (Garden City, NY: Doubleday, 1983) 18–27.

rhyme? paronomasia? chiasm? contrast of opposites? images?). What do these strategies direct one's attention to?

6. If there are repetitions, are they literal and exact? If there are variations, what is their meaning?

7. Do the components or topics recur elsewhere? In which book? In the Bible? Outside the Bible? In the same form or a different one? Are there signs of borrowing or imitation?

8. To what extent does my understanding correspond to the understanding of other readers (translations, commentators)? If there are differences, what are they due to?

～

Elements that refuse to be integrated in the picture are liable to be interpolations or corruptions. If they are interpolations—for what purpose were they added? If corruptions—how did they take place? (Reasoned suggestions for emendation; how did the corruption develop from the proposed original text?)

Bibliography

Adar, S. *Sippure Moše v^eHora'atam*. Jerusalem, 5712 [1952].
Ahad Ha-am [Asher Ginzberg]. "Moses." In *Selected Essays by Ahad Ha-ʿam*, translated from the Hebrew, edited, and with an introduction by Leon Simon, 306–29. Cleveland: Meridian; and Philadelphia: Jewish Publication Society of America, 1962.
Albo, Joseph. *Sefer ha-ʿIkkarim (Book of Principles)*. 4 vols. Edited by Isaac Husik. Philadelphia: Jewish Publication Society of America, 1946.
Albright, W. F. *From the Stone Age to Christianity: Monotheism and the Historical Process*. 2nd ed. Garden City, NY: Doubleday, 1957.
———. "Northwest-Semitic Names in a List of Egyptian Slaves from the Eighteenth Century B.C." *Journal of the American Oriental Society* 74 (1954) 222–33.
———. *Yahweh and the Gods of Canaan: A Historical Analysis of Two Contrasting Faiths*. Garden City, NY: Doubleday, 1968.
Alt, Albrecht. "Der Gott der Väter." In *Kleine Schriften zur Geschichte des Volkes Israel*, vol. 1, 1–78. Munich: Beck, 1953. (Orig. essay, 1929.) (ET = "The God of the Fathers." In *Essays on Old Testament History and Religion*, 1–77. Translated by R. A. Wilson. Oxford: Blackwell, 1966.)
Anderson, Bernhard W. "God, names of." In *IDB*, 2:407–17.
'Arbaʿah Perušim ʿal Peruš Raši . . .[includes Maharal, Mizraḥi and others]. 2 vols. Jerusalem: Dibre Ḥakamim, 1957–58.
Bakir, ʿAbd el-Mohsen. *Slavery in Pharaonic Egypt*. Supplément aux annales du Service des antiquités de l'Egypt 18. Cairo: Impre. de l'Institut Francais d'Archéologie, 1952.
Beer, Georg, with Kurt Galling. *Exodus*. Handbuch zum Alten Testament 1/3. Tübingen: Mohr/Siebeck, 1939.
Blau, Joshua. "Ḥ^atan damim." *Tarbiz* 26 (5617 [1957]) 1–3.
Bonnet, Hans. *Reallexikon der ägyptischen Religionsgeschichte*. Berlin: de Gruyter, 1952.
Brongers, H. A. "Die Zehnzahl in der Bibel und in ihrer Umwelt." In *Studia Biblica et Semitica: Theodoro Christiano Vriezen qui munere professoris theologiae per XXV annos functus est, ab amicis, collegis, discipulis dedicata*, 30–45. Wageningen: Veenman, 1967.
Brown, F., S. R. Driver, and C. A. Briggs. *A Hebrew and English Lexicon of the Old Testament*. Oxford: Clarendon, 1952.
Buber, Martin. *Moses: The Revelation and the Covenant*. 1946. Reprinted, New York: Harper, 1958. (Heb. ed. *Moše*, Jerusalem-Tel-Aviv, 1945.)
Cassuto, Umberto. *The Documentary Hypothesis and the Composition of the Pentateuch*. Translated by Israel Abrahams. Jerusalem: Magnes, 1961.

———. *Peruš ʿal Sefer Bᵉrešit*. Vol. 1, *Me'Adam ʿad Noaḥ*. Jerusalem: Magnes, 1959. (ET = *A Commentary on the Book of Genesis*. Part 1, *From Adam to Noah*. Translated by Israel Abrahams. Jerusalem. Jerusalem: Magnes, 1961.)

———. *Peruš ʿal Sefer Šᵉmot*. Jerusalem: Magnes, 1952. (ET = *A Commentary on the Book of Exodus*. Translated by Israel Abrahams. Jerusalem: Magnes, 1967.)

———. "Rešit Ha-historiografia Bᵉyisraʾel." *Eretz Israel* 1 (1951) 85ff. ET = "The Beginning of Historiography among the Israelites." In U. Cassuto, Biblical and Oriental Studies, 1, Bible, pp. 7-16. Translated by Israel Abrahams. Jerusalem: Magnes, 1973).

Chavel, Charles B. *Peruše haTora lᵉRabbenu Moše ben Naḥman (Ramban)*. Jerusalem: Magnes, 1962.

Childs, Brevard S. "The Birth of Moses." *JBL* 84 (1965) 109ff.

Coats, George W. "Despoiling the Egyptians." *VT* 18 (1968) 450ff.

Cogan, Mordechai. "A Technical Term for Exposure." *JNES* 27 (1968) 133-35.

Colson, F. H. *Philo: With an English Translation*. Vol. 6. Loeb Classical Library. Cambridge: Harvard University Press, 1968-1981.

Couroyer, Bernard. "Quelques égyptianismes dans l'Exode." *RB* 63 (1956) 209-19.

———. "Le doigt de dieu." *RB* 63 (1956) 481-95.

———. "Un égyptianisme biblique: 'Depuis la fondation de l'Égypte.'" *RB* 67 (1960) 42-48.

Cross, Frank M. Jr., *The Ancient Library of Qumran and Modern Biblical Studies*. Garden City, NY: Anchor, 1961.

Dillman, August. *Die Bücher Exodus und Leviticus*. Leipzig: Hirzel, 1880.

Driver, G. R. "Sacred Numbers and Round Figures." In *Promise and Fulfillment: Essays Presented to Professor S. H. Hooke in Celebration of His Ninetieth Birthday, 21st January, 1964*, edited by F. F. Bruce, 62-90. Edinburgh: T. & T. Clark, 1963.

———. "Playing on Words." In *Fourth World Congress of Jewish Studies, Papers*, 121-29. Jerusalem: Magnes, 1967.

Driver, S. R. *The Book of Exodus, in the Revised Version: With Introduction and Notes*. Cambridge Bible for Schools and Colleges. Cambridge: Cambridge University Press, 1911.

———. *An Introduction to the Literature of the Old Testament*. 9th ed. International Theological Library. New York: C. Scribner, 1913.

———. *A Treatise on the Use of the Tenses in Hebrew and Some Other Syntactical Questions*. 3rd ed. Oxford: Clarendon, 1892.

Dumermuth, Fritz. "Folkloristisches in der Erzählung von den ägyptischen Plagen." *ZAW* 76 (1964) 323-25.

Edgerton, William F. "The Government and the Governed in the Egyptian Empire." *JNES* 6 (1947) 152-60.

———. "The Strikes in Ramses III's Twenty-Ninth Year." *JNES* 10 (1951) 137-45.

Eerdmans, B. D. "The Name Jahu." *OTS* 5 (1945) 1-29.

Ehrlich, Arnold B. *Mikra ki-Pheschuto*. Vol. 1, *Pentateuch*. Berlin: Papfeloyer, 1899

———. *Randglossen zur hebräischen Bibel*. Vol. 1, *Genesis und Exodus*. Leipzig: Hinrichs, 1908

Eising, Hermann. "Die ägyptische Plagen." In *Lex tua veritas: Festschrift für Hubert Junker zur Vollendung des siebzigsten Lebensjahres am 8. August 1961, dargeboten von Kollegen, Freunden und Schülern*, edited by Heinrich Gross and Franz Mussner, 75-88. Trier: Paulinus, 1961.

Eissfeldt, Otto. *The Old Testament: An Introduction*. Translated by Peter R. Ackroyd. New York: Harper & Row, 1965.
ʾEnṣiqlopedia Miqraʾit. Vols. 1–5. Jerusalem, 1950–1968.
Epstein, J. N., and Ezra Zion Melamed, editors. *Mᵉkilta dᵉR. Šimʿon bar Yoḥay*. Jerusalem: Mekitse Nirdamim, 5715 [1955].
Erman, Adolf. *The Literature of the Ancient Egyptians*. Translated by Aylward M. Blackman. London: Methuen, 1927. Reprinted as *The Ancient Egyptians: A Sourcebook of Their Writings*. Introduction by William Kelly Simpson. Harpers Torchbooks. New York: Harper & Row, 1966.
Fohrer, Georg. *Überlieferung und Geschichte des Exodus: Eine Analyse von Ex 1–15*. BZAW 91. Berlin: Töpelmann, 1964.
Freedman, David Noel, and Edward F. Campbell. "The Chronology of Israel and the Ancient Near East." In *The Bible and the Ancient Near East: Essays in Honor of W. F. Albright*, edited by George Ernest Wright, 203–28. Garden City, NY: Doubleday, 1961.
Friedlander, Gerald. *Pirḳê de Rabbi Eliezer (The chapters of Rabbi Eliezer, the Great): According to the Text of the Manuscript Belonging to Abraham Epstein of Vienna*. New York: Bloch, 1916.
Gardiner, Alan H. "Adoption Extraordinary." *Journal of Egyptian Archaeology* 26 (1940) 23–29.
Goldbaum, Frederic J. "Two Hebrew Quasi-Adverbs: לכן and אכן." *JNES* 23 (1964) 132–35.
Goldman, Solomon. *From Slavery to Freedom*. The Book of Human Destiny 3. New York: Abelard-Schuman, 1958.
Grdseloff, Bernhard. "Édôm, d'après les sources égyptiennes." *Revue de l'histoire juive en Égypte* 1 (1947) 69–99.
Greenberg, Moshe. *The Ḫab/piru*. American Oriental Series 39. New Haven: American Oriental Society, 1955.
———. "The Thematic Unity of Exodus III–XI." In *Fourth World Congress of Jewish Studies, Papers*, 151–54. Jerusalem: Magnes, 1967.
———. "Yᵉḥezqel 20 vᵉhagalut Haruḥanit [Ezekiel 20 and the Spiritual Exile]." In *ʿOz LᵉDavid*, 433–42. Jerusalem: Kiryat Sefer, 1964.
Greenup, A. W. "Peruš R. Mᵉyuḥas ʿal Šᵉmot." *Ha-Ṣofe Lᵉḥokmat Yisraʾel* 13, pp. 1–81, 121–82. Budapest: Kohn Mor Vacz, 1929.
Gressmann, Hugo. *Mose und Seine Zeit: Ein Kommentar zu den Mose-Sagen*. Forschungen zur Religion und Literatur des Alten und Neuen Testament 18. Göttingen: Vandenhoeck & Ruprecht, 1913.
Griffiths, J. Gwyn. "The Egyptian Derivation of the Name Moses." *JNES* 12 (1953) 225–31.
Groot, J. de, "The Story of the Bloody Husband (Exodus iv 24–26)." *OTS* 2 (1943) 10–17.
Gunn, Battiscombe. "On the Supposed Mention of the Egyptian God Re in Exodus." *Egyptian Religion* 1 (1933) 33–34.
Habel, Norman. "The Form and Significance of the Call Narratives." *ZAW* 77 (1965) 297–323.
Halevy, A. A. "Lᵉlimmud Ha-ʾaggada Ha-historit." In *Horaʾat Ha-tora Šᵉbᵉʿal Pe: Yalqut Maʾᵃmarim*, edited by Joseph Heinemann, 125ff. Jerusalem: Magnes, 5720 [1960].
Haran, Menahem. "Qavvim Lᵉteʾur ʾᵉmunatam šel Haʾavot." In *ʿOz LᵉDavid*, 40–70. Pirsume ha-Ḥevrah le-ḥeḳer ha-Miḳra be-Yiśraʾel 15. Jerusalem: Kiryat Sefer,

1964. Reprinted in *Ha-Historia šel ʿAm Yisraʾel*, edited by Benjamin Mazar, vol. 2, 111–24. Tel Aviv: Jewish History Publications and Massada, 1967. (ET = "The Religion of the Patriarchs." In *The World History of the Jewish People*, edited by Benjamin Mazar, 2:219–45. New Brunswick, NJ: Rutgers University Press, 1970.)

Helck, Wolfgang. "T̲kw und die Ramses Stadt." *VT* 15 (1965) 35–48.

Herrmann, Siegfried. "Israel in Ägypten." *Zeitschrift für ägyptische Sprache und Altertumskunde* 91 (1964) 63–79.

———. "Der Name JHW^3 in den Inschriften von Soleb." In *Fourth World Congress of Jewish Studies, Papers*, 213–16. Jerusalem: Magnes, 1967.

Heschel, Abraham Joshua. *The Prophets*. New York: Harper & Row, 1962.

Hort, Greta, "The Plagues of Egypt." *ZAW* 69 (1957) 84–103; 70 (1958) 48–59.

Hyatt, J. Philip. "Yahweh as 'The God of My Father.'" *VT* 5 (1955) 130–36.

Jacob, Benno. "The Childhood and Youth of Moses, the Messenger of God." In *Essays in Honour of the Very Rev. Dr. J. H. Hertz, Chief Rabbi of the United Hebrew Congregations of the British Empire, on the Occasion of His Seventieth Birthday, September 25, 1942 (5703)*, edited by Isidore Epstein et al., 245–59. London: Goldston, 1942.

———. "Gott und Pharaoh." *MGWJ* NF 32 (1924) 118–26, 202–11, 268–89.

———. "Mose am Dornbusch." *MGWJ* NF 30 (1922) 11–33, 116–38, 180–200.

———. *Das Zweite Buch der Tora: Exodus, übersetzt und erklaert*, Aus dem Nachlass des 1945 verstorbenen Verfassers herausgegeben von E. I. Jacob. Ms. microfilm in Hebrew University, Jerusalem. (Since published as *Das Buch Exodus*. Herausgegeben im Auftrag des Leo Baeck Instituts von Shlomo Mayer; unter Mitwirkung von Joachim Hahn und Almuth Jürgensen. Stuttgart: Calwer, 1997. ET = *The Second Book of the Bible, Exodus*. Translated with an Introduction by Walter Jacob, in association with Yaakov Elman. Hoboken, NJ: Ktav, 1992.)

James, T. G. H. et al. *A General Introductory Guide to the Egyptian Collections in the British Museum*. London: Trustees of the British Museum, 1964.

Janssen, J. M. A. "A traverse les publications égyptologiques récentes concernant l'Ancien Testament." In *L'Ancien Testament et l'Orient: Études Présentées aux VIes Journées Bibliques de Louvain (11–13 Septembre 1954)*, 29–63. Orientalia et Biblica Lovaniensia 1. Leuven: Leuven University Press, 1957.

Joüon, Paul. *Grammaire de l'hébreu biblique*. 2nd ed. Rome: Pontifical Biblical Institute Press, 1947. (ET = Joüon, Paul, and T. Muraoka. *A Grammar of Biblical Hebrew*. Subsidia Biblica 27. Rome: Pontifical Biblical Institute Press, 2006.)

Josephus. *Antiquities of the Jews*.

———. *Against Apion*.

Kadushin, Max. *Organic Thinking: A Study in Rabbinic Thought*. New York: Jewish Theological Seminary of America, 1938.

———. *The Rabbinic Mind*. New York: Jewish Theological Seminary of America, 1952.

Kahana, Avraham. *Šᵉmot. Tanak ʿim Peruš Maddaʿi*. Zitomir: n.p., 1903.

Kasher, Menahem. *Torah Shelemah*. Vols. 3/2, 8–13. Jerusalem: Kasher, 1945–1954.

Kaufmann, Yehezkel. *The Religion of Israel*. Abridged and translated by Moshe Greenberg. Chicago: University of Chicago Press, 1963.

Kittel, Rudolf. *Geschichte des Volkes Israel*. Vol. 1. Handbücher der alten Geschichte. Gotha: Perthes, 1923.

Kittel, Rudolf, and Paul Kahle, editors. *Biblia Hebraica*^{3}. Stuttgart: Württembergische Bibelanstalt, 1949.

Köhler, Ludwig, and Walter Baumgartner. *Lexicon in Veteris Testamenti Libros.* Leiden: Brill, 1958.
Kosmala, Hans. "The 'Bloody Husband.'" *VT* 12 (1962) 14–28.
Labuschagne, C. J. "The Emphasizing Particle *gam* and its Connotations." In *Studia Biblica et Semitica: Theodoro Christiano Vriezen qui munere professoris theologiae per XXV annos functus est, ab amicis, collegis, discipulis dedicata*, 193–203. Wageningen: Veenman, 1967.
Lambert, Mayer. "Notes exégétiques." *Revue des études Juives* 39 (1899) 299–303.
Laurentin, A. "We ʿattah—Kai nun." *Biblica* 45 (1964) 168–97.
Lauterbach, J. Z., editor. *Mekilta de-Rabbi Ishmael.* Schiff Library of Jewish Classics. Philadelphia: Jewish Publication Society of America, 1933–35.
Letteris, Meir Halevy, editor. *Sefer Torah Nᵉbiʾim Ukᵉtubim.* New York: Hebrew Publishing Company, n.d.
Lindblom, Johannes. "Noch einmal die Deutung des Jahwe-Namens in Ex. 3:14." *Annual of the Swedish Theological Institute* 3 (1964) 4ff.
Loewenstamm, Samuel E. *Masoret Yᵉṣiʾat Miṣrayim Bᵉhištalšᵉlutah.* Jerusalem: Magnes, 5725 [1965]. (ET = *The Evolution of the Exodus Tradition.* Translated by Baruch J. Schwartz. Jerusalem, 1992).
Lohfink, Norbert. "Die priesterschriftliche Abwertung der Tradition von der Offenbarung des Jahwenamens an Mose." *Biblica* 49 (1968) 1–8.
Luzzatto, S. D. *Peruš Šadal . . . ʿal Hᵃmiša Ḥumše Torah.* Edited by P. Schlesinger. Tel Aviv: Devir, 1966.
Malamat, Abraham. "King Lists of the Old Babylonian Period and Biblical Genealogies." *Journal of the American Oriental Society* 88 (1968) 163–73.
Margulies, Mordecai, editor. *Midrash Haggadol on the Pentateuch: Exodus* (Heb.). Jerusalem: Mosad Harav Kook, 5716 [1956].
May, Herbert G. "The Patriarchal Idea of God." *JBL* 40 (1941) 113–28.
McCarthy, Dennis J. "Moses' Dealings with Pharaoh: Ex. 7,8—10,27." *Catholic Biblical Quarterly* 27 (1965) 336ff.
McNeile, A. H. *The Book of Exodus with Introduction and Notes.* Westminster Commentaries. London: Methuen, 1908.
Meek, T. J. *Hebrew Origins.* New York: Harper, 1960.
Montet, Pierre. *L'Égypte et la Bible.* Cahiers d'archéologie Biblique 11. Paris: Delachaux & Niestlé, 1959.
———. *Everyday Life in Egypt in the Days of Ramesses the Great.* Translated by A. R. Maxwell-Hyslop and Margaret S. Drower. New York: St. Martin's, 1958
Morgenstern, Julian. "The Bloody Husband (?) (Exod. 4:24-26) Once Again." *Hebrew Union College Annual* 34 (1963) 35ff.
———. *Rites of Birth, Marriage, Death and Kindred Occasions among the Semites.* Cincinnati: Hebrew Union College Press, 1966.
Mowinckel, Sigmund. "The Name of the God of Moses." *Hebrew Union College Annual* 32 (1961) 121–33.
Nims, C. F. "Bricks without Straw?" *BA* 13 (1950) 22–28
Noth, Martin. *Exodus.* Translated by J. S. Bowden. Old Testament Library. Philadelphia: Westminster, 1962.
———. *Überlieferungsgeschichte des Pentateuch.* Stuttgart: Kohlhammer, 1948. (ET = *A History of Pentateuchal Traditions.* Translated by Bernhard W. Anderson. 1972. Reprinted, Chico, CA: Scholars, 1981.)

Oppenheim, A. Leo. "Assyriological Notes to the OT." *Jewish Quarterly Review* 36 (1945/6) 171ff.
———. *The Interpretation of Dreams in the Ancient Near East*. Transactions of the American Philosophical Society N.S. 46/3. Philadelphia, 1956.
Patai, Raphael. *Sex and Family in the Bible and the Middle East*. Garden City, NY: Doubleday, 1959.
Pedersen, Johannes. *Israel: Its Life and Culture*. 4 vols. in 2. Translated by A. Møller and A. I. Fausbøll. London: Oxford University Press, 1926–40.
Pope, Marvin H. "Number, Numbering, Numbers." In *IDB*, 3:561–67.
———. "Seven, Seventh, Seventy." In *IDB*, 4:294–95.
Pritchard, James B., editor. *The Ancient Near East in Pictures*. Princeton: Princeton University Press, 1954.
———. *Ancient Near Eastern Texts Relating to the Old Testament*. 2nd ed. Princeton: Princeton University Press, 1955.
Qafiḥ, Yosef David. *Peruše Rabbenu Saʿadya Gaʾon ʿal Hattora*. Jerusalem: Mosad ha-Rav Kook, 1963.
———. *Sefer Maʾor ha-ʾafelah lᵉRabbenu Nᵉtanʾel ben Yᵉšaʿya*. Jerusalem, Ha-Agudah le-Hatsalat Ginze Teman, 1957.
Rad, Gerhard von. "History and the Patriarchs." *Expository Times* 72 (1961) 213–16.
Redford, Donald B. "Exodus 1:11." *VT* 13 (1963) 401–18.
———. "The Literary Motif of the Exposed Child." *Numen* 14 (1967) 209–28.
Rudolph, Wilhelm. *Der "Elohist" von Exodus bis Josua*. BZAW 68. Berlin: Töpelmann, 1938.
Rylaarsdam, J. Coert. "Exodus: Introduction and Exegesis." In *Interpreter's Bible*, edited by George Arthur Buttrick, 1. Nashville: Abingdon, 1952.
Sadaqa, A. and R. *Jewish and Samaritan Version of the Pentateuch*. Tel Aviv, 1964.
Schild, E. "On Exodus iii 14—I AM THAT I AM." *VT* 4 (1954) 296–302.
Schleiff, Arnold. "Der Gottesname Jahwe." *Zeitschrift der deutschen morgenländischen Gesellschaft* 90 (1936) 696–702.
Seeligmann, I. L. "Menschliches Heldentum and göttliche Hilfe: Die doppelte Kausalität im alttestamentlichen Geschichtsdenken." *Theologische Zeitschrift* 19 (1963) 385ff.
Segal, M. H. *Masoret u-Viqoret*. Jerusalem: Kiryat Sepher, 1957.
Smend, Rudolf. *Erzählung des Hexateuch auf Ihre Quellen Untersucht*. Berlin: Reimer, 1912.
Speiser, E. A. *Genesis*. Anchor Bible 1. Garden City, NY: Doubleday, 1965.
Stadelman, Rainer. *Syrisch-palästinensische Gottheiten in Ägypten*. Probleme der Ägyptologie 5. Leiden: Brill, 1967.
Talmon, Shemaryahu. "The 'Bloody Husband.'" *Eretz Israel* 3 (1954) 93–96.
Thierry, G. J., "The Pronunciation of the Tetragram." *OTS* 5 (1948) 1–42.
Thomas, D. W., "A Note on *wayyedaʿ ʾᵉlohim* in Exodus II.25." *Journal of Theological Studies* 49 (1948) 143ff.
Vaux, Roland de. *Ancient Israel: Its Life and Institutions*. 2 vols. Translated by J. McHugh. New York: Macmillan, 1961.
Volz, Paul, and Wilhelm Rudolph. *Der Elohist als Erzähler: Ein Irrweg der Pentateuchkritik? An der Genesis Erläutert*. BZAW 63. Giessen: Töpelmann, 1933.
Vriezen, Th. C. "Exodusstudien: Exodus I." *VT* 17 (1967) 334ff.
Wijngaards, J. N. M. "הוֹצִיא and הֶעֱלָה: A Twofold Approach to the Exodus." *VT* 15 (1965) 91–102.

Winnett, F. V. *The Mosaic Tradition*. Toronto: University of Toronto Press, 1949.
Wright, G. Ernest. "Modern Issues in Biblical Studies: History and the Patriarchs." *Expository Times* 71 (1960) 292-96.
Yalqut Šim'oni. Repr. New York: Pardes, 1944.
Yoyotte, J. "L'Égypte ancienne et les origines de l'anti-judaïsme." *Revue de l'histoire des religions* 163 (1963) 133-43.
Zimmerli, Walther. *Ezechiel*. 2 vols. Biblischer Kommentar. Neukirchen Kreis Moers, 1955-69. (ET = *Ezekiel: A Commentary on the Book of the Prophet Ezekiel*. 2 vols. Translated by Ronald E. Clements and James D. Martin. Hermeneia. Philadelphia: Fortress, 1979, 1983.)

———. "Ich bin Jahwe." In *Geschichte and Altes Testament*, edited by W. F. Albright, 179-209. Beiträge zur historichen Theologie 16. Tübingen: Mohr/Siebeck, 1953. (ET = "I Am Yahweh." In *I Am Yahweh*, edited by Walter Brueggemann, 1-28. Translated by Douglas W. Stott. Atlanta: John Knox, 1982.)

Scripture Index

Hebrew Bible

Genesis

1:1—2:3	150	15:17	59
1:1	53n78	16:13	66
1:28	16	16:16	115
2:1–4	53	17:1	104, 106n109
3:3–19	76n42	17:2	29
3:16b	24	17:6	29
4:1	36	17:14	90n73
9:1	16	17:15–21	76
9:7	16	17:24–25	115
9:18	42	18	77
10	10	18:1	57n2
10:21	23n24	18:17–19	70
11:26ff.	118n123	18:18	30
12	118n123	18:20–21	43
12:1ff.	76n43	18:23–33	76
12:1–3	76n42	19:13	43
12:1	118n123	20:7	70
12:8	66, 104	20:11	26
13:1	17	20:12	31
14:13	23	21:8–21	52n77
14:22	104	21:8	35
15	76	21:9ff.	37
15:2	104	21:16	33, 38
15:3	97	22:1–14	52n77
15:7	103, 104	22:2	76n42, n43
15:8	104	22:11	59
15:13–16	44	22:17	29
15:14	70	22:22–23	31
		23:7	97n88
		24	39
		24:1–27	130
		24:2	75n39

24:3	104	41:44	18, 104
24:5ff.	75	41:46	115
24:10	75n39	42:9ff.	39
24:35–48	130	42:18	26
24:39–40	75	42:20	39, 39n55
25:20	115	42:21	39
25:26	115	43:7	39
25:27	35	43:32	23, 24, 35, 125, 163
26:3	67	44:19–20	40
26:4	30	45:8	146
26:16	17	45:9	74
26:24	103	46:3	103
26:25	66	46:4	18
27:20	104	46:8–27	15
27:27	104	46:8	15
28:3	30	46:9–10	108
28:13	103, 104	46:31	134
28:14	30	46:34	35, 125, 163
29–30	15	47:6	19
29:2ff.	39	47:13–26	158–59
29:5ff.	40	47:21	18
29:32	36, 38	47:23–26	20
31:3	67	47:27	42n64
31:33b–34	31	47:27b	16, 52–53
32	89	48:4	30
32:5	74	48:15	57n1
32:6	40	48:20	15
32:23–33	68n28	48:28	15
32:25ff.	89	49	15
32:25	88n67	50:5–6	18
32:27	89	50:16	40
32:29	89n69	50:24–25	18, 78n47
32:30	89	50:26	16
32:31	89		
33	89		
33:10b	89	*Exodus*	
33:11	89		
34:25	25	1–19	3
35:11	30, 104, 106n109	1–15	93n83
35:22b–26	15n1	1–2	13, 48–55
37:21	39	1	30, 48, 102n98
37:24	39	1:1—2:10	48n73
41:1–7	130	1:1—2:25	15–55
41:17–24	130	1:1–22	15–30, 48n73

SCRIPTURE INDEX

1:1–7	15–16, 27, 50n75, 52	2:1–10	30–37, 45, 48n73, 51, 160
1:1	2, 15, 158	2:1	31, 32
1:5ff.	142	2:2–3	33
1:5a	16, 16n3	2:2	31, 32
1:5b	16, 16n3	2:3	26n41
1:6–7	2, 42	2:4	31, 52
1:6	16, 17, 52	2:6	23, 34n41, 37
1:7	16, 27, 29, 55n80	2:7–9	52
1:8–14	16–22, 47, 52	2:7	23, 46
1:8–12	27, 53, 55n80, 97n88	2:8–14	26
1:8	27	2:10–11	50n75
1:9–12	17	2:10	38n54, 45, 46
1:9–10	21	2:11—4:31	48n73
1:9	16, 19, 26, 27, 80	2:11—4:23	48n73
1:10	19n10, 27, 29, 83	2:11–22	37–41, 45, 51
1:11ff.	102	2:11	23, 38, 38n54, 45, 54, 119n126
1:11–12	83	2:12	38
1:11	26, 54, 119n126	2:13	23, 38
1:12	27, 28, 29	2:15	38–39, 39n54, 50n75, 52, 94n85
1:13–14	21, 27, 28, 50n75, 53, 54, 55, 102n98, 118	2:15b	86
1:13	55n80	2:16	39
1:14	28	2:17	39, 40n58
1:15—2:10	54n79	2:18	40, 41, 87n64
1:15–22	22–26, 50n75, 51, 85n61	2:19	37, 39
		2:22	37, 45, 46, 48n73, 86, 87n63
1:15–21	28	2:22b–25	45n70
1:15–20	27	2:23–25	41–45, 48n73, 52, 53
1:15–16	21		
1:15	27	2:23	42, 42n64, 53, 54, 95n85, 117n122
1:17	85n61	2:23ab–25	54, 81
1:20–21	85n61	2:23b–25	85n61, 86, 117, 118
1:20	27		
1:20a	27	2:24–25	45
1:21–22	27	2:24	44, 113
1:21	28, 51	2:24a	117n122
1:22	19n10, 22, 27, 28, 48n74, 54	2:24b	117n122
		2:25	45, 46, 48n74
2	48	3:1—7:13	56–119
2:1–25	30–47	3:1—6:1	115–19
2:1–22	46, 118		

SCRIPTURE INDEX

3–4	13, 107	3:13–22	64
3:1—4:17	56–85	3:13–15	67n26
3	48	3:13–14	116
3:1ff.	48n73	3:13	65n20, 66, 75, 78, 103n100
3:1–10	56–61	3:14–22	75
3:1–6	84, 86	3:14–17	78
3:1–5	75	3:14–15	106n109
3:1	42, 48	3:14	67, 67n26, 78, 84, 103n100
3:2–6	60	3:14a	67
3:2–4	58	3:14b	67, 67n26, 68
3:2	82	3:15–16	116
3:2a	57n2	3:15	61, 66n24, 67, 68, 78, 82, 103n100
3:2b	57n2	3:15b	66
3:3	82	3:16ff.	100
3:4	59, 82, 83	3:16–18a	96
3:6–10	78	3:16–17	64n19, 81, 85
3:6	43, 59, 64, 77n44, 103, 106, 116	3:16	65n20, 82
3:7–10	75, 80	3:17	12, 81, 82, 107
3:7–9	113	3:18–22	82, 85
3:7–8	61, 81, 83, 85	3:18–19	97, 102
3:7	61, 78, 80, 82, 83	3:18	23, 72n35, 82, 83n57, 97
3:8	12, 19, 64n19, 80, 81, 82, 107	3:18a	96
3:8a	63	3:18b–20	94, 95
3:9–15	82, 83, 84, 85, 85n61	3:19–22	70
3:9	61, 78, 80, 82, 83, 83n57	3:19–20	88
3:10	61, 62, 62n11, 63, 78, 80, 82	3:19	82, 88, 99, 100, 111n116
3:11–12	61–64	3:20	71, 87, 88, 95
3:11	62, 62n11, 75, 78n46, 103n100	3:21–22	70
3:11a	62n10	3:21	134
3:11	63, 103	4	116
3:12–15	82	4:1ff.	94
3:12	62–63, 62n11, 63, 67, 75, 78, 78n46, 81n53, 83n57, 84	4:1–17	71–74, 85
3:12a	62, 62n13	4:1–9	63, 96
3:12b	58, 62n13, 63, 66, 69, 88	4:1	71n34, 72, 75, 82, 111
3:13ff.	66, 84n60, 85	4:2–9	75
		4:2–3	116
		4:2	87
		4:5	82

4:8–9	94	4:29–30	82
4:9b	72	4:30	108
4:10	75, 78, 117	4:31	107
4:11–12	75	5–15	13
4:12	67, 78	5	42n63, 72, 88, 102n98, 115, 116, 116n121, 119
4:13	67n27, 73, 76, 78, 83n57		
4:14–17	76	5:1–5	96–98
4:14	96	5:1	23, 82, 96, 110, 116
4:15–16	96		
4:15	67, 72, 78, 116, 117	5:2	113, 136, 143
		5:3	23, 43, 82, 83n57
4:16	96, 108, 114	5:4	97, 119n126
4:17	48, 74, 81, 87, 92, 94	5:5	17, 97, 97n88, 119n126
4:18–26	86–96	5:6ff.	102n98
4:18–20	86–87, 86n62, 92, 93	5:6–23	54, 102, 102n98
		5:6–21	98–99
4:18	40, 86, 86n62, 94, 95, 118n124	5:6–19	99
		5:8	98
4:19–26	90n75	5:9–21	101
4:19–20a	94, 96n86	5:10–20	99
4:19	42, 94, 95, 95n85, 96	5:10	102n97, 158
		5:13	21
4:20	86, 87, 87n63, 92, 95	5:17	98
		5:20	102
4:20b	94, 96n86	5:22–23	77, 77n44, 82, 99
4:21–23	87–88, 92, 93, 94	5:23	113
4:21	88, 92, 94, 95, 149n31	6	107
		6:1–12	114
4:22–23	88, 94, 95, 96, 97, 134, 154	6:1	82, 99, 119
		6:2ff.	55
4:23	88, 90, 90n75, 92, 101	6:2—7:13	103–20
		6:2—7:7	119
4:24ff.	87n63, 92	6:2–12	119
4:24–26	45n70, 88–92, 94	6:2–9	103–9
4:24	90, 90n73, 90n75	6:2–8	107, 113, 115, 116
4:24a	96	6:2–3	85n61, 106n109, 116
4:25	87n63		
4:27—6:1	96–102	6:2	103, 106n109, 113, 118, 118n123, 118n124
4:27–5:5	102		
4:27ff.	82, 95		
4:27–31	96	6:3–5	104
4:27	57, 87, 96	6:3	65n21, 66, 106

6:3a	58n6	7:3	109, 110, 111n116, 129
6:4–5	113		
6:4	117n122	7:4	119n126
6:5	117n122	7:5	103, 105, 107, 110, 113, 114, 119n126, 129, 135, 153
6:5a	117n122		
6:6ff.	104		
6:6–8	12, 106		
6:6	103, 106, 113, 117n122	7:6–7	115
		7:7	31, 42, 115
6:7	11, 103, 107, 113	7:8—9:15	79
6:8	81, 103, 106, 113	7:8–13	111–13, 115
6:9	114, 116	7:8–9	115
6:11	148	7:9ff.	148
6:12	114, 116, 155	7:10–13	116n121
6:12b	116	7:10–12	138
6:13ff.	118n123	7:10	120
6:13–30	108–9	7:11–12	148
6:13	108, 114, 118	7:11	79, 124
6:14ff.	32	7:13	148
6:14–25	114	7:14—11:10	120–54
6:14	108	7:14–25	120–22
6:20	31	7:14	116
6:22ff.	84n60	7:15	148n29
6:25b	108, 109	7:16	101, 153
6:26–28	108	7:17–18	121
6:26–27	109, 114	7:17	121, 135, 147, 148n29
6:26	114		
6:27	109, 114	7:17a	123
6:28–30	114	7:19–20a	153
6:28	109	7:19	121, 147
6:29	108, 109, 113, 117, 155	7:20	120, 121, 147
		7:21a	121
6:30	108, 114	7:21b–22	153
7	116	7:21b	121
7:1–7	109–11, 117n122	7:22	79, 110, 115, 147, 148
7:1–6	114		
7:1–5	108	7:24	121
7:1–2	116	7:25	122
7:1	114, 117n122	7:26—8:11	123–24
7:2–6	154	7:26	101, 122, 138
7:2	116, 148, 150	7:28	147, 152
7:3–5	128	7:29	123
7:3–4	95, 135	7:30	149n30
		8:1–3	153

8:1	147
8:2	147
8:3	115, 148
8:4	123
8:5	77n44, 123, 126, 145
8:6	123, 135, 140n22
8:7	123
8:8b	124n6
8:11	110, 115, 123, 148, 149
8:12–15	124
8:12	147
8:12b	154
8:13	126, 147
8:14–15	115
8:14	148
8:15	110, 136n18, 148
8:16–28	124–26
8:16	101
8:17	125, 152
8:18	125, 126, 135, 139
8:20	125
8:21	43
8:22–23	145
8:22	81, 162, 163
8:24	132
8:25	123, 124, 125, 131, 144, 145
8:27	124, 125
8:28	110, 154
9:1–7	126
9:1	101
9:3	66n24, 126
9:4	125, 139
9:6	125, 126, 152
9:7	110, 144, 154
9:8–12	126–27, 148
9:9–10	126
9:12	110
9:13–35	127–29
9:13–16	129
9:13	101
9:14–16	130
9:14	128, 136, 140n22
9:15–16	152, 152n36
9:15	147
9:16	110, 136
9:18	128, 140
9:19	126, 152
9:20	110
9:22–23	148, 148n29
9:22	126
9:23	148, 148n29
9:24	128, 140
9:24a	148n29
9:25	126
9:25a	148n29
9:26	126
9:27	100
9:28	129
9:29	99, 136, 140n22
9:30	129, 131, 136n18, 145
9:32	126
9:34	129, 154
9:35	110, 148
10:1–20	129–32
10:1–2	152
10:1	109, 110, 111, 130, 134, 138, 154
10:2	130, 136
10:3–6	74n38, 130
10:3–4	130
10:3	101, 136n18
10:4	126
10:5	147
10:5b	152
10:6	128, 140
10:7	110
10:8	101
10:10	18, 132, 144, 145
10:12–13	148
10:13	148
10:14	128, 140
10:15	147
10:16	100
10:17	147, 153, 154

10:19	154	12:43–49	93n82, 93n83
10:20	110, 148	13:5ff.	9
10:21–29	132–35, 142	13:5	61
10:21–23	148	13:8	9
10:21	141	13:11–16	8n1
10:22	148	13:17	63n15
10:23	122, 126	13:18	17, 63n15
10:24ff.	154	13:21	59, 63n15
10:24–26	148n28	14:8	110
10:24	18, 101, 145	15:2	61n9
10:27	110, 148	16–18	13
10:28ff.	148n28	16:7	97
11	114	16:8	97
11:1ff.	88	17:1	63n15
11:1–3	132–35, 154	17:7	126
11:1	88, 130, 134	17:14	9
11:2–3	82	18	40, 87
11:2	70, 71	18:2ff.	94
11:3	134	18:2	94n83
11:4ff.	134	18:2b	90
11:4–8	132–35	18:3–4	86, 87
11:4–7	134	18:4	43, 87
11:4	88n66, 134	18:5	57
11:6	128	18:10–11	41
11:7	126	18:27	57
11:7b	141	19–24	13
11:8	134, 134n15	19–20	3
11:9–10	114, 135, 117n122, 154	19	58
		19:4ff.	11
11:9	135n17	19:4–6	81, 107
11:10	110, 114	19:4	57
11:26ff.	118n123	19:9	64n18
12:12	134, 141, 150n33, 161	20–40	3
		20:2	11
12:14ff.	9	20:8–11	53
12:17	119n126	20:20	77
12:31–32	132	20:26	60n7
12:31	101, 131, 134	21	23
12:33	99	21:2	23n24
12:35	70	23:10ff.	12
12:36	134	23:13	66
12:38	17	23:17	131
12:40	31	24	58
12:42	119n126	24:4ff.	64

SCRIPTURE INDEX 183

24:4–5	62n13
24:4	9
25–31	13
25:8	2
29:9ff.	10
29:12	128
29:43	2
29:45	2
32–34	13
32:8	12
32:14	77
33:18	77n44
33:19	67
34:3	57
34:14	59
34:23	131
34:27–28	9
34:30	77n44
35–40	14
40:36–37	63n15

Leviticus

1:1	2
8–9	2
10:2	59
10:4	108
10:11	73
13:46	12
17:3ff.	12
19:23	12
20:19	31
20:24	61
23:43	9
25	53
25:42	53
25:43	53
25:46	53
25:53	53
25:55	53
26	12

Numbers

1:7	109
1:48	42n64
9:4ff.	12
9:15–23	2
10:11	57
10:29	40
10:30	57
12:3	86
12:7	74, 75n39
12:8	77n44
14:12	17
14:13	17
14:20	77
15:32ff.	12
16	108
16:12	134
16:13b	38
16:30	77n44
17:20	71
22:6	17
22:22ff.	89n69
26:8	87n63
26:11	108
26:59–60	32
26:59	31, 31n37
27:17	57
31:7	25
31:23	59
33:2	9

Deuteronomy

1:22ff.	109n113
1:42	109n113
1:46	67n27
2:2	109n113
2:9	109n113
2:16–17	109n113
2:16	109n113
2:17	109n113
2:30	146n26
4:12	58n5

4:20	45n70
4:24	59
4:34	17
4:36	77
4:38	17
6:16	43
6:20–25	7
6:20	8n2
6:23	12
7:1	17
9:1	17
9:3	59
9:14	17
11:10	21
13:2ff.	71
13:6	11
15:13–14	70
18:18	74
20:13–14	25
24:8	73
25:7	134
25:18	26
26	9n3, n4
26:3–10	8n1
26:7	43
28	12
29:3	146n26
29:9ff.	10
31:9	9
31:17	126
31:22	9
31:23	67
31:26	9
33:10	73
33:16	58, 58n4
34:10	74

Joshua

1:5	67
3:7	67
5:2–12	93n82
5:5	93n82
5:15	60
8:2	69
10:40	135n17
11:20	146n26
22:31	67n25
24	10
24:2	23n24
24:3	23n24
24:14	44

Judges

4:11	40
5:4ff.	58
6:11	78
6:12	58, 67
6:14ff.	63
6:14	58, 78, 95
6:16	58, 63n16, 67, 74, 95
6:17ff.	95
6:20	58
6:22	58
6:23	58
6:36ff.	95
6:36–40	74
6:39ff.	95
7:7	95
7:9–15	95
8:24	70
9:17	67n25
10:11–13a	104
11:13	17
13:24	35
19:30	18
20:18–26	45
21:11	25

1 Samuel

1:10	21
1:20	36
1:27	70
2:20	70

2:25	111	21:2	23
2:27–29	104		
2:34	62n12		
3:4–10	74	## 1 Kings	
3:5–6	60n8		
4	23, 45	1:10ff.	59
4:17	104	3:19	67n25
6:6	146n26	9:19	20n11
10:15–16	86	9:20	23
10:22b	86	11:15	25
11:9	74	11:31–39	82
12:8	78	12:15	82, 146
12:11	78	14:6	78
12:23	77	14:7–16	82
13–14	23	14:7–9	104
14:10	62n12	14:21	109
15:1	78	15:2	109
15:15	67n25	15:5	67n25
16:1–3	42	15:29	82
16:1	78	16:1–4	82
16:2–3	69	16:12	82
17:50	135n17	18:1	118n123
18:25	74	18:24–25	66
23:13	67n27	18:36	123
24:1	45	18:37	111
25:6	74	19	58
29	23	19:11ff.	59
		19:13	60
		21:19–26	82
## 2 Samuel		22:27	74
		22:42	109
5:14	32		
6:20	60n7		
7:11–12	26	## 2 Kings	
7:27	61		
7:28–29	61	4:18	35
7:28	61	4:27	21
7:29	61	4:28	70
8:18	40n61	5:10	160
12:24–25	32	5:11	121
14:26	42n65	9:17–18	74
15:13	23	9:25–37	82
15:20	67n27	19:29	62n12
15:30	60n7	20:5	61n9
19:25	40	20:8	71

20:9	62n12	4:13ff.	76n43
23	10	5:5–6	104
23:26–27	45n69	6:7	105
23:34	36	7:4	105
24:17	36	12:15	105
		16:7	16
		20:1–29	104
Isaiah		20:5–6	106
6:2	60	20:5	105
6:8	78	20:6b	107
14:14–15	100	20:7–8	44
36:20	100	20:9	44, 105
37:30	62n12	20:25	111
38:7	62n12	22:30	77
41:24	23n20	24:17	60n7
44:25	79	29:3	138
48:10	45n70	32:32	35
52:6	105	34:2ff.	57n1
63:11	36	34:4	53

Jeremiah		*Hosea*	
1:6–9	74	1:9	67n26
1:7	78	2:2	19n10
4:4	59	12:10	11
9:24–25	35	13:4	107
11:4	45n70		
15:1ff.	77n45	*Amos*	
16:21	105		
18:13	67n25	3:7	70
23:1	57n1	5:22–25	81n54
31:29	22	7:15	56
35:6	23n24		
44:29	62n12	*Jonah*	
		1:9	23
Ezekiel			
1:1—3:15	74	*Micah*	
1	74		
2:3	78	7:14	57n1
2:4	78		
3:5	78		
3:6	78		

Zephaniah

3:6–7	129
3:8	59

Malachi

3:2	59

Psalms

18:26	69
20:8	66
23:1	57n1
29	59
31:9	61
36:7	43
50:11ff.	81n54
50:21	67n26
68:17	58
78:1	155
78:44–51	147
78:45ff.	125, 152n36
78:70–72	56
79:5	59
79:6	65
79:13	57n1
80:2	57n1
105:24	17
105:28–36	147n27
105:30	123
105:31	125
105:45	8n1
106:23	77
112:6	26n29
114:1–2	11
116:4	66
116:13	66
116:17	66
135:13	68
136:4	79

Proverbs

14:10	21
20:11	47

Job

9:18	21
21:14–15	100
22:28	124
42:5	45

Song of Songs

8:6	59

Ruth

1:6	44
1:22	135n17
4:11	26

Ecclesiastes

2:22	66n24
7:7	70

Esther

1:12	59

Daniel

3:15	100
4:1	138

Nehemiah

8:7–8	73

1 Chronicles

2:1	15
3:5	32
4:18	23
17:6	57n1
18:17	40n61

2 Chronicles

17:8–9	73
17:12	20n11
32:28	20n11
35:22	45n69

Index of Ancient and Premodern Sources

Ancient Near Eastern Sources

Akkadian

Code of Hammurabi, 57n1
Creation Epic (*Enuma Elish*), 37n48, 66n22, 74n38
Esarhaddon: Fight for the Throne, 57n1
Flood Story, 138n20
Hymn to the Sun-God, 57n1
Legend of Sargon, 159, 159n9
Oracles Concerning Esarhaddon, 103n103, 104n104

Aramaic

Petition for Authorization to Rebuild the Temple of Yaho at Elephantine, 162n20

Egyptian

Amen-hotep II: Memphis and Karnak Stelae, 24n25
Charms against Snakes, 79n50, 112n118
Circumcision in Egypt, 35n42
Divine Oracle to Thut-Mose IV Through a Dream (Sphinx Stela), 103n101
The God and His Unknown Name of Power, 66n22
Hyksos in Egypt, 163n23
Hymns to the Gods as a Single God, 57n1
In Praise of the City Ramses, 20n12
Instruction of Ani, 35n45
Journal of a Frontier Official, 23n23
Papyrus Jumilhac (Isis hides Horus), 34, 159
Prophecy of Nefer-Rohu (Nefer-ti), 125, 125n10
Ramses III: Lists, 24n25
Report of a Frontier Official, 20n13, 158n5
Repulsing of the Dragon and Creation, 79n49
Universalist Hymn to the Sun, 57n1

Hittite

Song of Ullikummis, 74n38

Sumerian

Lipit-Ishtar Lawcode, 57n1

Ugaritic

Aqht, 23n20
Baal Cycle, 74n38
Keret, 74n38, 138n20

Ancient Biblical Texts and Translations

Qumran texts, 3
Samaritan Pentateuch, 3n3, 17, 28,
    48n74, 59, 61, 88n66, 97n88,
    98n93, 115, 130, 134
Septuagint, 3, 13, 16n3, 20, 22, 39,
    40n58, 42, 59, 87, 88n67,
    105n107, 125
Targum Jonathan, 41, 87
Targum Yerušalmi, 59
Targum Onkelos, 40n61, 57, 87,
    88n67, 98n93, 105n107
Targums, Palestinian, 88, 89n72, 90
Vulgate, 87n63

Classical and Hellenistic Sources

Herodotus, 25, 35
    II, 38   162
    II, 41   163
    II, 42   163
    II, 45   163
Josephus, 20n14, 22, 37
    Against Apion
      1.26   163
    Antiquities
      2.9.1   20
      2.9.2   22, 25
      2.9.5   35
      2.9.6–10.2   36
      2.12.4   66
      2.13.3–4   116n121
      2.14.3   125
      2.14.5   132n14
Philo
    Life of Moses
      1.25   71
Philo of Byblus, 92

New Testament

Acts
    7:22   36

Mishnah and Babylonian Talmud

Mishnah
    Abot 2.5(6)   38n51
    Eduyyot 2.10   122
    Nidda 5.3   91
    Taanit 2.4   43n51
Babylonian Talmud
    Menaḥot 85a   80
    Nedarim
      22b   11
      32b   91
    Sotah 11b   25
    Taanit 20b   157n2
    Yoma 85b   90n73

Midrashic Literature

B^ereshit Rabba, 40, 125

INDEX OF ANCIENT AND PREMODERN SOURCES 191

M^{e}kilta, 3n2, 11n6, 17n6, 40n61,
    93n82, 109n113
M^{e}kilta d^{e}Rashbi, 78
Š^{e}mot Rabba, 16n2, 19n10, 22,
    24n27, 25, 29n34, 32, 33, 34,
    36, 38, 38n51, 38n53, 41,
    44, 59, 60, 62, 62n12, 67n26,
    68n29, 70, 71n34, 72n35, 73,
    78n47, 87, 89n70, 89n71,
    89n72, 99, 100, 102n97,
    102n98, 106n109, 106n110,
    111, 113, 121, 121n2, 122,
    125n9, 128, 157n2,
Sekel Tob, 29, 31, 47, 62, 73, 100,
    106, 121, 122, 126, 135n16
Wayyiqra Rabba, 38n51, 78
Midrash Haggadol, Exodus, 21, 36,
    38, 67, 73, 77n44, 81, 120n1,
    121
Pirqe d^{e}Rabbi Eli'ezer, 93
Tanḥuma, 137
Torah Shelema (Kasher), 90n73,
    90n75, 93n81

Medieval and Premodern Jewish Commentators/Writers

Abarbanel, Isaac, xii, 18, 22, 33,
    36n46, 41, 47, 69, 78, 99,
    110n115, 112, 114, 123,
    124n6, 125, 126n11, 127,
    131, 131n13, 133, 141n23,
Albo, Joseph, 110n115
Baḥya ben 'Ašer, 70, 109n113, 138
Bekor Šor, Joseph, 34n41, 42, 70, 97,
    108, 117, 118, 120n1, 122,
    126, 127
Ḥizquni (Ḥizqia ben Manoaḥ), 42,
    45n70, 60, 70, 71n33, 88, 89,
    90, 108, 121

Ibn Ezra, Abraham, 2, 8n2, 36,
    39n57, 40, 42, 42n63, 58,
    59, 62n12, 63n17, 64, 86, 88,
    88n67, 89, 89n71, 90, 90n73,
    90n75, 91n78, 93n83, 94n84,
    94n85, 96, 104, 109n113,
    110n115, 120n1, 121, 122,
    132, 140
Kimḥi, David, 42, 45n70, 90n75,
    104, 111
Maharal (Judah Loew ben Bezalel),
    94n84
Maharzu (Ze'ev Wolf Einhorn),
    38n51
Maimonides, Moses, 110n114,
    111n116
Malbim (Meir Leibush ben Yeḥiel
    Michael), 17, 47n72, 73
Ma'or ha-'^{a}felah, 58n6
Meiri, Menaḥem b. Solomon, 43n67
Meṣudat David, 45n70
Meyuḥas ben Elijah, 105, 108, 110,
    134
Pseudo-Rashi, 43–44n67
Qafiḥ, Joseph, 34
Ralbag (Levi ben Gershom
    [Gersonides]), 114, 138
Ramban (Moše ben Naḥman
    [Nachmanides]), 10n5, 35,
    43, 44n68, 48n74, 58n4,
    61n9, 64n18, 67n26, 86n62,
    87n63, 87n65, 88n66, 94,
    94n85, 106n108, 106n109,
    111n116, 127, 128, 130, 133,
    135n16, 144
Rashbam (Š^{e}muel ben Meir), xii, 16,
    19, 42, 44, 48n74, 53n78, 64,
    66n24, 69n32, 88, 89, 89n69,
    90, 94n85, 97, 98, 105, 107,
    108, 110, 120n1, 121, 124,
    138
Rashi (Š^{e}lomo Yiṣḥaqi), 19n10, 38,
    40, 45n70, 45n71, 48n74, 57,
    68n29, 69, 87n65, 89n71, 94,
    99n95, 104, 105, 106n109,
    108, 109, 109n113, 126, 129
Saadya ben Joseph Ga'on, 19n10,
    34, 39n55, 90, 91, 110n115

Shadal (Šᵉmuel David Luzzatto), 21,
    22, 26, 39n55, 45n70, 45n71,
    58n4, 62n12, 62n13, 69,
    90n74, 93n83, 135,
Tosefot Yom Tov, 91, 122

www.ingramcontent.com/pod-product-compliance
Lightning Source LLC
Chambersburg PA
CBHW031817220426
43662CB00007B/687